westermann

Exploring History
2

Edited by
Dr. Christa Lohmann

Written by
Dr. Matthias Bode
Rolf J. Kröger
Dr. Deanna Nebert
Dr. Barbara Nerlich
Thomas Söhrnsen

westermann GRUPPE

© 2019 Bildungshaus Schulbuchverlage Westermann Schroedel Diesterweg Schöningh Winklers GmbH
Braunschweig, www.westermann.de

Das Werk und seine Teile sind urheberrechtlich geschützt. Jede Nutzung in anderen als den gesetzlich zugelassenen bzw. vertraglich zugestandenen Fällen bedarf der vorherigen schriftlichen Einwilligung des Verlages. Nähere Informationen zur vertraglich gestatteten Anzahl von Kopien finden Sie auf www.schulbuchkopie.de.

Für Verweise (Links) auf Internet-Adressen gilt folgender Haftungshinweis: Trotz sorgfältiger inhaltlicher Kontrolle wird die Haftung für die Inhalte der externen Seiten ausgeschlossen. Für den Inhalt dieser externen Seiten sind ausschließlich deren Betreiber verantwortlich. Sollten Sie daher auf kostenpflichtige, illegale oder anstößige Inhalte treffen, so bedauern wir dies ausdrücklich und bitten Sie, uns umgehend per E-Mail davon in Kenntnis zu setzen, damit beim Nachdruck der Verweis gelöscht wird.

Druck A^3 / Jahr 2021
Alle Drucke der Serie A sind im Unterricht parallel verwendbar.

Redaktion: Christoph Meyer
Druck und Bindung: Westermann Druck GmbH, Braunschweig

ISBN 978-3-14-**111816**-2

01 THE WEIMAR REPUBLIC — 6

The End of the War and the November Revolution 1918 8
Culture of Remembrance:
Dealing with Historical Figures 12
The Treaty of Versailles 14
Historical Workshop:
Historic and Historical Maps 18
The Weimar Constitution 20
Years of Unrest 1919–23 23
The Stresemann Era: Stabilizing the Republic 28
The Golden Twenties 30
The Great Depression: A Comparative Approach 34
The End of the Republic 1930–33 38
Summary:
The Weimar Republic 44

02 THE THIRD REICH — 46

Adolf Hitler and the Origins of Nazi Ideology 48
A Legal "Seizure of Power"? 52
Seduction and Violence 56
Everyday Life in Nazi Germany 60
The Economy in Germany 64
Hitler's Foreign Policy – road to disaster 68
The Second World War 74
Societies at War 80
Culture of Remembrance:
A Controversy in England About the Right Way to Remember 86
From Loss of Rights to Mass Murder 88
Opposition and Resistance in Germany 94
Historical Workshop:
Analysing Monuments 98
Summary:
The Third Reich 100

03 THE COLD WAR AND GERMAN DIVISION — 102

Allied Cooperation and Rivalry 104
Flight and Expulsion from Eastern Europe 106
Culture of Remembrance:
Remembering the Past: Germans Expelled After World War II 110
Planning the Post-war World 112
The Four Powers in Germany 1946–48 114
Berlin Blockade and Allied Confrontation 1948/49 118
Founding Two German States 1949 121
Historical Workshop:
Analysing Films 126
Summary:
The Cold War and German Division 128

04 THE TWO GERMANIES WITHIN EUROPE — 130

Western and Eastern Integration? 132
The Adenauer Years 136
The Early Ulbricht Era 140
Building the Berlin Wall 144
West Germany in the 60s – a time of change? 146
East Germany after 1961: Losing a second chance? 150
A New Government, a New Ostpolitik 152
The Limits of Growth 156
A Dictatorship to Live With? 160
A New Cold War – and a new détente 164
The Crisis of the SED Government 168
German Unity – a question of speed? 172
Social Upheaval in United Germany 176
Culture of Remembrance:
A Monument to German Freedom and Unity? 178

Europe 1945–1967: United in Diversity 180
Broadening and Deepening 182
After the Cold War: From Cooperation to New Nationalism 184

Summary:
The Two Germanies within Europe 188

05 SUPERPOWER RIVALRY — 190

Superpower Rivalry	192
The Cuban Crisis 1962 – 13 days on the edge	196
American Involvement in Vietnam 1962–75	200

Historical Workshop:

Analysing Eyewitness Reports	204
The Soviet Union and Eastern Europe 1955–69	206
From Co-operation to the Collapse of Communist Europe	210

Summary:

Superpower Rivalry	214

06 21ST CENTURY CHALLENGES — 216

The USA and Russia – from cooperation to a new Cold War	217
Islamism and the "War on Terror"	220
Refugees	223
Energy and Climate Change	225
Globalization	227
What's Left?	229

Glossary	230
Index	236
Picture Credits	240

The Weimar Republic

M 1 Philipp Scheidemann Proclaims the Republic
9 November 1918

M 3 Potsdamer Platz in the 1920s

M 2 Vampire Vacuum Cleaner
Advertisement for AEG, 1929

M 4 "Our Last Hope: Hitler"
National Socialist Election Poster, 1932

01 THE WEIMAR REPUBLIC
The First German Democracy, 1918–1933

The first republic in Germany started in a time of trouble and collapsed within only fifteen years.

As World War I ended in 1918, German political and military leaders had to deal with a dangerous situation. There were worries that the Russian Revolution from 1917 might spread to Germany, too. Sailors and soldiers were already beginning to revolt. People were tired of war and wanted it to end. The emperor was forced to abdicate. A provisional government had to end the war and bring the German troops home in an orderly manner. The country had become politically and socially unstable.

The war had lasted longer and was far more destructive than anyone had imagined. At the peace conference in Versailles, the Allies demanded that Germany pay for the damages the war had caused. These demands made difficult conditions for democratic German governments and held back economic recovery in Europe.

With the emperor gone and further changes in the leadership, Germany needed a new constitution. The new Weimar Constitution was considered a model for democratic government.

In the early years of the republic, inflation became a serious problem. Political murders, right-wing lies, and attempted overthrows of the government added to uncertainty. However, after 1923 the republic grew stronger and gradually re-established the German diplomatic role in world affairs.

The Golden Twenties saw a sudden increase of creativity and cultural freedom. That ended with the Great Depression, which had dramatic effects in both the USA and Germany.

As political and economic pressure on the republic grew after 1929, various governments proved incompetent. The republic ended with the appointment of Adolf Hitler as Chancellor in January 1933.

This chapter deals with many questions such as:
- How did the first German democracy come about at the end of World War I?
- What problems did the Treaty of Versailles create for Germany?
- What were the main principles of the Weimar Constitution?
- What made the republic unstable in the first years of its existence?
- How did political leaders stabilize the republic after 1923?
- What were the "Golden Twenties" like in Germany?
- How did the Great Depression affect the USA and Germany?
- Why did the Weimar Republic collapse?

The Weimar Republic

M 1 Soldiers at the Brandenburg Gate
Photograph, 9 November 1918

The End of the War and the November Revolution 1918

At the end of World War I, Germany was destabilized. Politically and militarily, the country had to adapt to great changes.

The Russian Revolution Affects Germany

In Russia at the end of the 19th century industrialization caused social problems and people started to demand more democracy. Over two million Russians died or were wounded in the First World War, which led to more political unrest. By 1917 Russians were tired of war and worried about food shortages. In mid-March the autocratic tsar abdicated, making Russia a republic. A provisional government ran the country until elections for a constituent assembly could be held later in the year. Meanwhile, military discipline on the front broke down. In April, the German government secretly helped the **Bolsheviks**, radical revolutionaries led by Lenin, return to Russia after twenty years in exile. Bolshevik goals were "peace, land and bread". The Bolsheviks overthrew the provisional government in November. They signed a peace treaty with Germany at **Brest-Litovsk** in February 1918. The treaty was humiliating, but it ended the war for Russia. However, this German success on the Russian front caused problems when **councils of workers and soldiers** (such councils are called **soviets** in Russian) tried to bring Bolshevik ideas to Germany.

The November Revolution in Germany

By October 1918 the German *Supreme Command* asked the Allies for an **armistice**. At the same time the military tried to shift responsibility for the lost war to political

Vocabulary

Supreme Command: highest military staff

mutiny: a refusal by a group of soldiers or sailors to accept orders

M 2 Prince Max of Baden
Photograph, 1918

leaders. General Erich Ludendorff insisted that deputies from the Reichstag be included in the government. On 3 October Chancellor Max von Baden agreed and formed a new government which included deputies from the parliament for the first time. By 9 November *mutinies* in Wilhelmshaven and Kiel and uprisings in other German cities reached Berlin. There thousands of demonstrators demanded an end to the war and William II's abdication. They hoped it would be easier to get an armistice without the emperor. When William refused to abdicate, Max von Baden announced the abdication anyway. He gave the chancellorship to Friedrich Ebert, the leader of the largest political faction in the Reichstag – the Social Democrats.

During the excitement and confusion in Berlin on 9 November, two different political leaders proclaimed two different republics. At about 2 p.m., Philipp Scheidemann (SPD) proclaimed the German republic from a balcony of the Reichstag. That was followed at about 4 p.m. by Karl Liebknecht, who proclaimed a free socialist republic, first from the roof of a car in front of the Berlin City Palace, then about an hour later, from a balcony over a portal of the palace.

M 3 **Philipp Scheidemann**
Photograph, 1918

Historical Terms

Bolshevik: Bolschewik
Treaty of Brest-Litovsk: Frieden von Brest-Litowsk
council of workers and soldiers: Arbeiter- und Soldatenrat
soviet: (russ.) Rat
armistice: Waffenstillstand
Council of People's Representatives: Rat der Volksbeauftragten
Ebert-Groener Pact: Ebert-Groener Pakt
All-German Assembly of Councils: Allgemeiner Kongress der Arbeiter- und Soldatenräte
Spartacist Uprising: Spartakusaufstand
Free Corps: Freikorps

Friedrich Ebert Looks for Calm in Chaos

Ebert had to take control of a revolutionary situation. He had not been appointed to office legitimately. His Social Democratic Party had divided during the war. He led the mainstream Majority Social Democrats who wanted to establish a parliamentary democracy. The more radical Independent Social Democrats preferred to establish councils of workers and soldiers, as had happened in Russia. Although both factions joined the cabinet, the **Council of People's Representatives**, Ebert agreed to let the councils of the workers and soldiers meet independently.

The Ebert-Groener Pact

On the evening of 10 November General Groener of the Supreme Command called Ebert on the telephone. Groener said that the army would support Ebert's government in fighting leftists in Germany. In return, the officer corps would stay in command of the army without political supervision. Despite what he had already promised the councils of workers and soldiers, Ebert accepted Groener's offer in what is known as the **Ebert-Groener Pact**. The long-term effect of the pact left the German officer corps largely outside of political control. Ebert then set about organizing his government. His most important task was to end the war. Matthias Erzberger (Centre Party) led the parliamentary delegation which had already been sent to France, where an armistice was signed on 11 November 1918.

New Elections are Set

In December an **All-German Assembly of Councils** met. A majority agreed to set elections for a constituent assembly on 19 January 1919. Delegates to the meeting who disagreed because they wanted a soviet system called for a boycott of the elections and rose up against the government – the **Spartacist Uprising**. This revolt was quickly put down. Groups of decommissioned soldiers, called **Free Corps**, found the Communist leaders Rosa Luxemburg and Karl Liebknecht and murdered them. By the time the elections to the National Assembly were held, the revolution had ended.

M 4 **Spartacist Uprising in Berlin**
Fighting in the streets of the newspaper district.
Photograph, 5 January 1919

The End of the War and the November Revolution 1918

M 5 "Long live the socialist republic!"
Sailors on the battleship Prinz Regent Luitpold in Kiel.
Photograph, early November 1918

M 6 Appeal to the Population of Schleswig-Holstein

After sailors mutinied in Kiel, civilians joined the revolt and took control of the city government. The first workers' and soldiers' council stated its goals:

"Political power lies in our hands.
A provisional provincial government will be formed; it will establish a new order in cooperation with the existing authorities.
5 Our goal is a free, socially-minded people's republic.
In those parts of the province where workers' and soldiers' councils do not yet exist, we call on the population of the city and the countryside to follow our example and stand united behind the new people's government and support
10 its work on behalf of the common good.
At first, our main task will be to secure the peace and heal the damage created by the war.
Issues that extend beyond the jurisdiction of the provincial administration remain, of course, under the authority of
15 state and Reich legislation. We are willing to work together, in the customary ways, with the entire civil service, as long as it supports the new course.
We are determined to meet any opposition with all the public power at our disposal.

People of Schleswig-Holstein! An old democratic dream of
20 freedom and unity, for which many of the best of you fought and suffered, will now become reality on a new and higher level! Kiel, 7 November 1918
The Workers' and Soldiers' Council"

Kieler Stadtarchiv/KstA; transl. by Frederick Reuss at German Historical Institute: http://germanhistorydocs.ghi-dc.org/pdf/eng/AUFRUF_1918_ENG.pdf [July 9, 2018].

M 7 Two Abdications

a) Prince Max von Baden's Announcement of William II's Abdication, 9 November 1918:

"The Kaiser and King has decided to renounce the throne. The Imperial Chancellor will remain in office until the questions connected with the abdication of the Kaiser, the renouncing by the Crown Prince of the throne of the German Empire and of Prussia, and the setting up of a regency have
5 been settled.
For the Regency he intends to appoint Deputy Ebert as Imperial Chancellor, and he proposes that a bill shall be brought in for the establishment of a law providing for the immediate *promulgation* of general suffrage and for a
10

Vocabulary

promulgation: making sth. known officially

constitutional German National Assembly, which will settle finally the future form of government of the German Nation and of those peoples which might be desirous of coming within the empire."

Quoted from: Charles F. Horne, Walter F Austin, Leonard Porter Ayres (eds.), Source Records of the Great War Vol. VI, New York: National Alumni 1923, at: http://www.firstworldwar.com/source/abdication_maxvonbaden.htm [July 7, 2018].

b) William II's Own Abdication Proclamation, 28 November 1918:

"I herewith renounce for all time claims to the throne of Prussia and to the German Imperial throne connected therewith.

At the same time I release all officials of the German Empire and of Prussia, as well as all officers, non-commissioned officers and men of the navy and of the Prussian army, as well as the troops of the federated states of Germany, from the oath of fidelity which they tendered to me as their Emperor, King and Commander-in-Chief.

I expect of them that until the re-establishment of order in the German Empire they shall render assistance to those in actual power in Germany, in protecting the German people from the threatening dangers of anarchy, famine, and foreign rule.

Proclaimed under our own hand and with the imperial seal attached.

Amerongen, 28 November 1918

Signed WILLIAM"

Quoted from: Charles F. Horne, Walter F Austin, Leonard Porter Ayres (eds.), Source Records of the Great War Vol. VI, New York: National Alumni 1923, at: http://www.firstworldwar.com/source/abdication.htm [July 7, 2018].

M 8 "No Revolution at All"

R. R. Palmer, an American historian, characterizes the November Revolution in Germany:

"No industries were nationalized. No property changed hands. No land laws or agrarian reforms were undertaken […] the East Elbian Junkers remained untouched in their landed estates. There was almost no confiscation even of the property of the former Kaiser and other ruling dynasties of Bismarck's federal empire. The very statues of emperors, kings, princes and grand dukes were left standing in the streets and squares. Officials, civil servants, police agents, professors, schoolteachers of old imperial Germany remained at their respective duties. The army […] remained the old army in miniature, with all its essential organs intact, and lacking only in mass. […] The officers were predominantly of the old aristocratic families – as always. Never had there been a revolution so mild, so reasonable, so tolerant. There were no terror, no fanaticism, no stirring faith, no expropriation, no émigrés. There had in truth been no revolution at all, in the sense in which France, England, the United States, Russia, and other countries, either recently or in the more distant past, had experienced revolutions."

R. R. Palmer, A History of the Modern World, New York: Knopf 1965, pp. 759f.

Tasks

1. **The Russian Revolution Affects Germany**
   a) Give reasons for the outbreak of the Russian Revolution in 1917 (text).
   b) Show why German support for Russian revolutionaries became problematic later (text).
2. **The November Revolution in Germany**
   a) List the goals of the Kiel council of workers and soldiers (M6).
   b) Assess the legality of Max von Baden's actions in November 1918 (M7a, text).
   c) Explain the difference between the two proclamations of abdication (M7a and b).
   d) Find out more about the mutinies in Wilhelmshaven or Kiel (M5).
   e) Report to your class on public events to remember the mutinies today.
3. **Friedrich Ebert Looks for Calm and the Ebert-Groener Pact**
   a) Describe Ebert's problems in November 1918 (text).
   b) Analyse his solutions to these problems.
4. **Parliamentary Elections Set**
   a) Outline the political situation before the parliamentary elections on 19 January 1919 (text).
   b) Assess the decision by some of the leftists to boycott the elections.
5. **"No Revolution at All"**
   a) Compare and contrast Palmer's assessment of the revolutionary situation in Germany in 1918–19 with your own opinion of it (M8, text).

Dealing with Historical Figures

Since their deaths Rosa Luxemburg and Karl Liebknecht have been honoured by the left wing as martyrs to communism. Demonstrations (called LLL demonstrations after Lenin was added in 1924) were held during the Weimar Republic from 1919 to 1933. In the Nazi era these demonstrations were forbidden. They resumed in East Germany in 1946 and are held yearly on or around 15 January, continuing to the present day.

Biography

Rosa Luxemburg (1871–1919)
was born in Congress Poland, studied in Switzerland for a degree as a doctor in law, and became a German citizen in 1897. She joined various leftist political parties and founded the Communist Party of Germany together with Karl Liebknecht on 1 January 1919. Her criticism of Lenin, published in 1922, has become famous: "Freedom only for the supporters of the government, only for the members of a party … is no freedom at all. Freedom is always the freedom of the one who thinks differently." She took part in the Spartacist Uprising and was murdered by members of a Free Corps on 15 January 1919.

Biography

Karl Liebknecht (1871–1919)
was born in Leipzig, became a doctor in law in 1897 and opened a practice in Berlin. In his political career he was elected to the Berlin city council assembly, the Prussian House of Representatives and then to the Reichstag. Liebknecht was a famous opponent of militarism. In December 1914, he gave the only vote in the Reichstag not to approve new credit to pay for the war. He proclaimed a free socialist republic for Germany on 9 November 1918. Together with Rosa Luxemburg he founded the Communist Party of Germany on 1 January 1919. He took part in the Spartacist Uprising and was murdered by members of a Free Corps on 15 January 1919. The press secretary for the Free Corps reported that Liebknecht had been "shot while trying to escape" and that Luxemburg had been "killed by an angry crowd".

M 1 Monument for Rosa Luxemburg in Berlin
The monument is on the Katharina-Heinroth-Ufer next to the Lichtenstein Bridge, where Luxemburg's body was thrown into the Landwehr Canal.

The architects Ralf Schüler und Ursulina Schüler-Witte designed both monuments (M1, M2) in 1987. Photograph, 2015

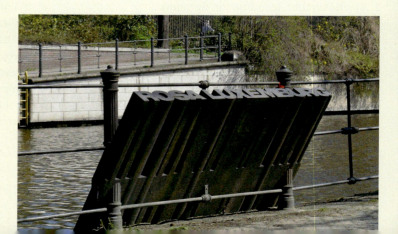

M 2 Monument for Karl Liebknecht in Berlin
This memorial is near the New Lake in the Tiergarten, where Liebknecht was shot. Photograph, 2015

M 3 Former State Council Building in (East) Berlin
The portal from the City Palace, which was torn down after 1945, was built into the façade of the State Council Building of East Germany. This was the balcony from which Karl Liebknecht proclaimed the free socialist republic of Germany on 9 November 1918. Photograph, 2015

Tasks

1. **Describing the Monuments (M1 – M3)**
   a) Assess the importance of the monument's location.
   b) Look for inscriptions or symbols which are used on the monument.
   c) Describe the impression the monument makes on you.
2. **Finding Information**
   a) Find out as much about the monument as you can: architect, date built, sponsors, reasons for building it, name or title of the monument, its artistic style.
   b) Find out who supported building the monument and who paid for it.
   c) Note whether the monument is used in ceremonies or formal occasions, who maintains it, and any nicknames it has.
   d) Explain why people visit the monument today.
3. **Interpreting the Monument**
   a) Assess the importance of the monument to visitors today.
   b) Estimate which groups will be enthusiastic about the monument today and which groups will not.
   c) Formulate what the monument stands for and your response to it in your own words.

M 1 "Down with the dictated peace!"
Demonstration against the Treaty of Versailles in front of the Berlin City Palace, May 1919. Photograph, 1919

The Treaty of Versailles

In addition to difficult domestic problems, Germany had to deal with the consequences of losing World War I.

Problems at the Peace Conference

Paris was where the winners met to decide how to organize Europe after the First World War. The Treaty of Versailles dealt with Germany and led to great bitterness. The peace conference in Versailles lasted from January until June 1919. No one told the Germans about the treaty's conditions until 7 May, when the German delegation got an ultimatum. Although Germany had become a republic and Wilson's Fourteen Points had given Germans hope that the peace conditions might be milder, this was not the case. The representatives of the three main powers in Paris, Woodrow Wilson (President of the USA), Georges Clemenceau (French Prime Minister), and David Lloyd George (British Prime Minister) refused to make concessions. The German government hesitated over the terms – Chancellor Philipp Scheidemann resigned, saying he would rather see his hand dry up than sign the treaty. The Allies refused to set a deadline for longer than 23 June. They put pressure on the German government to accept the conditions by threatening to go on with the war if necessary. Finally, a new German delegation to Versailles signed the treaty on 28 June 1919.

M 2 "War Guilt" according to the Treaty of Versailles

Article 231: The Allied governments affirm, and Germany accepts, the responsibility of Germany and her allies for causing all the loss and damage to which the Allied governments and their peoples have been subjected as a result of war.

Quoted from: John Traynor, Europe 1890–1990, London: Nelson Thornes Ltd. 1991, p. 108.

Historical Terms

What the Peace Treaty with Germany Looked Like – in brief

The major provisions of the treaty were:

financial

• Germany was responsible for the outbreak of the war and had to pay reparations (the total sum to be set later), according to Art. 231

territorial

• Alsace and Lorraine were returned to France

• the Saar coalfields were given to France (a plebiscite on national status was set for 1935)

• Eupen and Malmedy were ceded to Belgium

• Posen was ceded to Poland as part of the "Polish corridor"

• regional plebiscites (Schleswig 1920–21, Silesia 1921, Memel 1920, East Prussia 1920) would be set to determine national status

• Danzig became a Free City under the protection of the League of Nations

• the left bank of the Rhine and a fifty kilometre strip on the right bank were demilitarized (Allied troops should remain for fifteen years)

• Germany and Austria were forbidden to unite

colonial

• Germany lost all its colonies (they were divided among the Allies)

military

• the German army was reduced to 100,000 men

• the navy and air force were disbanded

• weapons and munitions were destroyed

• the German emperor William II should be turned over to the Allies for trial as a war criminal

In all, Germany lost about ten per cent of its population and thirteen per cent of its land area.

Historical Terms

League of Nations:
Völkerbund

The League of Nations

President Wilson's plan for world peace called for an international organization to prevent wars in the future. The idea was approved in Paris, and the new **League of Nations** set up its headquarters in Geneva. However, the US Senate disagreed with Wilson and refused to ratify either the agreement to join the League or the Treaty of Versailles. Communist Russia was not admitted as a member of the League. Germany was not allowed to join until 1926. Today the League of Nations is considered the forerunner of the United Nations.

M 3 "The League of Nations … and what it really looks like"
Cartoon by Arpad Schmidhammer, 1920

The Treaty of Versailles

M 4 "Versailles"
"Even you have the right of self-determination: Would you like your pockets emptied before or after your death?"
The American President Wilson, French Prime Minister Clemenceau, a symbolic German, and British Prime Minister Lloyd George are shown. Cartoon by Thomas Theodor Heine, 3 June 1919

Vocabulary
useful phrases
guillotine
to pull a lever

Vocabulary
the blade falls
to execute, execution, executioners
a condemned man
with hands tied behind his back

M 5 The Kiss of Peace
Cartoon by T. Th. Heine from "Simplizissimus", 1919

Vocabulary
to default: to fail to pay money owed

M 6 Reparations: A German Legend

Canadian historian Margaret MacMillan estimates the sum of reparations Germany actually paid:

"In Germany the Diktat ('dictated treaty') took the blame for all that was wrong with the economy: high prices, low wages, unemployment, taxes, inflation. [...] Germans ignored the fact that fighting the Great War had been expensive, and that losing it had meant they could not transfer the costs to anyone else. They also did not grasp, as most people have failed to do since, that reparations payments never amounted to anything like the huge amounts mentioned in public discussions. [...] Even with payment schedules that were revised downwards several times, however, the Germans continued to argue that reparations were intolerable. With a rare unanimity in Weimar politics, virtually all Germans felt they were paying too much. Germany regularly *defaulted* on its payments, for the last time and for good in 1932. [...]

In the final reckoning Germany may have paid about 22 billion gold marks (£1.1 billion, $4.5 billion) in the whole period between 1918 and 1932. That is probably slightly less than what France, with a much smaller economy, paid Germany after the Franco-Prussian War of 1870–1871."

Margaret MacMillan, Peacemakers, London: John Murray 2001, pp. 490f.

Tasks

1. **Problems at the Peace Conference**
   a) Find examples showing the attitudes of the winning powers at the peace conference (text).
   b) Explain why the German government was disappointed by the peace conference.
2. **What the Peace Treaty with Germany Looked Like**
   a) Choose three principles of the treaty you think are the most important (text).
   b) Compare and contrast your principles with your classmates' choices.
3. **The "War Guilt" Clause**
   a) Point out the consequences of Article 231 for Germany (M2).
4. **Looking at the Cartoons**
   Work as partners.
   a) Describe one of the cartoons (M3–M5).
   b) Compare your cartoon with your partner's.
5. **Reparations: A German Legend**
   a) Summarize the text briefly in your own words (M6).
   b) Discuss Margaret MacMillan's views on the German reparations in class.

Historic and Historical Maps

The terms "historic" and "historical" maps are often used interchangeably, but they have different meanings. Historic maps were made in the past and give the perspective of that time. Historical maps were made later to explain historical events or developments. A map of Germany drawn in 1871 is a historic map. A map of Germany drawn in 2008 to show the country as it was united in 1871 is a historical map.

Maps often seem to present events and developments objectively. However, careful examination of a map can reveal the impressions and ideas which contributed to the drawing of the map at the time more clearly. In the case of the controversial Treaty of Versailles, this is not surprising.

"Germany's Mutilation", the map showing the results of the First World War, was made to be used in schools in the 1920s. It shows a quite different perspective on the treaty than the modern historical map, "Germany after the First World War", from a contemporary textbook.

M 1 "Deutschlands Verstümmelung"
"Germany's Mutilation", a classroom wall map sent to schools by the German government in 1928.

M 2 Germany After the First World War – borders of the German Reich

Historical Workshop

Map Analysis Workshop

1. Describing the maps
a. Compare the extract shown and the scale of both maps. Note any differences.
b. Look at the legends of both maps and make a table of the information given. Note any differences.
c. Pay attention to the colouring, the lines drawn and the script used. Concentrate on the area around Danzig and East Prussia. Note the differences you find.
d. Compare the titles of both maps. Note the differences.

2. Assessing the maps
a. State the purpose of each map.
b. Determine which map is historic and which is historical. Give reasons for your choice.
c. Consider whether the historical map could also become a historic map.

3. Evaluating the maps
a. Decide which map shows more information about the Treaty of Versailles.
b. Determine the attitude to the Treaty of Versailles each title reveals.
c. Show how to use the map "Germany's Mutilation" as a primary source.
d. The map "Germany's Mutilation" does not contribute to reconciliation. Comment on this statement.

M 1 Women Wait to Vote
For the first time women could vote and be elected in the 1919 elections to the National Assembly. Photograph, Berlin, 1919

Historical Terms

proportional representation: Verhältniswahlrecht
emergency powers: Notverordnung
referendum: Volksentscheid
direction of policy: Richtlinienkompetenz
initiative: Volksbegehren

M 2 "The Constitution of the German Reich"
Title page of the edition sent to schools, 1919

The Weimar Constitution

A new constitution was written quickly, because the 1849 Constitution of Germany could be used as a model. After the unrest of the November Revolution, the National Assembly tried to include as many groups as possible in the new political system.

The National Assembly in Weimar

Despite the Spartacist call to boycott elections, 83% of the voters took part in the election on 19 January 1919. Because Berlin seemed too dangerous, the new National Assembly met in Weimar on 6 February. At first the assembly elected the Social Democrats Friedrich Ebert President and Philipp Scheidemann Chancellor of the Republic. Scheidemann led a coalition government of Social Democrats, the Centre Party, and German Democrats. It had the support of 76% of the voters and was called the "Weimar Coalition". The assembly had a solid democratic majority in 1919, but parliaments elected later slowly saw this majority disappear. From February 1919 until January 1930, twenty different government coalitions were formed – each lasting on average only 239 days.

Principles of the Constitution

The constitution was divided into two parts. The first described the structure and responsibilities of the Reich. The second set out the basic rights and obligations of German citizens. The main constitutional principles laid out a system of federal states, the separation of powers, and an electoral system based on **proportional representation** – parliamentary seats were won according to the number of popular votes each party received. For each 60,000 votes, a parliamentary mandate was created. In addition to a catalogue of human and civil rights, a new "right to work" (Article 163) and the "right of workers and employers to co-determine business policy in their firms" (Article 165) were included. For the first time in Germany all children had to go to school – for eight years of elementary school, and then for further schooling until the age of 18 (although these requirements

M 3 Friedrich Ebert
First President of the Republic, 1919–1925

M 4 Paul von Hindenburg
Last President of the Republic, 1925–1934

were never actually put into practice). The National Assembly accepted the constitution by a vote of 262 to 75 on 31 July 1919.

The President

Structurally, the President had broad powers. Like the emperor in the former German Empire, the President of the Republic appointed and dismissed governments, appointed judges to the highest court, dissolved the Reichstag, acted as commander-in-chief of the military and as head of state in international affairs. The President also had special **emergency powers** (Article 48) and could call for a **referendum** on a law passed by the Reichstag. He was elected directly for a term of seven years.

The Government and Plebiscites

The Chancellor and each of his ministers had to have the confidence of the Reichstag to stay in office. The President appointed and dismissed the Chancellor and the cabinet ministers. The constitution stated that the Chancellor determined the **direction of policy**.

The federal states were represented in the Imperial Council ("Reichsrat"). However, the council played only a small role in advising on and approving laws which were passed.

Popular participation was a basic element of the Weimar constitution. Both men and, for the first time, women over the age of twenty could vote. The Reichstag was elected proportionally, the President directly. Citizens could approve or disapprove of laws passed by the Reichstag, if the President called for them to do so or if five per cent of the voters petitioned for a direct vote on the measure (referendum). In addition the people could propose a law directly, if ten per cent of the voters petitioned for a plebiscite (**initiative**). In these ways the President as well as the people voting directly could interfere with the Chancellor's direction of policy.

Tasks

1. The National Assembly in Weimar
   a) Explain the meaning of the term "Weimar Republic" (text).
   b) List the political parties which made up the Weimar Coalition.
   c) Characterize the political direction of the Weimar Coalition.

The Weimar Constitution

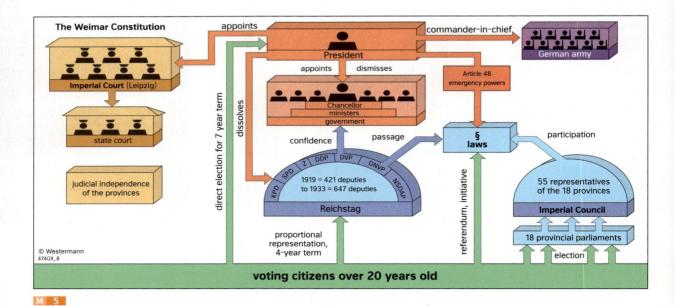

M 5

M 6 Excerpts from the Weimar Constitution

Article 25: The President has the right to dissolve the Reichstag, but only once for the same reason. New elections, at the latest, are held 60 days after the dissolution.
Article 48: If a state does not fulfil the obligations laid upon it by the Reich constitution or the Reich laws, the President may use armed force to cause it to oblige. In case public safety is seriously threatened or disturbed, the President may take the measures necessary to re-establish law and order, if necessary using armed force. In the pursuit of this aim he may suspend [...] civil rights [...] partially or entirely.
The President has to inform the Reichstag immediately about all measures undertaken which are based on paragraphs 1 and 2 of this article. The measures have to be suspended immediately if the Reichstag demands so.
Article 53: The Chancellor, and, at his request, the ministers, are appointed and dismissed by the President.
Article 54: The Chancellor and the ministers, in order to exercise their mandates, require the confidence of the Reichstag. Any one of them has to resign, if the Reichstag votes by explicit decision to withdraw its confidence.

Transl. by Alexander Ganse (2001), at: www.zum.de/psm/weimar/weimar_vve.php#Third%20Chapter [July 10, 2018].

Tasks

1. **Principles of the Constitution**
   a) List the main organs of the government and their functions (M5, text).
   b) Explain how majority representation is different from proportional representation (text).
2. **The President**
   a) List the functions of the President (text).
   b) Show the additional powers of the President according to Articles 25 and 48 of the Weimar Constitution (M6).
3. **The Government and Plebiscites**
   a) List the functions of the Chancellor (text, M6).
   b) Explain how the functions of the President could conflict with the functions of the Chancellor and the Reichstag (text, M6).
   c) Discuss how plebiscites could create political problems (text).
4. **The Weimar Constitution**
   a) The Weimar Constitution has been called the most democratic constitution Germany has ever had. Discuss this argument with your classmates (text, M5, M6).
   b) Assess strengths and weaknesses of the Weimar Constitution.

Years of Unrest 1919–23

At first the Weimar Republic had dramatic political and economic difficulties. Right-wing extremists and attempts to overthrow the government destabilized the country.

Attacking the Republic: Political Murder

The National Assembly agreed in 1919 not to question the patriotism of any politician who signed the Versailles Treaty. But German nationalists and right-wing extremists fought intensely against all such "traitors". They called the signers "November criminals". Political leaders who tried to *comply* with the conditions of the Versailles Treaty were called "fulfilment politicians".

Right-wing terrorists systematically murdered those they accused of treason, including Matthias Erzberger and Walther Rathenau. Others, like former Chancellor Philipp Scheidemann and the journalist Maximilian Harden, left public life after they were badly injured in assassination attempts. After Rathenau's murder in 1922, Chancellor Joseph Wirth accused the nationalists in the Reichstag, "There [pointing to the right] is the enemy, who drips his poison into the people's wounds. There stands the enemy – and there is no doubt: This enemy stands on the right!"

Punishment for right-wing attacks could be mild, because many policemen and judges had sworn loyalty to the German emperor before 1918. They often sympathized with anti-republican ideas.

M 1 **Walther Rathenau**
German Foreign Minister, murdered by right-wing radicals on 24 June 1922

The "Stab in the Back" Legend

One of the most harmful lies told during the Weimar era was that republican leaders had helped to defeat the army during the war. The former Chief of the Supreme Military Command, General Paul von Hindenburg, stated this "stab in the back" myth in testimony he gave to a parliamentary committee investigating the question of Germany's war guilt. It quickly was taken up by nationalists and right-wing extremists. The myth was repeated many times. It defamed the Republic and its leaders.

Historical Terms

stab in the back legend: Dolchstoßlegende

Vocabulary

to comply: to act according to an agreement, order, or plan

The Kapp Putsch

In March 1920 Free Corps soldiers attempted a coup d'état led by Wolfgang Kapp. The acting Chief of the General Staff, General von Seeckt, refused to defend the government, saying the army would be destroyed if regular troops fired on former comrades. Nevertheless, the Republic defended itself:

A general strike in Berlin brought the city to a halt. The coup d'état failed within five days. However, the attempt set off left-wing unrest, especially in the Ruhr. Ebert had to turn to Seeckt to restore order in the Ruhr, using regular troops and some Free Corps members.

In Bavaria a right-wing movement led by Gustav von Kahr forced the elected minister-president to resign and installed an anti-republican government. The Republic did not fall in the Kapp Putsch, but its future was still uncertain.

Year of Crises – 1923

In 1923 several crises in the Weimar Republic raised the question once again whether democracy in Germany would continue.

The Occupation of the Ruhr and Hyperinflation

In December 1922 the Allied commission in charge of reparation payments reported the German government in default. This gave the French and Belgian governments the excuse to move troops into the Ruhr area and occupy it in January 1923. Chancellor Wilhelm Cuno (no party) called for **passive resistance**. The French government removed German workers who did not cooperate and hired its own workers instead. France also took over financial and industrial resources and punished strikers with *intimidation* and arrest. The German government had to support the Germans who were punished and their families. During the occupation 85% of German coal supplies fell into foreign hands, while unemployment spread throughout other parts of Germany. The economic burden of supporting the Ruhr population was too expensive.

Germany had financed the First World War by borrowing money, rather than raising taxes. When the war was lost, this debt had to be paid along with reparations. Also, the government had to pay pensions for war invalids, widows, and orphans. The Ruhr occupation and the German support of passive resistance added even more to the debt. German leaders printed more money to pay the government's debts. This led to the most dramatic case of inflation in an industrialized economy in modern times.

The crisis ended when the German government changed its course. On 13 August 1923 Gustav Stresemann (German People's Party, DVP) became Chancellor of a "Grand Coalition" (Social Democratic Party of Germany, SPD; Centre, Zentrum; German Democratic Party, DDP and DVP). German reparation payments to France and Belgium began again. The Ruhr occupation ended. Stresemann introduced a new currency, which stopped the cycle of **hyperinflation**. However, a parliamentary vote of no confidence brought down the government in November 1923. Stresemann kept a role in the government as Foreign Minister until he died in 1929.

M 2 "Twenty Billion Marks"
German banknote from 1 October 1923

Vocabulary

intimidation: forcing sb. to do sth. by making him afraid

Historical Terms

passive resistance: passiver Widerstand
hyperinflation: Hyperinflation

Food item	Aug 1922	Sep	Oct	Nov	Dec	Jan 1923	Feb	Mar	Apr	Jun	23 July	24 Sep	26 Nov
	in marks										in thousands of marks	in millions of marks	in billions of marks
rye bread (kg)	16.40	16.40	24.50	53.00	158.00	300.00	390.00	500.00	510.00	1,440.00	16.00	10.00	0.52
potatoes (kg)	12.00	10.80	11.40	13.90	17.05	27.00	74.00	127.00	114.00	385.00	9.00	2.20	0.14
whole milk (L)	15.00	23.00	50.00	91.00	202.00	241.00	432.00	587.00	765.00	1,103.00	6.10	6.80	0.30

Statistics, from: Nils Freytag (ed.), Quellen zur Innenpolitik der Weimarer Republik 1918–1933, Darmstadt: Wissenschaftliche Buchgesellschaft (WBG) 2010, p. 100.

M 3 Development of Food Prices in Munich 1922–23

Info

Further Political Disturbances in 1923

The Ruhr occupation and hyperinflation destabilized Germany. Even after currency reform, Germans feared that their income and savings could disappear without warning once more. They worried that democracy could be unstable and insecure – a problem which had long-term effects.

Also in 1923 separatists in the Rhineland and in the Palatinate tried to secede from Germany, while communist uprisings occurred in Saxony, Thuringia, and Hamburg. In Munich, a little-noted "Beer Hall Putsch" was led by an unknown right-wing extremist, Adolf Hitler. All these uprisings were put down quickly, but it was clear that the Republic had to solve serious problems.

The "Stab in the Back" Legend

M 4 Election Poster of the German National People's Party, 1924

Tasks

1. **Attacking the Republic: Political Murder**
   a) Make a report on either Walther Rathenau (M1) or Matthias Erzberger and how their murderers were punished.
   b) Assess the role of political murder in the Weimar Republic (text).

2. **The "Stab in the Back" Legend**
   a) Explain what the "stab in the back" was (text).
   b) Interpret the election poster (M4).
   c) Comment on the effect of the legend on public opinion in Germany during the Weimar Era.

Year of Crises – 1923

M 5 "Productive Confiscator"
A French soldier guards a coal shipment in the Ruhr Area, 1923. Colourized photograph

M 6 "No, You Can't Make Me"
Poster of the German government during the Ruhr occupation, 1923

M 7 The Year 1923 from Lord D'Abernon's diary

The English ambassador to Berlin wrote 1929 in his diary about German events in 1923:

"Berlin, December 31, 1923. – Thus ends a year of crisis. The dangers from without and within have been such as to threaten the whole future of Germany. A mere recital of the trials will give an indication of how grave the peril, how severe the storm. Though I have lived through the period and have taken an active part in some of the events, I have not always at the moment realised the fatefulness of the position. Looking back, one sees more clearly how near to the precipice this country has been.

In the twelve months from January till now, Germany has lived through the following dangers:

The Ruhr Invasion. The Communist Rising in Saxony and Thuringia. The Hitler Putsch in Bavaria.

An unprecedented financial crisis.

The Separatist Movement in the Rhineland.
Any one of these, if not overcome, would have brought about fundamental change, either in internal conditions or external relations. If successful, each and any would have wrecked all hope of general pacification. Political leaders in Germany are not accustomed to receive much public laudation; those who *have seen* the country *through* these perils deserve more credit than is likely to be their portion."

Edgar Vincent Viscount D'Abernon, An Ambassador of Peace: Lord D'Abernon's Diary, London: Hodder and Stoughton 1929–1931, Vol. II, p. 290.

M 8   Anecdotes of Hyperinflation

a) A woman who ran a Quaker relief centre, which offered help to the poor:

"[There was] the widow of a policeman who was left with four children. She had been awarded three months of her late husband's salary. The papers were sent on, as required, to Wiesbaden. There they were again checked, rubber-stamped and sent back to Frankfurt. By the time all this was done, and the money finally paid out to the widow, the amount would only have paid for three boxes of matches."

b) A worker in a transport firm in Berlin:

"I vividly remember pay-days at that time. I used to have to accompany the manager to the bank in an open six-seater Benz which we filled to the brim with bundles and bundles of million and milliard mark notes. We then drove back through the narrow streets quite unmolested. And when they got their wages, the workmen did not even bother to count the number of notes in each bundle."

c) The memories of a German writer:

"One fine day I dropped into a café to have coffee. As I went in I noticed the price was 5000 marks – just about what I had in my pocket. I sat down, read my paper, drank my coffee, and spent altogether about one hour in the café, and then asked for the bill. The waiter duly presented me with a bill for 8000 marks. 'Why 8000 marks?' I asked. The mark had dropped in the meantime, I was told. So I gave the waiter all the money I had, and he was generous enough to leave it at that."

d) A man who was a student at the time:

"You very often bought things you did not need. But with those things in hand you could start *to barter*. You went round and exchanged a pair of shoes for a shirt, or a pair of socks for a sack of potatoes. And this process was repeated until you eventually ended up with the things you actually wanted."

M 9   Children Playing with Worthless Banknotes
Photograph, 1923

e) A currency dealer:

"It was in many ways a cheerful time for the young. When I grew up we were taught to save money and not throw it away. But in the worst days of the inflation this principle was turned upside down. We knew that to hold on to money was the worst thing we could do. So this allowed us, with a good conscience, to spend whatever we had available."

Quotes taken from: Greg Lacey and Keith Shephard, Germany 1918–1945. A Study in Depth, London: John Murray 1997, pp. 24f.

Vocabulary

to see through: to help through
to barter: to exchange goods, not pay with money

Tasks

1. **Poster: "No, You Can't Make Me"**
   a) Interpret the poster's political message (M6).
   b) Show how passive resistance in the Ruhr raised the German government's debt (text).
3. **Year of Crises – 1923**
   a) Draw a mind map of the dangers to the Republic in 1923 (text).
   b) Assess the English ambassador's opinion of the German situation in 1923 (M7).
4. **Hyperinflation**
   a) Explain what led to hyperinflation (text).
   b) Show which groups profited from hyperinflation and which lost, giving reasons for your opinion (text, M2, M3, M8, M9).
   c) Assess the long-term effect of hyperinflation on the Weimar Republic.

Vocabulary

to win sb. over: to make sb. agree or see the truth about sth.

rapprochement: restoring harmony and friendly relations

M 1 Foreign Ministers Gustav Stresemann (Germany) and Aristide Briand (France) after signing the Treaty of Locarno in 1925

Historical Terms

fulfilment policies: Erfüllungspolitik

M 2 German Nationalist Election Poster
for 20 May 1928 parliamentary Elections.
Nationalists and extremists despised Stresemann's successes, especially what they termed his acceptance of French hegemony along the Rhine. He was forced to rely on the Social Democratic opposition to support his foreign policy.

The Stresemann Era: Stabilizing the Republic

After briefly serving as Chancellor from August until November 1923, Gustav Stresemann then became Foreign Minister. Nationalists and the right wing criticized him (as they had criticized the ministers before him) for pursuing **fulfilment policies**. Stresemann was a realist who saw the limits of German foreign policy after losing the war. Although he had been a monarchist, he changed his political ideas and became a reasoned supporter of the Republic ("Vernunftrepublikaner").

Foreign Policy

One of Stresemann's first goals was to reach an agreement on reparation payments. Charles Dawes, an American finance expert, and the Allied Reparations Commission suggested lowering payments – the Dawes Plan (1924). Stresemann accepted the plan.

Stresemann actively *won over* French Foreign Minister Aristide Briand as his partner in international affairs. Both men had the interests of their own countries in mind. Briand wanted German agreement to the borders of France. He did not think that punishing Germany encouraged her agreement. Stresemann wanted to end German diplomatic isolation after World War I. He tried to put relations with Germany's neighbours on friendly terms. The foreign ministers compromised on problems such as borders and reparations to achieve their goals. As they dealt with one another, they became friends. The first result of this personal friendship was the Treaty of Locarno in 1925. At Locarno representatives of France, Britain, Belgium, Italy, and Germany agreed to a European security pact and recognized the western German borders as permanent. That meant that Alsace-Lorraine and Eupen-Malmedy would remain under French and Belgian rule. This was the first step after 1918 to bring Germany back into the European concert of powers. Stresemann continued these efforts and saw Germany become a full member of the League of Nations in 1926. He and Briand were awarded the Nobel Peace Prize in the same year. However, nationalists in both countries criticized the two men for their cooperation.

Stresemann's course of German *rapprochement* continued in the 1928 Kellogg-Briand Pact, which banned war as a political instrument. Problems with the Dawes Plan arose by 1928 and an international commission once again set up a plan for payment – the Young Plan (1929). It suggested payments for 59 years (until 1988), when remaining reparations would be renegotiated. In return, the military occupation of the Rhineland was to end in 1930. Nationalists led by the press tsar Alfred Hugenberg (German National People's Party, DNVP) and extremists, especially Adolf Hitler (National Socialist German Workers' Party, NSDAP), organized a plebiscite against the Young Plan, which the cabinet had accepted. Stresemann died on 3 October 1929, still working to assure public support for it. The plebiscite against the Young Plan failed in December 1929.

End of the Stresemann Era

Stresemann's death and the Wall Street crash of October 1929, which led to the Great Depression, ended the years of political and economic stability in Germany. The Republic had lost its strongest political guardian. Later the Stresemann years seemed to be the most successful years of the Republic.

Info

The US Moratorium on Reparations

Although the Young Plan had won public support, the question of reparations became less important as the Great Depression arrived in Europe. When Americans recalled their loans from Germany, the German government could not pay even the reduced reparations set up by the Young Plan. In 1931 U.S. President Herbert Hoover declared a one-year moratorium on reparation payments. That led the French and British governments to refuse payment on their American war loans. In 1933 Chancellor Adolf Hitler refused to pay reparations any further.

M 3 "You will have hard labour for three generations!"
Political poster against the referendum on the Young Plan, 1929

Tasks

1. **The Stresemann Era: Stabilizing the Republic**
   a) List three ways Stresemann stabilized German foreign relations (text).
   b) Discuss your list with your classmates.
2. **Poster "Locarno?"**
   a) Interpret the poster (M2).
   b) Explain why Stresemann's policies were unpopular with German nationalists.
3. **The Young Plan**
   a) Describe the Young Plan briefly and the controversy it caused in Germany (text, M3).
   b) Analyse the effect of the Young Plan referendum on the German government in 1929.
4. **The Friendship Between Briand and Stresemann**
   a) Assess the friendship between Briand and Stresemann in making foreign policy for their countries (text).
   b) Discuss how important personal friendships can be in diplomatic affairs.

The Golden Twenties

After World War I there was a decade of modernization and economic growth. Moral standards became less strict. Many young people had served in the military. Many had lost friends and relatives in the war. They often decided that life was too short and simply tried to enjoy it. In North America these years were known as the "Roaring Twenties". By the mid-1920s Europe was also affected. Here the years were called the "Golden Twenties", or in France the "années folles" – the "Crazy Years". Women had new roles in society, and there were new trends in art, architecture, culture, music and fashion.

The Flapper

Women got the right to vote in many countries around 1918. Along with having political rights, young women became so independent in economic, social and sexual matters that they shocked their parents. A symbol of the age was the "flapper" – a young woman with *bobbed* hair, wearing a loose-fitting dress, high heels, and make-up, dancing the Charleston. More and more women in cities worked in offices for better pay, so companies advertised new household machines to free them from housework.

Film and Literature

New mass media, such as radio and cinema, became cheaper and popular. In Germany films showed new ideas to a large audience. Robert Wiene used *Expressionism* to emphasize horror in "The Cabinet of Dr. Caligari", a classic German film of the era. "The Blue Angel" (1930) starred Emil Jannings and Marlene Dietrich in a film based on Heinrich Mann's novel "Professor Unrat". In it boring German middle-class values were criticized. The thriller "M" (1931) was directed by Fritz Lang and starred Peter Lorre and Gustaf Gründgens. Its plot criticized capital punishment when *vigilantes* punish a child murderer. German films were creative in the twenties. They were also a successful business – as early as 1925 over two million tickets to cinemas were sold.

Literature blossomed during the twenties. The German author Kurt Tucholsky satirized people and events in many short texts, which can be read quickly in the classroom today. Erich Maria Remarque criticized military service and the war effort in "All Quiet on the Western Front" ("Im Westen nichts Neues", 1929), which shocked conservatives. Alfred Döblin, author of "Berlin Alexanderplatz" (1929), experimented with Expressionist techniques in his socially critical novel. Other authors tried to stay away from political commentary: Thomas Mann, the German Nobel prize winner in literature in 1929, declared himself an "unpolitical" man in 1918. His brother Heinrich said that it was impossible for an author to avoid politics in his writings. Thomas Mann later changed his opinion, but by that time the Weimar Republic was failing.

Music

New forms of music were fashionable. Jazz became popular, and the film "The Jazz Singer", starring Al Jolson, was a hit in Germany. Singing groups such as "the Comedian Harmonists" were very successful. Variety shows, cabarets and nightclubs put on various types of musical entertainment, and young people especially enjoyed dancing.

M 1 A "Charleston" Dress
Edith Collin and Heinz Neumann dance the Charleston. They were considered Germany's best ballroom dancers at the time. Photograph, 1926

M 2 "The Cabinet of Dr. Caligari"
Film poster, 1919

Art and Architecture

Literature, theatre, painting, design, music and architecture used mixed approaches. In the Imperial era public architecture had concentrated on a Germanic "historic" style (whether or not the models for the buildings were actually historical). But in the twenties architects developed new styles. At first Expressionism dominated, but later Art Deco, the "New Objectivity", and the Bauhaus became more popular. Styles ranging from emotional engagement to extreme functionalism were seen.

In their paintings Käthe Kollwitz, George Grosz and Otto Dix criticized war and the upper social classes. They made art lovers who were used to more traditional approaches uncomfortable.

Technology and Science

Besides the changes in mass media, the most surprising ones were in transport. The automobile, although still expensive in Germany, was a luxury item many people wanted. Airplanes and air travel improved. In 1927 US pilot Charles Lindbergh even managed to cross the Atlantic alone. A year earlier the German engineer Hugo Junkers opened a new airline – the "Luft-Hansa AG".

Germans won Nobel prizes in the fields of relativity (Albert Einstein, physics, 1922), in the artificial production of chemical compounds (Carl Bosch, chemistry, 1931) and in quantum physics (Werner Heisenberg, physics, 1932), among others. German scientists in the Weimar Republic were a source of national pride.

The End of the Golden Twenties

On the whole the Golden Twenties were characterized by growing consumption, income and mass entertainment, much like our own times. While many young people criticized the old-fashioned ways of their elders in Germany, they often forgot that the unusual blossoming in the 1920s had its origins in the avant-garde of the Imperial era. The cosmopolitan atmosphere, particularly in Berlin, attracted artists and intellectuals who had had low social standing in Imperial circles, such as Jews, foreigners and homosexuals. However, when the Great Depression appeared, the Golden Twenties ended almost as abruptly as they had begun. When the National Socialists came to power, many artists and thinkers could no longer work in Germany and were forced to leave the country – either for religious or intellectual reasons or both.

Vocabulary

to bob: (here) to cut short
Expressionism: early 20th century artistic movement in which symbols or styles are distorted to show inner experience
vigilante: sb. who takes the law into his own hands

M 3 An Early Luft-Hansa Flight
Photograph, 1930

M 4 The Bauhaus
Designed by Walter Gropius in 1925 as an academy of art, the building is an example of functionality in architecture. Photograph, Dessau, about 1990

The Golden Twenties

M 5　Film Posters
"Metropolis" from 1926 (left) and "The Blue Angel" from 1920 (right)

Tasks

1. **The Golden Twenties and The Flapper**
   a) Point out what made the 1920s "golden" (text).
   b) Look at the photograph of the Charleston dress (M1). Explain its function.
   c) Compare and contrast the function of the Charleston dress with your own clothing.

2. **Film (as project work)**
   a) Work in groups on the German films mentioned in this unit:
   "The Cabinet of Dr. Caligari"
   "The Blue Angel"
   "M"
   "Metropolis"
   b) Describe the film you have chosen to the rest of your class.
   c) Compare and contrast the films.
   d) Decide which film you think is the best, giving reasons for your opinion.

3. **Literature**
   a) List the authors and books from the 1920s which you have read in school. Are any of the books (or authors) given in the text among them?
   b) Find a satire by Kurt Tucholsky to read and discuss in class.

4. **Music**
   a) Look up the 1927 American film „The Jazz Singer" on the Internet. Find out why its white star, Al Jolson, was made to look like a black singer in the film.
   b) Explain why jazz and singing groups like "the Comedian Harmonists" became popular in Germany in the 1920s (text).

M 6 Potsdamer Platz in the 1920s

M 7 Berlin: Germany's Cultural Mecca

The American historian Peter Gay on Berlin's status:

"[In 1924] Bertolt Brecht, already a well-known playwright, [...] moved from Munich to Berlin. The move is significant because it symbolizes the growing power of Berlin in the golden mid-twenties. As Germany's largest city, as the capital of Prussia and the Empire, Berlin had been the only possible choice for capital of the Republic. And Berlin came to engross not merely government offices and party headquarters, but the leaders of culture, at the expense of the provinces. Other major cities like Munich, Frankfurt, or Hamburg struggled to keep excellence in their universities, took pride in special institutes, cultivated continued high quality in their theatres and liveliness in their Bohemian quarters. But Berlin was a magnet. After years of resistance, Heinrich Mann gave way and moved there. 'Centralization,' he said in humorous resignation, 'is inevitable.' The city drew strength from its illustrious immigrants, and in turn gave strength to them. '[Max] Beckmann is unthinkable without Berlin,' one of his admirers noted in 1913, while, in 1924, another admirer turned the observation around: 'Beckmann [...] is the new Berlin.' The old Berlin had been impressive, the new Berlin was irresistible. To go to Berlin was the aspiration of the composer, the journalist, the actor; with its superb orchestras, its hundred and twenty newspapers, its forty theatres, Berlin was the place for the ambitious, the energetic, the talented. Wherever they started, it was in Berlin that they became, and Berlin that made them, famous [...]"

Peter Gay, Weimar Culture, New York: Harper & Row 1968, pp. 127f.

Tasks

1. **Art and Architecture**
   a) Point out what was modern about the building in M4.
   b) Look up one of these art works on the Internet and explain why it was controversial:
      - Käthe Kollwitz, "The Survivors" (1923) or "Never Again War" (1924)
      - George Grosz, "The Pillars of Society" (1926)
      - Otto Dix, "Metropolis" (1928)
2. **Technology and Science**
   a) Assess the difference the automobile and airplane made in people's lives (text).
   b) Look up the discoveries made by Albert Einstein, Carl Bosch, or Werner Heisenberg on the Internet (text) and report back to your class on them.
3. **Berlin in the Twenties**
   a) Explain why Berlin became a magnet (M7).
   b) Assess the role of Berlin in the Golden Twenties (M6, M7).
4. **After the Golden Twenties Ended**
   a) Find out about one person mentioned in the text and what happened to him or her after 1933: Emil Jannings, Marlene Dietrich, Fritz Lang, Peter Lorre, Gustaf Gründgens, Bertolt Brecht, Kurt Tucholsky, Erich Maria Remarque, Alfred Döblin, Thomas Mann, Heinrich Mann, Käthe Kollwitz, Geroge Grosz, Otto Dix, Albert Einstein, Carl Bosch, Werner Heisenberg.
   b) Report back to your class.

The Great Depression: A Comparative Approach

The Great Depression affected both the USA and Germany deeply. Solving the problems caused by the economic difficulties challenged both countries.

The Situation in the United States

The collapse of the *stock* market in the USA in 1929 was caused by over-production of consumer goods. Too many automobiles, radios and electric appliances were made and could not be sold. Too many workers did not earn enough to buy such goods, while people who earned more money had already bought them. In the summer of 1929 many investors decided to buy stock in a booming market. Later analysts called this boom a **speculative bubble**.

Some people borrowed money to speculate in stocks. In late October there was a panic on Wall Street. Many people lost their savings and some lost everything. On the worst day (29 October) some stocks lost up to 90% of their earlier value. As one eyewitness reported, traders on the New York Stock Exchange "hollered and screamed, they clawed at one another's collars. It was like a bunch of crazy men. Every once in a while, when Radio or Steel or Auburn would [go down], you'd see some poor devil collapse and fall to the floor."

Between 1929 and 1932 American industrial production and the gross national product were cut in half. Drought and lack of soil conservation made a "Dust Bowl" in the Middle West from the Canadian border to Texas. Many farmers gave up their homes and tried to find work somewhere else, usually farther west. When families moved on, parents and children took up unskilled jobs such as field workers. These children could no longer attend school. Although unemployment reached its highest level in 1933, the Great Depression lasted in the USA until World War II began.

In 1932 President Herbert Hoover stood for election against Franklin D. Roosevelt. Many voters blamed Hoover for not acting quickly at the beginning of the Great Depression. Roosevelt, the Governor of New York, had introduced unemployment insurance there and promised Americans a "New Deal". He won 57% of the votes. A large majority of Democrats also won seats in both houses of the US Congress. As President, Roosevelt set up public programs to give people jobs. One of the first was the Tennessee Valley Authority, which built dams to provide electricity, prevent flooding and modernize the rural area. National programmes to conserve the soil began; photographers and writers were paid to travel the country and describe regional problems to a wide audience. Roosevelt told the public about his plans in regular radio programmes – which he called Fireside Chats. He was a very popular politician and the only person elected to the presidency four times.

The Situation in Germany

Unemployment increased after the 1929 stock market crash. This led to deficits in the budget, because unemployed workers had to be supported – they no longer paid taxes, but instead cost the state money. Chancellor Brüning and his cabinet set a strict *austerity course*: They reduced expenses wherever possible to cut costs. Many Germans still worried about the hyperinflation from the early years of the republic. Then the government had overspent without financial backing. That experiment could not be repeated. Instead, the salaries of civil servants were cut

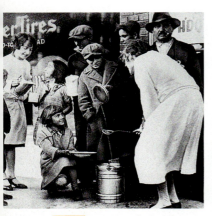

M 1 A Soup Kitchen in Chicago, 1929

These children of unemployed workers are given soup.

Vocabulary

stock: shares in a corporation or company

austerity course: economic policy to reduce government spending

M 2 Franklin D. Roosevelt (1882–1945)

Photograph, about 1938

by 25% and social spending was cut by 14%, but taxes and payments for social security increased. These measures set up a vicious circle: Workers with less income could no longer buy goods, so industrial production fell. That caused more workers to lose their jobs. They then paid fewer taxes, so social security costs rose. That made the authorities lower wages and salaries, which meant they had to raise taxes and social security payments, and so on.

By July 1931 a wave of bankruptcies caused German banks to fail. Unemployment increased from 2.6 million in February 1930 to 4.9 million in January 1931. Unemployment reached its highest point at 5.6 million in 1932. German trade unions and Social Democrats demanded public programmes to create jobs for the unemployed, but Brüning refused to change his austerity measures. He could see bitter social and political troubles coming up, but saw no alternative. Thus, an economic problem became a political crisis. People who still hoped for a democratic and parliamentary solution lost faith in the constitutional system entirely. More and more voters sought a new leadership with new ideas, thus paving the way for the Nazis.

M 3 Looking for Work
Photograph, 1930

Historical Terms

speculative bubble:
Spekulationsblase

M 4 Unemployed Seeking Work at the Hanover Employment Office, 1930
Note the graffiti urging voters to "Elect Hitler" and the swastikas (symbols of the Nazi Party) on the shed walls in the background of the photograph. Photographed by Walter Ballhause, who was unemployed himself at the time of this picture.

The Great Depression: A Comparative Approach

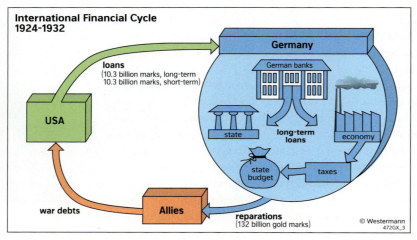

M 5 Diagram of the International Financial Cycle

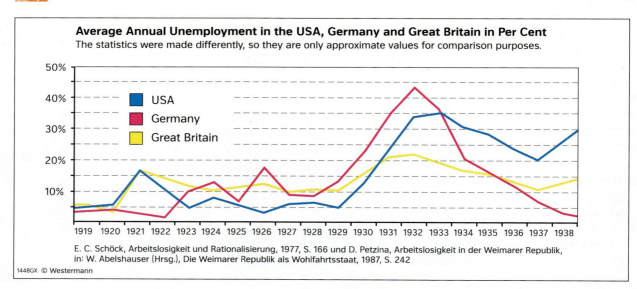

Tasks

1. **The Great Depression in the USA**
   a) List President Roosevelt's efforts to help Americans overcome the depression (text).
   b) Assess Roosevelt's success or failure in dealing with the Great Depression in the USA.
2. **The Great Depression in Germany**
   a) List Chancellor Brüning's efforts to help Germans overcome the depression (text).
   b) Assess Brüning's success or failure in dealing with the Great Depression in Germany.
3. **Dealing with Photographs**
   a) Point out what the photographs show briefly (M1, M3, M4).
   b) Analyse the message of the photographs.
4. **Diagram on International Finance**
   a) Use the diagram to show how international finance from 1924–32 was inter-related (M5).
   b) Explain what happens if one of the arrows in the diagram is interrupted.
5. **Average Annual Unemployment Diagram**
   a) Use the diagram to analyse unemployment in the USA and Germany from 1929 to 1938 (M6).

M 7 An American Report

Richard Waskin, a child in Detroit, remembers:

"Mostly I remember if it hadn't been for my mother who was an excellent *seamstress*, and she seemed to find jobs here and there with the department stores, I don't know how we would have made it, because my father was a common laborer, a factory worker, and there just wasn't [sic] any jobs at that time.
Sometimes during the winter […] when the snow fell in Detroit they called for people that they wanted to shovel the snow, and of course everybody didn't get hired – you just had to go out there and the foreman or whoever would be throwing the shovel and if you happened to catch it you're hired. And so my father would go out there and on occasion he would be hired and earn a couple of dollars or so for the day's work there. Otherwise it was kind of catch or catch can there […].
But another thing as a child that I remember was that you stood in the welfare line somewhere on Michigan Avenue – I don't remember just exactly where – and they were passing out sweaters for children and we were fortunate enough to get me a grey sweater, and I can remember how proud I was of having that sweater and how warm I felt with that thing on.
Shoes, of course, were a problem and many times I remember I wore out the soles down to the pavement, so to speak, and you had to put cardboard in there. But then my father he got hold of some shoe forms – metal ones – and he would buy leather. He would cut out the sole – with nails and a hammer on these shoe forms – he would put new leather on my shoes and probably on my brothers' also […]."

https://view.officeapps.live.com/op/view.aspx?src=https%3A%2F%2Fbcareyachs93012.weebly.com%2Fuploads%2F2%2F3%2F0%2F7%2F23072012%2Fgreat_depression__reminisscenes.doc [August 15, 2018].

Vocabulary

seamstress: woman who sews clothes

M 8 A German Report

Journalist Heinrich Hauser remembers:

"An almost unbroken chain of homeless men extends the whole length of the great Hamburg-Berlin highway. It is the same scene for the entire two hundred miles, and all the highways in Germany over which I travelled this year. They walked separately or in small groups with their eyes on the ground. And they had the queer, stumbling gait of barefoot people, for their shoes were slung over their shoulders. Some of them were guild members – carpenters with broad felt hats, milkmen with striped red shirts, and bricklayers with tall black hats – but they were in a minority. Far more numerous were those to whom one could assign no special profession or craft – unskilled young people for the most part who had been unable to find a place for themselves in any city or town in Germany, and who had never had a job and never expected to have one.

There was something else that had never been seen before – whole families who had piled all their goods into baby carriages and wheelbarrows that they were pulsing along as they plodded forward in dumb despair. It was a whole nation on the march.

I saw them – and this was the strongest impression that the year 1932 left with me – I saw them, gathered into groups of fifty or a hundred men, attacking fields of potatoes. I saw them digging up the potatoes and throwing them into sacks while the farmer who owned the field watched them in despair and the local policeman looked on gloomily from the distance. I saw them staggering towards the lights of the city as night fell, with their sacks on their backs. What did it remind me of? Of the war, of the worst period of starvation in 1917 and 1918, but even then people paid for the potatoes."

Transl. quoted from: Greg Lacey and Keith Shephard, Germany 1918–45. A Study in Depth, London: John Murray 1997, p. 47.

Tasks

1. **Eyewitness Reports on Life in the Great Depression in the USA and Germany**
   Work together as partners or in small groups.
   a) Read M9 or M10.
   b) Assess the problems with unemployment in Germany or the USA (M9 or M10).
   c) Comment on the effects of the Great Depression in the USA and in Germany.

The End of the Republic 1930–33

The Weimar Republic collapsed under the weight of many problems. The Great Depression increased economic problems; government coalitions became more and more instable; political extremists grew stronger.

The Failure of Parliamentary Government

In 1928 a second Grand Coalition (SPD, Centre, DVP, DDP, and BVP) took office under Chancellor Hermann Müller (SPD). The coalition managed foreign policy successfully. Its agreement to the Young Plan let the Allied occupation of the Rhineland end early in 1930 instead of 1934. The coalition won the referendum on the Young Plan in spite of nationalist and Nazi opposition. Domestic problems brought down the government. The cabinet could not agree on the question of unemployment insurance. Both employers and employees paid for the insurance, but after October 1929 the government could not pay for the growing numbers of unemployed workers. The parties did not agree on how to solve the problem: Social Democrats suggested raising insurance premiums from 3.5% to 4.0%, but the German People's Party wanted to reduce benefits. In March 1930 Heinrich Brüning (Centre) proposed a compromise solution, but Social Democrats could not agree. Instead the cabinet resigned. It was the government with a parliamentary majority which served for the longest continuous period of time in the Weimar Republic (636 days).

Government by Decree

President Hindenburg appointed Brüning Chancellor, telling him that he could rule by decree instead of having to depend on a parliamentary majority. However, the lack of parliamentary support meant that the influence of the President on the government increased. The Weimar Constitution gave the President the power to dissolve the Reichstag and call new elections (Article 25), appoint the chancellor (Article 53), and issue emergency decrees (Article 48). In a government which ruled by decree, the Reichstag no longer had to pass the laws. These constitutional features were originally made to be used only in crisis situations. However, after 1930 rule by decree became permanent. The move to consolidate power in the office of the President and outside of parliament led to the end of democracy.

Chancellor Brüning

Brüning's austerity measures were unpopular, but he could stay in office by presidential decree. When in 1930 Social Democrats, German Nationalists and National Socialists voted to set aside a presidential decree according to Article 48 of the constitution, Hindenburg dissolved the Reichstag and called new elections. These ended in political disaster: Hitler's National Socialists won 107 seats, far more than the 12 mandates the party had before. The German Nationalists won 41 seats and the Communists 76, so the extremists in the Reichstag were much stronger.

After the 1930 elections, Hindenburg reappointed Brüning Chancellor. The Social Democrats were caught: Either the party tolerated rule by presidential decree or it risked strengthening the extremist parties. Unemployment continued to grow, the financial crisis worsened. Government by decree became normal. In 1930 there were only five presidential decrees, but in 1932 there were sixty-six. At

---

Historical Terms

brownshirts:
Sturmabteilung, SA

M 1 "These are the enemies of democracy. Away with them!"
Social Democratic Election Poster, 1930

the same time, the Reichstag stopped passing laws. Communists and National Socialists called the Reichstag a "chatterbox".

Brüning's dismissal came in 1932, after Hindenburg stood for re-election as President. His major opponents were Adolf Hitler (National Socialist) and Ernst Thälmann (Communist). Because Hindenburg did not win an absolute majority, a second vote was necessary. Brüning worked to unite the democratic parties, including the Social Democrats, behind Hindenburg as the lesser evil. The election campaign, as in all elections from 1930 on, saw a return of violence in the streets like in the early years of the republic – Nazis and Communists fought each other in brutal street battles. As a result, Brüning's Minister of the Interior and of the Army, Wilhelm Groener, forbade the Nazi paramilitary organization, the **brownshirts**, on 13 April 1932. Hindenburg was angry about having to thank the Social Democrats for his victory and blamed Brüning for it.

The final blow came when Hindenburg had a personal conflict of interest. Brüning and his cabinet wanted to support many unemployed workers by first cancelling financial support for large unprofitable estates in eastern Germany and then settling workers on them. Hindenburg, who was an estate owner himself, did not agree with the idea of large landowners losing their property to unemployed workers. He refused to sign the emergency decree Brüning suggested and dismissed him on 30 May 1932.

Chancellors von Papen and von Schleicher

After appointing Chancellor Franz von Papen, Hindenburg disbanded the Reichstag and called for new elections on 31 July 1932. Papen set aside the edict forbidding the paramilitary Nazi brownshirts in June. The violence that came about was similar to the violence in a civil war – 300 people were killed and 1200 injured in street fighting. In the "Bloody Sunday" street battle in Altona alone (17 July 1932) eighteen people were killed and more than sixty injured. Papen used the incident as an excuse to dismiss the Prussian government by decree, claiming to prevent more violence. The decree in effect overthrew the Social Democratic Prussian government. The SPD considered calling for a general strike. But when millions were unemployed, a general strike was useless. It did not take place.

M 2 Heinrich Brüning
Chancellor from 30 March 1930 to 30 May 1932 (789 days)

M 3 Franz von Papen
Chancellor from 1 June to 17 November 1932 (170 days)

M 4 Kurt von Schleicher
Chancellor from 3 December 1932 to 28 January 1933 (57 days)

The elections did not bring a new parliamentary majority. The National Socialists won the most mandates – 230 seats – and became the largest faction in the Reichstag. Together with the Communists, the Nazis could block any measure proposed by the government. Papen's stated goal to "tame" the Nazis also failed. When offered a role in the Papen government, Hitler refused. He demanded to become Chancellor himself – a step neither Papen nor Hindenburg was willing to take.

Parliament met for the first time on 12 September in a stormy session, which ended with the Reichstag being dissolved. New elections were set for 6 November, but the results disappointed the National Socialists. Instead of the 37.4% from the July elections, the party only won 33.1% – 196 seats. This led to a crisis within the party; many members worried that Hitler had demanded too much. General Kurt von Schleicher convinced Hindenburg to appoint him in place of Papen (3 December). Schleicher tried to divide the Nazi leadership and win support from the trade unions, but he, too, failed. He resigned as Chancellor on 28 January 1933. When Papen suggested that Hitler replace Schleicher, Hindenburg hesitated. However, on 30 January 1933 he appointed Hitler Chancellor. That ended the Weimar Republic.

M 5 **"German Magic Works, Ltd."**

"There is no need to worry as long as chancellors are produced non-stop!"

Cartoon by Karl Arnold in "Simplicissimus", February 1933

The End of the Republic

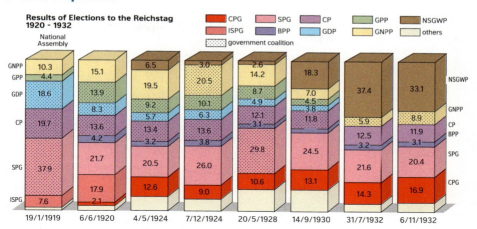

M 6 Results of Elections to the Reichstag 1920 - 1932

(CPG) **Communist Party of Germany:** Kommunistische Partei Deutschlands, KPD
(ISPG) **Independent Social Democratic Party of Germany:** Unabhängige Sozialdemokratische Partei Deutschlands, USPD
(SPG) **Social Democratic Party of Germany:** Sozialdemokratische Partei Deutschlands, SPD
(CP) **Centre Party:** Deutsche Zentrumspartei, Z
(BPP) **Bavarians People's Party:** Bayrische Volkspartei, BVP
(GDP) **German Democratic Party:** Deutsche Demokratische Partei, DDP
(GPP) **German People's Party:** Deutsche Volkspartei, DVP
(GNPP) **German National People's Party:** Deutschnationale Volkspartei, DNVP
(NSGWP) **National Socialist German Workers' Party:** Nationalsozialistische Deutsche Arbeiterpartei, NSDAP

M 7 "Our Last Hope: Hitler"
National Socialist Election Poster, 1932

M 8 "Back to Brüning. Against Fratricide – for Order and Renewal, Work and Bread"
Centre Election Poster, 1932

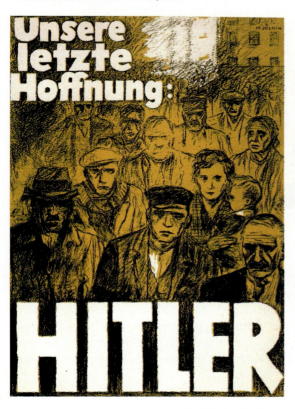

The End of the Republic

M 9 "They carry the firm's letters, but who carries its spirit?"
"Republik" – Caricature by Th. Th. Heine in "Simplicissimus", 1927

M 10 "The Tragic Death of German Democracy"

British historian William Carr places the collapse of the Weimar Republic in a broader context (1991):

"The collapse of the Weimar republic was a complex historical phenomenon into which many separate strands were interwoven; the shock of the great depression, the paralysing effects of unemployment on parties of the left, the *tenuous* roots of parliamentary democracy, the failure of the parties to grapple effectively with Germany's problems or even to coalesce against the Nazis, the power and drive of Hitler's movement, the antipathy of the middle class for democratic institutions, the vulnerability of the old president and the intrigues of his advisers and of pressure groups; all these factors, indigenous to the German situation, played a part in this tragedy. This does not exhaust the problem by any means. No country lives in a vacuum. [… In] the 1930s, the crisis of German democracy was not peculiar to that country, but a reflection of a more general crisis of democracy throughout the western world. Already in the second half of the 1920s, during a period of relative prosperity, there were ominous signs of impending crisis when parliamentary democracy was superseded by dictatorship in Italy, Spain, Portugal and Yugoslavia. The drift from democracy was greatly accentuated by the depression. Because parliamentary institutions seemed incapable of dealing boldly with mass unemployment, critics on right and left called into question the basic liberal concepts of freedom and the rule of law even in the well-established democratic countries. […] In short, the tragic death of German democracy can be properly understood only as part of a wider canvas."

William Carr, A History of Germany 1815–1990, London: Bloomsbury Academic/Hodder Arnold Publication 1991, p. 312.

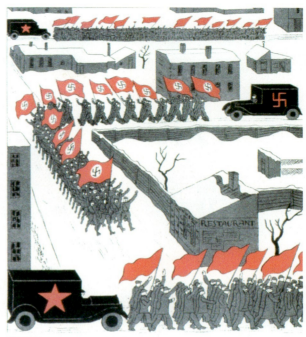

M 11 Emergency Decree

"Learning from recent events each demonstrating group must provide its own *hearse*." Erich Schilling, caricature from "Simplizissimus", 1932

Vocabulary

tenuous: weak

hearse: car carrying a coffin

Tasks

1. **The Failure of Parliamentary Government**
   a) Outline the successes and failures of the Grand Coalition of Chancellor Hermann Müller (text).
   b) Historians have criticized the Müller cabinet for resigning in March 1930. Agree or disagree, explaining the reasons for your opinion.

2. **Government by Decree**
   a) Explain what "government by decree" means (text).
   b) Comment on the decision to rule by decree.

3. **Political Posters**
   a) Discuss which poster (M1, M7, M8) you find the most effective, giving reasons for your opinion.

4. **Chancellors Brüning, Papen and Schleicher**
   a) Describe the photographs briefly (M2, M3, M4).
   b) Comment on the political stability of the republic from the men's times in office.

5. **Bar Chart on Elections 1919 – 1932**
   a) Make a list of government coalitions and their size of the vote from 1919 to 1932 (M6).
   b) Analyse the difficulty in finding parliamentary majorities from 1920 to 1932.

6. **"German Magic Works, Ltd." or "Emergency Decree"**
   a) Interpret the artist's message (M5 or M11).

7. **British Historian Carr on the End of the Weimar Republic**
   a) Point out the reasons Carr gives for the fall of the republic (M10).
   b) Comment on Carr's view, giving your own opinion.

8. **"Republic" – a caricature**
   a) Interpret the caricature (M9).

SUMMARY The Weimar Republic

1914 — First World War
1918 — Revolution begins/William II abdicates; Scheidemann proclaims the German republic
1922 — Hyperinflation

The Weimar Republic – the historical map

| 1926 | 1928 | 1930 | 1932 | 1934 |

The Golden Twenties

Wall Street Crash

Hitler appointed Chancellor

Summary

Confusion and panic characterized the start of the Weimar Republic. With civil war threatening, the military tried to blame the lost war on the civilian government. Chancellor von Baden named Friedrich Ebert (SPD) Chancellor. Ebert formed a cabinet with the leftist factions in the Reichstag. A parliamentary delegation sent to France worked out an armistice with the Allies. Free Corps members put down a Spartacist revolt and murdered its leaders Luxemburg and Liebknecht before elections to a National Assembly were held.

The Treaty of Versailles disappointed many Germans. It demanded high reparations, loss of German territory, demilitarization of the Rhineland, loss of all colonies, and limited the size of the army. The German government had to accept the terms they were given.

The Weimar Constitution was written to include many who had been excluded earlier. Plebiscites, referenda, initiatives, and proportional representation gave citizens tools to affect policy directly. The president had a powerful position. The chancellor determined the direction of policy; the Reichstag passed the laws. The weaknesses of the constitution became clear later.

In its early years, political murders, right-wing lies, and attempts to overthrow the government destabilized the republic. The occupation of the Ruhr led to hyperinflation, which wiped out savings and people's trust in government. But by 1924 the political situation stabilized.

Gustav Stresemann ended hyperinflation and improved German foreign relations, especially with France. International financial plans brought relief in reparations. The Treaty of Locarno (1925) provided for European security and better relations with Germany's neighbours. In 1926 Germany joined the League of Nations. Stresemann and Aristide Briand of France were given the Nobel Peace Prize together.

Creativity in fine arts, letters, and sciences blossomed in the Golden Twenties. This flowering ended with the Great Depression.

The last government coalition with a parliamentary majority under Chancellor Müller (SPD) resigned in 1930. The following chancellors, Brüning (C), von Papen, and von Schleicher, all ruled by presidential decree. Voters reacted by electing more extremists to the Reichstag. On 30 January 1933 Hindenburg appointed Adolf Hitler Chancellor. It was a tragic ending to the Weimar Republic. The greater tragedy followed.

DATES

9 November 1918: William II abdicates
30 January 1933: Hitler appointed Chancellor

HISTORICAL TERMS

Bolshevik
Treaty of Brest-Litovsk
council of workers and soldiers
soviet
armistice
Council of People's Representatives
All-German Assembly of Councils
Spartacist Uprising
Free Corps
League of Nations
proportional representation
emergency powers
direction of policy
referendum
initiative
stab in the back legend
passive resistance
hyperinflation
fulfilment policies
speculative bubble
brownshirts

PERSONS

Friedrich Ebert
Philipp Scheidemann
Rosa Luxemburg
Karl Liebknecht
Gustav Stresemann

HISTORY WORKSHOP

Historic and Historical Maps

The Third Reich

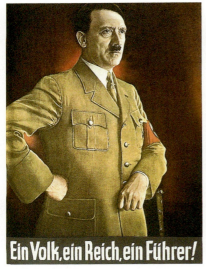

M 1 "One People, one Reich, one Führer!" Poster

M 2 Selection at the Ramp of Auschwitz, 1944

M 3 Standard-bearers of the Hitler Youth, 1936

M 4 "The Eternal Jew" Propaganda Poster, 1937

M 5 Coventry after the Bombardment

M 6 Hans and Sophie Scholl

02

THE THIRD REICH
1933 – 1945

The twelve years of Nazi dictatorship in Germany were an crucial period in the history of the 20th century and changed its course. The Nazis still have a hold on us – in daily news stories, in politics, in books and movies, even in the streets of Europe.

Today's Germany and Europe cannot be understood without knowledge of Adolf Hitler's Germany, the totalitarian state that plunged the world into another disastrous war and whose racist ideology climaxed in the genocide of the European Jews, the Holocaust. More than 50 million people were killed, millions of refugees had to leave their homes and many regions of Europe were completely destroyed.

The founding of the United Nations, the division of Germany and a new conflict, the Cold War, between the capitalist West and the communist East shaped the world after 1945. Until today the responsibility for the Second World War and the national sentiment of guilt have shaped the role of German politicians and citizens in Europe.

This chapter deals with many questions such as:
- What were the Nazis' beliefs and aims?
- How could Hitler set up a dictatorship?
- Why was the Nazi regime so popular among many Germans?
- How was unemployment reduced?
- What kind of opposition was there?
- What was life like in Nazi Germany?
- How did World War II break out?
- What led to German defeat?
- What did war mean to the peoples in Europe?
- How did the Nazis turn their racist ideology into mass murder?

Vocabulary

customs: the taxes that must be paid to the government when goods are brought in from other countries

application: a formal request for a job

anti-Semitic: showing hatred of Jews, unfair treatment of Jews

to conscript: to make sb. join the armed forces

shackles: two metal rings joined together by a chain and placed around a prisoner's wrists or ankles

to emerge: to appear or become known

scheme: a plan or system for doing or organizing sth.

social-Darwinist: applying Charles Darwin's theory of the "survival of the fittest" to mankind

Adolf Hitler and the Origins of Nazi Ideology

Between 1933 and 1945 Adolf Hitler took complete control of Germany and ruled the country as a dictator. Who was this man to dominate German politics and to bring about final disaster?

Early Life

Adolf Hitler was born on 20 April 1889, as the son of a *customs* official in the small Austrian town of Braunau. His parents died early and he moved to Vienna to study at the Academy of Fine Arts, but his *application* was rejected. It was in Vienna that Hitler came into contact with racist and *anti-Semitic* ideas. He was also impressed by the concept of Pan-Germanism, which wanted all Germans to live in one state. He made his living by selling paintings and postcards and when he ran out of money he was forced to live in a hostel for the homeless. In 1913 Hitler moved to Munich in Germany to avoid being *conscripted* into the Austrian Army.

When the First World War broke out Hitler joined the German army and fought at the western front. He was promoted to corporal and received the Iron Cross for bravery. In October 1918, Hitler was blinded in a British gas attack. He was sent to a military hospital and gradually recovered his sight. When Germany surrendered Hitler fell into a deep depression. In his book "Mein Kampf" he later wrote: "There followed terrible days and even worse nights – I knew that all was lost […] in these nights hatred grew in me, hatred for those responsible for this deed."

Entering Politics

Hitler became obsessed with his idea of revenge, especially laying blame on the German politicians who signed the armistice on 11 November 1918, the "November criminals", and on the Jews and Marxists in Germany for undermining the war effort. When Hitler learned about the terms of the Treaty of Versailles, he decided to enter politics. Like many Germans Hitler felt humiliated and wanted to see his

M 1 Hitler the Speaker
Photograph, Berlin, 4 April 1932

country throw off the *shackles* of the treaty and once again take its place in the world – the "rebirth" of Germany through a strong nationalist government.

In late 1919 Hitler joined the German Workers' Party (DAP) which became the **National Socialist German Workers' Party** (NSDAP) in 1920. Hitler soon *emerged* as the leading figure and wrote down the party's beliefs in the 25-Point Party Programme.

The Nazi Ideology

The 25 Points were a curious mixture of ideas with negative undertones. Nazism really was an anti-ideology: anti-democratic, anti-communist, anti-Semitic and anti-capitalistic. Thus the programme appealed to many dissatisfied voters at times of disorder and misery. However, many of the economic principles were never transformed into practical policy when the Nazis came to power, as they were, of course, completely unacceptable to the party's supporters in big business. Hitler's autobiographical work was written in 1924, while he was in prison for leading the Beer Hall Putsch in Munich. In "Mein Kampf" Hitler presents his world view, which after the Nazi takeover became the ideological basis of the new regime. Hitler's *scheme* was a system of prejudices. It contained a racist interpretation of world history, in which the Aryan race is presented as 'creating culture' and the Jewish race as 'destroying culture'. Hitler also adopted a *social-Darwinist* view of life in which the strong survive and the weak perish by natural selection. He believed in the superiority of the Aryan race and consequently insisted that the races should not be mixed so that the 'purity of blood' would be preserved.

Nazi ideology also demanded the use of force to make Germany a world power and conquer living space for the German master race in the east. In place of democracy Hitler demanded a one-party state that would be run on the **"leadership principle"**. At the top of the new German state was the Führer, who had unlimited power and the support of the Germans. Together they would create a **"people's community"**, which would put an end to rigid class divisions and privileges.

Historical Terms

National Socialist German Workers' Party: Nationalsozialistische deutsche Arbeiterpartei, NSDAP

"leadership principle": "Führerprinzip"

"people's community": "Volksgemeinschaft"

M 2 **Party Medal with Swastika**
Photograph

M 3 **"Pictures of German Races"**
Racial science at a German school, 1943

Adolf Hitler and the Origins of Nazi Ideology

M 4 "Basic Programme of the National Socialist German Workers' Party"
Facsimile, 1920

M 5 The Programme

Extracts from the 25 Points of the National Socialist German Workers' Party, 1920:

"1. We demand the union of all Germans into a Great Germany [...]
2. We demand that Germany be treated in the same way as other countries and that the Treaty of Versailles be annulled.
3. We demand land and territory (colonies) for our growing population.
4. Only those who are our fellow countrymen can become citizens. Only those who have German blood [...] can be our countrymen. Hence no Jew can be a countryman. [...]
6. The right to choose the government [...] shall belong only to citizens and they alone shall hold public office. [...]
8. All immigration of non-Germans must stop and all non-Germans who have entered Germany since 1914 shall leave the Reich immediately. [...]
11. All unearned income, and all income that does not arise from work, shall be abolished. [...]
13. We demand the nationalization of all *trusts*. [...]
15. We demand a generous increase in old-age pensions. [...]
20. In order to make it possible for every capable [...] German to obtain higher education [...] we demand that specially talented children of poor parents [...] be educated at the expense of the state. [...]
23. We demand a legal campaign against those who tell deliberate political lies through the press [...]. We demand legal action against those tendencies in the media, in art and literature that have a bad influence upon the life of our people, and that offensive organizations shall be dissolved. [...]
Common good before individual good. [...]
25. In order to achieve this programme, the party demands the creation of a strong central power of the state."

Adapted from: http://avalon.law.yale.edu/imt/nsdappro.asp [July 10, 2018].

M 6 Excerpts from Adolf Hitler's "Mein Kampf"

In 1925 Hitler outlined his political ideology and future plans for Germany in his book "Mein Kampf":

"All the great civilizations of the past became decadent because the originally creative race died out, as a result of *contamination* of the blood [...]. In other words, in order to preserve a certain culture, the type of manhood that creates such a culture must be preserved. But such a preservation goes hand-in-hand with the *inexorable* law that it is the strongest and the best who must triumph and that they have the right to endure.

He who would live must fight. He who does not wish to fight in this world, where permanent struggle is the law of life, has not the right to exist. Such a saying may sound hard; but, after all, that is how the matter really stands.

If we were to divide mankind into three groups, the founders of culture, the bearers of culture, the destroyers of culture, only the Aryan could be considered as the representative of the first group.

In order to form a correct judgment of the place which the Jew holds in relation to the whole problem of human civilization, we must bear in mind the essential fact that there never has been any Jewish art and consequently that nothing of this kind exists today. We must realize that especially in those two royal domains of art, namely architecture and music, the Jew has done no original creative work. When the Jew comes to producing something in the field of art he merely [...] steals the intellectual word of others. The Jew essentially lacks those qualities which are characteristic of those creative races that are the founders of civilization.

Therefore the Jewish intellect will never be constructive but always destructive.

The Jew has never been a nomad, but always a parasite, *battening* on the substance of others. If he occasionally *abandoned* regions where he had hitherto lived he did not do it voluntarily. He did it because from time to time he was driven out by people who were tired of having their hospitality abused by such guests. Jewish self-expansion is a parasitic phenomenon – since the Jew is always looking for new *pastures* for his race [...]. He is and remains a parasite, a *sponger* who, like a *pernicious* bacillus, spreads over wider and wider areas according as some favourable area attracts him. The effect produced by his presence is also like that of the vampire; for wherever he establishes himself the people who grant him hospitality are bound to be bled to death sooner or later."

http://gutenberg.net.au/ebooks02/0200601.txt [July 10, 2018] (Translation: James Murphy).

Vocabulary

trust: a group of companies that work together illegally to reduce competition, control prices etc.
contamination: making sth. dirty or no longer pure by adding a substance that is dangerous or carries disease
inexorable: (a process) that cannot be stopped or changed
to batten: to grow prosperous especially at the expense of others
to abandon: to leave
pastures: land or a plot of land used for grazing
sponger: a person who gets money, food, etc. from other people without doing anything
pernicious: destructive

Tasks

1. **The Programme of the NSDAP**
   a) Make a table of nationalist, socialist or racist ideas in the 25 Points (M5).
   b) Discuss which ideas are questionable.
2. **Hitler and the Question of Race**
   a) Read the excerpts from "Mein Kampf" (M6) and list the allegations against the Jews.
   b) In which way do Aryans and Jews, according to Hitler, differ?
   c) Do research on Jewish artists and authors during the Weimar Republic.
   d) Imagine you live in the Twenties and read Hitler's book. Write a letter to the editor of the Berliner Tageblatt in which you present your opinion on the question of race.
3. **Nazi Symbols**
   Find out on the Internet about the current use of Nazi symbols and present your results in class.
4. **Controversy over "Mein Kampf" in 2016**
   a) Since 2016 it is legal to publish Hitler's book in Germany. Collect arguments in favour of or against a publication.
   b) Discuss the influence "Mein Kampf" might have on today's youths.

M 1 An American View

Only a few days after the Enabling Act was passed the New York Times published the cartoon "To the Dark Ages", New York Times, 2 April 1933

A Legal "Seizure of Power"?

Establishing a Dictatorship

After Adolf Hitler's appointment to Chancellor on 30 January 1933, the NSDAP quickly consolidated its power. Using President Hindenburg's constitutional rights Hitler completely transformed Germany into a police state and achieved absolute power for himself. But how could he create a dictatorship in only a few months?

Two important laws helped him to remove the opposition. When the Reichstag building burnt down, Hitler blamed the Communists and asked President Hindenburg to sign the Decree for the Protection of People and State. This emergency decree ("Reichstagsbrandverordnung") of 28 February took away many of the basic rights of the German people, censored papers, limited meetings and allowed the police to arrest leading Communists.

In this atmosphere of fear new elections to the Reichstag took place on 5 March 1933. The NSDAP only won 43.9 per cent of the vote, but Hitler could claim the majority in parliament with the help of the seats won by the DNVP.

On the "Day of Potsdam" on 21 March 1933, the Nazis used the opening of the new Reichstag to demonstrate not only the unity of the nation but also the historical continuity between old Germany and the Third Reich. The ceremony at the Potsdam Garrison Church in the presence of President Hindenburg, former Crown Prince William and leading generals was arranged to show that the Nazis could be trusted. Dressed in civilian clothes rather than uniform, Hitler bowed with respect to the old Field Marshal and apparently to the old Prussian traditions and values of honour, loyalty and love of country. The German public followed the events in Potsdam on the radio and over public loudspeakers.

Historical Terms

"Enabling Act":
"Ermächtigungsgesetz"

"Seizure of Power":
"Machtergreifung", Machtübernahme

But the new Chancellor wanted to free himself of all constitutional restrictions and any form of parliamentary control. So he introduced a second law, the **"Enabling Act"**, on 23 March 1933. In an atmosphere of terror it was passed by a two-thirds majority in the Reichstag. Only the Social Democrats – many Communist deputies had already been arrested – voted against this act, which deprived the Reichstag of all its powers. It enabled the government to pass laws without parliamentary consent, thus abolishing the basic democratic principle of the separation of powers.

M 2 **Otto Wels**
Chairman of the SPD, Photograph, 1932

Bringing Germany into Line – the "Gleichschaltung"

Now that the Nazis could make their own laws, they reorganized the German political system and German society under Nazi control. This process was called "Gleichschaltung". Step by step the Nazis eliminated any form of opposition in the first months after their **"Seizure of Power"**.

In April 1933 Hitler *dismantled federalism* by appointing state governors and abolishing the state parliaments. In May the trade unions were replaced by the German Labour Front ("Deutsche Arbeitsfront", DAF). Their offices were occupied by the SA ("Sturmabteilung", the paramilitary organization of the NSDAP), their leaders arrested and strikes forbidden. Also, the political parties were brought into line. The KPD and a little later the SPD were banned. Their offices were closed down and their leaders put in concentration camps. In July a Law Against the Creation of Parties provided that the NSDAP was the only remaining party and thus Germany became a one-party state. The civil service was also put under control by dismissing any civil servant from office who was not Aryan or did not pledge his unconditional loyalty to the Nazi state.

The "Night of the Long Knives"

By 1934 Hitler had destroyed democracy, but big business, the former aristocracy and the army remained intact. The SA under Ernst Röhm wanted to push ahead with the Nazi revolution, calling for socially radical policies and a new "People's Army". Hitler rejected these demands, knowing that he would need the support of the army and the industrialists in the wars to come. On 30 June 1934, in the "Night of the Long Knives", he ordered the SS ("Schutzstaffel") to execute Röhm, who had become a threat to his power, and hundreds of other SA leaders or political opponents without trial. A few months later grateful Reichswehr generals ordered all soldiers to swear loyalty to the person of Adolf Hitler rather than to the nation or the constitution.

M 3 **"Heil Hitler!"**
Photo Collage of the events of 30 June 1934 by John Heartfield

Hitler – The "Führer"

The death of 86-year-old President Paul von Hindenburg on 2 August 1934 removed the final obstacle to Hitler's complete power over Germany. A law combined the offices of Chancellor (the head of government) and President (the head of state); Adolf Hitler was *henceforth* addressed as Leader and Chancellor ("Führer und Reichskanzler") and was both head of state and commander-in-chief of the armed forces. The day of the President's death, a plebiscite was ordered for the German people to approve the combination of the two offices. Germany's voters *went to the polls* and about 90 per cent approved. Only eighteen months after the fateful 30 January 1933 the "Gleichschaltung" was completed and Hitler had unchallenged power in Germany. A mixture of laws, acts of violence and a system of propaganda had paved the way for him.

Vocabulary

to dismantle: to end an organization or system in an organized way
federalism: a system of government in which the individual states of a country have control over some affairs
henceforth: from then on
to go to the polls: to vote

A Legal "Seizure of Power"?

M 4 "Reichstag Fire Decree"

"Decree of the Reich President for the Protection of the People and the State, February 28, 1933". In virtue of Article 48(2) of the German Constitution, the following is decreed as a defensive measure against Communist acts of violence endangering the state:

"Article 1: Sections 114, 115, 117, 118, 123, 124, and 153 of the Constitution of the German Reich are *suspended* until further notice. Therefore, restrictions on personal liberty, on the right of free expression of opinion, including freedom of the
5 press, on the right of assembly and the right of association, and violations of the privacy of postal, telegraphic, and telephonic communications, *warrants* for house searches, orders for *confiscations*, as well as restrictions on property, are also *permissible* beyond the legal limits."

Transl. quoted from: United States Holocaust Memorial Museum. Decree of the Reich President for the Protection of the People and the State, translated from Reichsgesetzblatt I, 1933, p. 83, https://www.ushmm.org/wlc/en/article.php?ModuleId=10007889 [July 10, 2018].

M 5 The Passing of the Enabling Act

Since the Reichstag building had been burnt down, the new Reichstag met in the Kroll Opera House. Wilhelm Hoegner (SPD) was an eyewitness and described the atmosphere in which the members met to vote on the Enabling Act on 23 March 1933.

"The wide square in front of the Kroll Opera House was crowded with dark masses of people. We were received with wild choruses: 'We want the Enabling Act!' Youths with swastikas on their chests eyed us *insolently*, blocking our
5 way, in fact made us *run the gauntlet*, calling us names like 'Centre pig', 'Marxist sow'. The Kroll Opera House was crawling with armed SA and SS men. […] When we Social Democrats had taken up our seats at the extreme left, SA and SS men lined up at the exits and along the walls behind
10 us in a semicircle. Their expressions *boded* no good."

Wilhelm Hoegner, Der schwierige Außenseiter, München: Isar-Verlag 1959; transl. quoted from: Josh Brooman, Germany 1918–45. Democracy and Dictatorship (Longman History Project), London: Longman 1996, p.60.

M 6 March-in of the SA to Intimidate the Members of the Reichstag, 23 March 1933

M 7 "Enabling Act"

Excerpts from the Speech by the Social Democrat Otto Wels against the Passage of the Enabling Act (23 March 1933):

"After the persecutions that the Social Democratic Party has suffered recently, no one will reasonably demand or expect it to vote for the Enabling Act proposed here. […] Never before, since there has been a German Reichstag, has
5 the control of public affairs by the elected representatives of the people been eliminated to such an extent as is happening now, and is supposed to happen even more through the new Enabling Act. Such *omnipotence* of the government must have serious negative consequences as
10 the press, too, lacks any freedom of expression. […]
The Weimar Constitution is not a socialist constitution. But we stand by the principles *enshrined* in it, the principles of a state based on the rule of law, of equal rights, of social justice. In this historic hour, we German Social Democrats
15 […] pledge ourselves to the principles of humanity and justice, of freedom and socialism. No Enabling Act gives you the power to destroy ideas that are eternal and *indestructible*. […]
We greet the persecuted and the oppressed. We greet our
20 friends in the Reich. Your *steadfastness* and loyalty deserve admiration. The courage of your *convictions* and your unbroken optimism guarantee a brighter future."

In: Paul Meier-Benneckenstein, Axel Friedrichs (eds.), Dokumente der deutschen Politik, Bd. 1: Die Nationalsozialistische Revolution 1933, Berlin: Junker und Dünnhaupt 1935, pp. 36–38; transl. by Thomas Dunlap quoted from: http://germanhistorydocs.ghi-dc.org/pdf/eng/English_6.pdf [July 11, 2018].

Vocabulary

to suspend: to officially stop sth. for a time

warrant: a legal document that is signed by a judge and gives the police authority to do sth.

confiscation: the act of officially taking sth. away from sb.

permissible: (here) acceptable

insolently: in an extremely rude way that shows a lack of respect for somebody

to run the gauntlet: phrase referring to an old army punishment where a man was forced to run between two lines of soldiers hitting him

to bode: (here) to be a bad sign

omnipotence: having total power; able to do anything

to enshrine in: to state

indestructible: impossible to destroy

steadfastness: strength and firmness

conviction: a strong opinion or belief

arsonist: sb. who starts fire deliberately, esp. in buildings

M 8 Hitler Shaking Hands with President von Hindenburg on the "Day of Potsdam", 21 March 1933
Postcard, based on a painting by Carl Langhorst (1867–1950)

Tasks

1. **The Steps to Dictatorship**
   a) List the steps Hitler took on his way to dictatorship (text).
   b) Draw a diagram of Hitler's functions in August 1934 (text).

2. **Crushing the Opposition – the Reichstag Fire**
   a) Find out about the trial and fate of the *arsonist* Marinus van der Lubbe.
   b) Assess the effects of the "Reichstag Fire Decree" (M4) on the Reichstag elections of 5 March 1933.

3. **Manipulating the Population – "the Day of Potsdam"**
   a) Explain the message of the postcard (M8). Focus on the way it presents the two characters.
   b) Based on the author's text and the analysis of the postcard (M8) explain the importance of the "Day of Potsdam".

4. **The "Enabling Act" and the Idea of a Legal Revolution**
   a) Read the excerpt from Otto Wels' speech (M7). With a partner write a fictitious interview with Wels about his decision to oppose Hitler.
   b) Show what happened to Otto Wels after his speech.
   c) The passing of the Enabling Act established the Nazi dictatorship. Some historians speak of a legal revolution. The two words "legal" and "revolution" appear to contradict each other. With a partner find arguments against and in favour of this idea and discuss the extent to which the Nazis came to power by legal means.

5. **An American View**
   a) Describe the cartoon (M1) and express its message.
   b) Discuss in class how the transformation of a democratic Germany into a totalitarian state could have been avoided. By which means?

Vocabulary

to supervise: to control and make sure that everything is done correctly

denunciation: (here) the act of reporting sb. to the police

to foster: to encourage, promote

demigod: a ruler or other person who is treated like a god

omnipresent: present everywhere

saviour: a person who rescues sb./sth. from a dangerous or difficult situation

to boost: to make sb. feel more positive or confident

to appease: to make people calmer or less angry by giving them what they want

opportunist: person who uses every chance to get an advantage for himself

Historical Terms

Secret State Police: ("Geheime Staatspolizei", "Gestapo")

"Degenerate Art": "Entartete Kunst")

M 1 Prisoners in the Concentration Camp Oranienburg (near Berlin)
Photograph, 1933

Seduction and Violence

Why did many Germans accept Nazi rule? They lost their individual liberties, experienced the transformation of democracy into a dictatorship, but did not seem to worry. There were many reasons why most Germans were willing to go along with Nazi policies. To understand them different aspects should be considered: the economy, foreign policy and the changes Hitler caused in people's lives.

Control and Terror

Total control over people's lives was essential to Hitler's dictatorship and it was executed by two organizations: the Nazi party and the police. By 1938 the NSDAP had about five million members who *supervised* every citizen and reported suspicious behaviour to the police. There were Block Leaders who had eyes and ears in every block of flats. They kept card files on every household and *denunciation* became part of daily life. The police forces included the Gestapo, the **Secret State Police**. It was created in 1933 and had the right to take anyone into "protective custody" without the need of a trial. In addition the SS, which was established in 1925 to provide bodyguards for Hitler and was led by Heinrich Himmler, became the most powerful organization within the National Socialist state after the SA lost its power. SS members wore black uniforms and were extreme supporters of Nazi ideology. Their cruelty and terror left deep traces in Germany and Europe. They ran the concentration camps and worked closely with the Gestapo. Political prisoners and members of persecuted minorities like Gypsies, Jews or homosexuals faced brutal interrogations, torture and sometimes death. The Nazi state created an atmosphere of fear and intimidation and the number of prisoners in concentration camps rose steadily.

Propaganda and Hitler Myth

Joseph Goebbels and his Ministry of Propaganda wanted to gain control over the minds of the German people and worked hard to unite the nation behind the aims of the regime. Different means were employed. The mass media – the press, radio, theatre and the cinema – were censored and coordinated by Reich "chambers". Every day editors were given a briefing by the Propaganda Ministry on what could be published, broadcast or shown. People's radios ("Volksempfänger") were sold very cheaply so that by 1942 about 70 percent of all households owned one. Pictures or movies from mass rallies at Nuremberg ("Reichsparteitage") were also used to *foster* people's loyalty to Hitler. Spectacular parades symbolized the strength of the people's community and the solidarity between the German people and the Nazi Party.

The Propaganda Ministry also organized large exhibitions like the German Art exhibition, which was held each year from 1937 on and attracted over three million visitors. **"Degenerate Art"** essentially referred to abstract and surrealist art that Hitler hated. While modern styles of art were prohibited, the Nazis supported paintings and sculptures that promoted racial superiority and national ideals.

Another important area of propaganda was Hitler himself. The myth of the Führer as a *demigod* was created and became *omnipresent*. Hitler's picture was everywhere, and he was portrayed as Germany's *saviour*. Photographs showed Hitler as a hero who devoted his life to the German people. Others presented him

M 4 **Adolf Hitler's 48th Birthday**
Photograph, Berlin, 20 April 1937

as a "man of the people" or idolized by crowds. This cult of personality was also practised in the "German salute" while saying "Heil Hitler". By 1938 Hitler's popularity was at its peak.

Benefits from Nazi Rule

Many Germans, who were not among the persecuted minorities, felt they benefited from the regime. They only saw that unemployment decreased and German prestige increased through the Berlin Olympics in 1936 and Hitler's foreign policy. Instead of despair and hopelessness, optimism and self-confidence returned.

Despite low wages, longer working hours and a lack of consumer goods, most people felt better off than before. Robert Ley, leader of the German Labour Front, once said: "It is more important to feed the souls of men than their stomachs." Two programmes to care directly for the workers' interests were set up. "The Beauty of Labour" ("Schönheit der Arbeit", SDA) aimed to improve conditions at work, such as cleanliness, lighting or noise levels. "Strength through Joy" ("Kraft durch Freude", KDF) was another attempt to improve the status of workers. The government organized a wide variety of leisure activities including sports, cultural visits or vacation trips on ocean liners. Hitler himself had the idea *to boost* people's morale by introducing a new "people's car" (the "Volkswagen"), which every worker should be able to afford. Although only a few Germans ever enjoyed a KDF holiday and the new Volkswagen factory mostly produced army vehicles, all these campaigns helped *to appease* the working class and secure their support.

As in any dictatorial system, the Nazis offered advantages to those who willingly accepted the party's rule. In some professions, it was impossible to avoid joining the party, for example, teachers in public schools. However, for many professionals and well-educated people, becoming a Nazi was a move toward a successful career – a chance which thousands of *opportunists* took.

M 3 **"Strength through Joy"**
Poster, about 1938

Seduction and Violence

M 4 "Rally for Freedom"
Photograph, Nuremberg, 1935

M 5 "Your KDF-car"
Germans were encouraged to buy the people's car with a savings plan. Poster, 1938

M 6 "All Germany Listens to the Führer on the People's Receiver."
The Nazis, eager to encourage radio listenership, developed an inexpensive radio receiver to make it possible for as many as possible to hear Nazi propaganda.

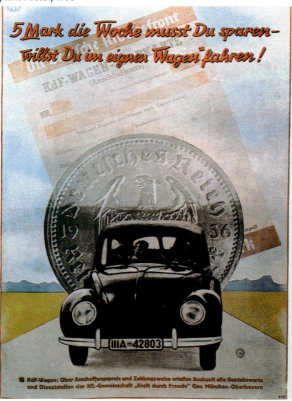

M 7 Roll-call in the Concentration Camp Dachau
Photograph, 1936

M 8 Control

An American Visitor to Germany Described the Methods of Control in 1939:

"The National Socialist Secret Police made silent arrests. Late at night and early in the morning they took man after man […] The door-bell or knocker sounded. There stood two, or at most three, tall men with pairs of pistols in their belts […] The chosen hour was one at which they would find the wanted man relaxed, surprising him at a meal or in bed. Other members of the household behaved as if hypnotized. They had no faith that he would have any chance of freeing himself by any legal means […] Their minds were filled with memories of what they knew of others who had been taken in this way – disappearing forever, returned in a closed *coffin*. Or, if let out alive, coming back starved in body and crazed in mind. Yet, they did nothing. Family and friends let their man go […]."

Quoted from: Josh Brooman, Germany 1918–45. Democracy and Dictatorship (Longman History Project), London: Longman 1996, p. 84f.

Vocabulary

coffin: a box in which a dead body is buried

Tasks

1. **Lost Individuality and Terror**
   a) Describe and compare the two photographs (M4, M7).
   b) Describe the photograph (M2) and analyse it with regard to its propaganda value.
   c) Study the report (M8) and explain the reaction of the family members.
2. **Benefits?**
   a) Analyse the propaganda posters (M3, M5, M6).
   b) Discuss why many Germans accepted Nazi rule.

Everyday Life in Nazi Germany

Women and the Family

The Nazis opposed women's emancipation and the feminist movement. During the Weimar Republic women had gained the right to vote, worked in all professions and studied at university. But the Nazis had a different view of the role of women. Nazi propaganda showed the family as the centre of life, and women as the centre of family life. Women were expected to stay at home and look after their children. Action was taken to reduce the number of women working in the professions. Women doctors, teachers and civil servants were forced to give up their careers. Their job was to keep the home nice for their husband and family. Minister Goebbels said, "The mission of women is to be beautiful and to bring children into the world." Organizations like the National Socialist Womanhood ("NS-Frauenschaft") offered cookery, child care and racial hygiene courses.

A number of laws to encourage women to have more children were introduced. The Law for the Encouragement of Marriage gave newly *wed* couples a loan of 1,000 marks, and allowed them 250 marks for each child they had. The Nazi slogan "I have donated a child to the Führer" glorified mothers as did the Mother's Cross for women who had more than four children. Unmarried women could volunteer to have a baby from an Aryan member of the SS.

The Nazis even ran campaigns to influence women's appearance and behaviour. Women were supposed to wear simple peasant-style clothes, hair in *plaits* or buns and flat shoes. They were not expected to wear make-up or trousers, dye their hair or smoke in public.

One of the main reasons for encouraging women to return to the home in 1933–34 was to create jobs for unemployed men. But concern for the interests of business and fear of losing industry's cooperation with the government prevented all women from being *dismissed*. As war approached, more workers were needed and women were increasingly allowed or even encouraged to go to work. NS ideology and reality did not match and never had.

The Nazification of Schools

In Nazi eyes the young were particularly important. To create a racial state and win living-space ("Lebensraum") in the east, the Nazis needed young people who were *indoctrinated* in ideology and who believed in the ideals of discipline, sacrifice and obedience.

M 1 Mother's Cross
A mother could be awarded a bronze, silver, or gold cross, depending on the number of her children. Eight would entitle the woman to a gold cross, six for silver, and four for bronze.

M 2 "The Aryan Family"
Painting by Wolfgang Willrich (1897–1948)

M 3 League of German Maidens
Photograph, 1938

In 1934 the Ministry of Education in Berlin took control of all schools in Germany. All teachers who were Jewish or were regarded as anti-Nazi lost their jobs. All other teachers had to take an oath of loyalty to Hitler and join a Nazi Teachers' League. Textbooks were rewritten and a new national *curriculum* was introduced. The number of sport lessons was doubled. Boxing became *compulsory* for boys and those who failed fitness tests could be expelled from their schools. In subjects like history, biology, German or maths, Nazi ideas were paid special attention. The achievements of the Weimar Republic were ignored and all disasters blamed on the Communists and the Jews. As the quality of learning suffered, fewer students entered the universities. Between 1932 and 1941, the number of students in higher education fell from 127,580 to only 40,986.

Organizing Youth

Outside school, the Nazi Party set up the Hitler Youth ("Hitlerjugend", HJ) to teach Nazi principles. Hitler's aim was to produce a young German, who was "as swift as a greyhound, tough as leather and hard as Krupp steel". Under the leadership of Baldur von Schirach, the Hitler Youth included almost 60 per cent of German boys by 1935. One year later it changed from a party to a state organization that all young "Aryan" Germans were expected to join. All rival organizations were banned, and at the outbreak of the Second World War in 1939, membership became *mandatory*. Critical parents were warned that their children could be taken away from them and put into orphanages or other homes unless they enrolled. In 1939 the Hitler Youth numbered almost 9 million.

The life of young people became increasingly *regimented*. Boys at 10 joined the Young Folk ("Jungvolk") and were involved in activities such as hiking and camping. They learned about Nazi ideology and military matters. Between the ages of 14 and 18 they enrolled in the Hitler Youth, which had a much stronger emphasis on military training and discipline. Summer camps were held including rifle training and team-building activities. Youngsters learnt *to endure* anything, to do their best: records were kept of what they did, competitions were held constantly to see which group was the best. For many children the Hitler Youth offered an opportunity to enjoy real leisure activities for the first time, but they had to live a life of Nazi conformity.

The Young Maidens ("Jungmädel") and the League of German Maidens ("Bund Deutscher Mädel", BDM) were the female equivalents of the Hitler Youth. They, too, had uniforms made up of a white blouse and a blue skirt. The girls were trained for comradeship, *domestic duties*, and motherhood. Outdoor activities were organized to make girls fit, strong mothers. At the age of 18 most of the girls in the BDM did a year's service on farms ("Landjahr"), helping both in the house and in the fields.

In the last months of the war, when the German army was defeated, it was to the *adolescents* of the Hitler Youth that Hitler turned for the defence of the Reich. Many of them could not wait to serve and die for their Führer and fatherland.

However, despite the Nazis' efforts, not all young Germans were brainwashed and believed everything they were taught. *Contemporary* sources show mixed feelings and attitudes. Some enjoyed the activities, the comradeship and proudly wore their uniforms, but the Hitler Youth did not appeal to others. They disliked the military drill and the pressure of daily duties. Some even formed their own groups like the "Swing Kids" or the "Edelweiss Pirates".

M 4 The Hitler Youth
Photograph, 1938

Vocabulary

wed: married

plaits: hair divided into three parts and twisted together

to dismiss: to remove sb. from the job

to indoctrinate: to teach ideas in such a way that neither opposition nor criticism is possible; to brainwash

indoctrination: the act of indoctrinating

curriculum: the subjects that are included in a course of study or taught in a school

compulsory: sth. that must be done because of a law or a rule

mandatory: compulsory, required

to regiment: to control strictly

to endure: to suffer sth. painful or unpleasant without complaining

domestic duties: work connected with home or family

adolescent: teenager

contemporary: belonging to the same time

Everyday Life in Nazi Germany

M 5 "The Child Alone … Gives Meaning to the Whole Life-Struggle"

In his speech to the NS Women's League on 8 September 1934 Hitler summed up his ideas of the role of women:

"The *sacrifices* which the man makes in the struggle of his nation, the woman makes in the *preservation* of that nation in individual cases. What the man gives in courage on the battlefield, the woman gives in *eternal* self-sacrifice, in
5 eternal pain and suffering. Every child that a woman brings into the world is a battle, a battle waged for the existence of her people. And both must therefore *mutually* value and respect each other […] So our women's movement is not […] the fight against men, but […] the common fight together
10 with men. For the new National Socialist […] has gained the trust of millions of women as fanatical *fellow-combatants*, women who […] did not set their sights on the rights which a Jewish intellectualism put before their eyes (liberation, emancipation), but rather on the duties *imposed* by nature
15 […] Whereas the programs of the liberal, intellectualist women's movements contained many points, the program of our National Socialist Women's movement has in reality but one single point, and that point is the child, that tiny creature which must be born and grow strong and which
20 alone gives meaning to the whole life-struggle […]."

Frankfurter Zeitung, September 9, 1934; Transl. quoted from: Jeremy Noakes and Geoffrey Pridham (eds.), Nazism, 1919–1945, Vol. 2: State, Economy and Society 1933–1939. Exeter: University of Exeter Press, 2000, pp. 255–56. http://www.germanhistorydocs.ghi-dc.org/docpage.cfm?docpage_id=2330 [May 24, 2018].

M 6 "You, too, Belong to the Führer"
Poster, 1937

Vocabulary

sacrifice: the fact of giving up sth. for the benefit of others
preservation: the act of keeping sth. in its original state or in good condition
eternal: everlasting

Vocabulary

mutually: (adv.) by two or more people felt or done in the same way
fellow-combatants: people who fight together
to impose: to force sth. on sb.

Tasks

1. The "Perfect Family" and the Role of Women
   a) Analyse how the painting (M2) illustrates the "perfect Nazi family".
   b) Hitler's speech (M5) was printed in many papers, also in the United States. From the perspective of an emancipated woman, write a letter to the editor in which you comment on Hitler's ideas.
   c) List the differences between the Nazi concept of a family and the one of today's society (text).

Info

Competition

This is what boys of the German Young Folk had to know or do for a Badge of Achievement ("Leistungsabzeichen"):

1. Ideology
- Life of the Führer
- Germans abroad
- Lost territories
- Flag oath
- Hitler Youth songs

2. Athletic achievements
- Running: 60 metres – 10 seconds
- Long jump: 3.25 metres
- Ball throwing: 35 metres
- Pull up on the horizontal bar: twice

3. Hiking and camping
- A day's hike of 15 kilometres with a light pack (not over 5 kilos)
- Participation in a camp, living in tents for at least three days
- Put up a tent
- Construct a cooking pit
- Know the names of the most important trees
- Use a map of the stars to orient yourself
- Know the most important symbols on a 1:25,000 map

4. Target practice
- Shooting with an air-gun, distance 8 metres in sitting position

M 7 "Youth Serves the Führer"
Poster, 1935

M 8 Maths and War

Tasks from a mathematics textbook, 1941:

"A bomber aircraft on take-off carries 12 dozen bombs, each weighing 10 kilos. The aircraft takes off for Warsaw, the international centre for Jewry. It bombs the town. On take-off with all bombs on board and a fuel tank containing 100 kilos of fuel, the aircraft weighs about 8 tons. When it returns from the crusade, there are still 230 kilos left. What is the weight of the aircraft when empty?"

Transl. quoted from: Chris N. Trueman, "Nazi Education", The History Learning Site: https://www.historylearningsite.co.uk/nazi-germany/nazi-education [July 11, 2018].

Tasks

1. **Education to Follow – the indoctrination of the youth**
    a) Describe the composition of the posters (M6, M7). What do they show and what is left out?
    b) Which effect should they have?
    c) What are your feelings when you look at these young people?
    d) Show what sources (M3, M4, M8) reveal about the Nazis' ideas of education.
    e) Compare the maths exercise (M8) with exercises in your textbook.
    f) Find out about the Swing Kids and the Edelweiss Pirates on the Internet or in an encyclopedia.

Vocabulary

grants: money given by the government

barracks: buildings for soldiers to live in

interest: the extra money that you pay back when you borrow money

memorandum: proposal on a particular subject

self-sufficient: able to produce everything you need without the help of others

to extract: to obtain a substance from sth. by using a chemical process

expenditure: amount of money spent

bond: document promising that the government will pay back money that it has borrowed with interest

to deceive: to make sb. believe sth. that is not true

The Economy in Germany

On 2 February 1933, only three days after Hitler had taken office, he addressed the German people in a speech on the disastrous economic situation in Germany. He demanded that "within four years unemployment must be finally overcome" and ended by saying, "Now, people of Germany, give us four years and then pass judgement upon us."

What followed was assessed by the German writer Sebastian Haffner (1978): "Among these positive achievements of Hitler the one outshining all others was his economic miracle. […] In January 1933, when Hitler became Reich Chancellor, there were six million unemployed in Germany. Only three years later, in 1936, there was full employment. Crying need and mass hardship had generally turned into modest but comfortable prosperity."

Statistics on unemployment seem to prove Haffner's conclusion, but in the end Hitler's economic policies systematically wrecked the German economy because they were only intended to prepare for war.

Combating Unemployment

Hitler's measures to battle unemployment had already been developed by previous governments, but the Nazis expanded these job creation programmes. One was

M 1 The Fight against Unemployment
Propaganda Poster, The Reich Ministry for Employment, 1934

the National Labour Service ("Reicharbeitsdienst", RAD), which became compulsory for men between the ages of 18 and 25. They were put into uniform and had to serve six months in work camps. The RAD used men to build a network of motorways (the Autobahn), drain marshes, plant forests or construct dikes to protect coastal areas from flooding. With hundreds of thousands of young men working on these projects, the jobless figures dropped sharply.

A Law to Reduce Unemployment gave government *grants* for building bridges, new homes, hospitals and *barracks*. Buildings like the new Olympic Stadium in Berlin (1936) not only provided work for many men but also impressed people and were a visible sign of Germany's power.

Ignoring the Versailles Treaty

Hitler restored compulsory military service in 1935. All men had to serve for two years and by 1939 about 1.4 million men were in the army, so they were not counted as unemployed.

But the official statistics tell only part of the story. They do not take into account political opponents and members of persecuted minorities who lost their jobs and did not appear in the unemployment statistics. German emigrants are ignored as well as many women who were pushed out of skilled jobs. From June 1933 *interest*-free loans were offered to young women who withdrew from the labour market in order to get married.

Rearmament and Autarky

Hitler's measures to lower unemployment and prepare Germany for war went hand in hand. In a 1936 *memorandum* on the Four Year Plan, Hitler demanded the German armed forces to be ready for attack and the economy fit for war within four years. The plan was designed to speed up armament and make Germany *self-sufficient* in raw materials through the development of artificial replacements. This process was known as "autarky". Although German companies developed a method of *extracting* oil from coal or producing artificial rubber, quantities were too small to make Germany independent from imports.

As a result of German rearmament, the production of consumer goods decreased. In a speech on 17 January 1936, Minister of Propaganda Joseph Goebbels stated, "We can do without butter, but, despite all our love of peace, not without arms." A little later Hermann Goering, commander of the air force and minister in charge of the Four Year Plan, announced in a speech, "Guns will make us powerful; butter will only make us fat." The shortage of consumer goods and falling real wages led to complaints – people did not see an increase in their living standards.

There was another problem: the rising number of soldiers needed barracks and equipment like guns, tanks, ships and aircraft. So the share of defence spending in total government *expenditure* – 4% in 1933 – rocketed to 50% by 1938. As the government did not have the money to finance job creation and armament programmes, it turned to deficit spending. The regime issued *bonds*, which were to be repaid after a successful war. In 1939 the level of national debt was unprecedented in German history.

The results of Hitler's efforts to combat unemployment look very impressive at first sight, and helped to stabilize the regime. But the economic upswing in Germany turned out to be an illusion which *deceived* the people. The price had to be paid later.

M 2 "Reichsarbeitsdienst"
The picture shows workers assigned to build the "Reichs Autobahn", 1934.

The Economy in Germany

M 3 Hitler Sets the Goal

In the secret memorandum on which Göring's Four Year Plan was based, Hitler wrote in 1936:

"We are overpopulated and cannot feed ourselves from our own resources. The solution ultimately lies in extending the living space of our people, that is, in extending the sources of its raw materials and foodstuffs. It is the task of the political leadership one day to solve this problem [...]."

Transl. quoted from: "Unsigned Memorandum" (August 1936), in: Documents on German Foreign Policy: From the Archives of the German Foreign Ministry. Washington, DC: United States Government Printing Office, 1957–1964. Series C (1933–1937), The Third Reich: First Phase, Volume 5: March 5–October 31, 1936. Document Number 490, pp. 853–62. http://germanhistorydocs.ghi-dc.org/docpage.cfm?docpage_id=2279 [July 11, 2018].

M 4 Index of Wages 1928–1938

The term "index" means that the wages in one year, in this case 1936, are taken to be 100. The other years are measured against this.

Year	Index of Wages
1928	125
1933	88
1934	94
1936	100
1938	106

Stephen Lee, Weimar and Nazi Germany, Oxford: Heinemann 1996, p. 63.

M 5 Unemployment in Germany

Unemployment in Germany	Total
January 1933	6 million
January 1934	3.3 million
January 1935	2.9 million
January 1936	2.5 million
January 1937	1.8 million
January 1938	1.0 million
January 1939	302,000

Chris N. Trueman, "The Nazis and the German Economy", The History Learning Site: https://www.historylearningsite.co.uk/nazi-germany/the-nazis-and-the-german-economy [July 11, 2018].

M 6 State Finances

German finances in billion RM	1933	1935	1937	1939
Tax and customs revenue	6.8	9.3	13.4	23.1
State spending	8.1	13.1	18.9	42.2
of which military spending	0.7	5.2	10.8	25.9
national debt	11.7	14.6	25.4	42.6

Eberhard Aleff, Das Dritte Reich, Hannover: Verlag für Literatur u. Zeitgeschehen 1970, p. 124.

M 7 Report on the Condition and Mood of Industrial Workers in Germany

The Sopade Report was commissioned by the exile leadership of the SPD (September 1938):

"Central Germany, September 1938: Among industrial workers there are many who do not give a damn about the successes of the Hitler system and have only scorn and contempt for the whole show. Others, however, say: 'Well, there are a lot of things Adolf does not know [...] and which he does not want'. [...] But one is never quite sure with them whether they mean it seriously or only want to protect their backs. Naturally, there are also many who have become unpolitical. In particular, a large number of the skilled workers who were unemployed for a long time are not enthusiastic Nazis. They often complain about the fact that they earn much less now than in say 1929 but, at the end of the day, they always say: 'It's all the same to us; at least we have work'. The further one goes down into the poorer sections the more opposition there is. But even now—although they know there is a labor shortage—they are all scared of losing their jobs. The years of unemployment have not been forgotten.

Those who are still Nazis in the plant are subdued. One has the feeling that many of them only stay in the Party to get an easier life. [...] The fact that one's wages continually buy less and less and that the *slave driving* gets worse and worse every day cannot be denied by even the 'oldest fighter' [...].

The mood in the plants is one of depression. It's true that even in the old days work was no fun and was regarded by many as a necessary evil. But in those days one had the feeling: if you don't like something you can get it off your chest frankly and in public [...]. Now one goes into the plant with a heavy heart because one is always afraid of saying a word too many and landing oneself in a spot. There is a dark cloud over one's whole life. One even looks forward less to getting home than in the old days because there is no longer any relaxed comradeship with friends and neighbors. Before, one always used to meet like-minded people in the workers sport and education associations, for a game of chess, or in the People's House. Now one leaves the factory, runs a few errands, goes home, reads the headlines in the paper, and goes to bed, and next morning the same monotonous cycle begins again. Those who have their 'duty' to perform whether in the SS, SA, Party, or Welfare are even worse off. They have *to slave away* in the evenings as well and moan a lot, particularly if they have been doing heavy physical work during the day. Most of them would gladly give up their posts. But they lack the courage to do so."

Transl. quoted from: Jeremy Noakes and Geoffrey Pridham (eds.), Nazism 1919–1945, Vol. 2: State, Economy and Society 1933–1939. Exeter: University of Exeter Press, 2000, pp. 179f.

Vocabulary

slave driving : make other people work very hard
to slave away: work hard

M 8 "Hurrah, the Butter is Gone!"
Collage by John Heartfield, Workers Illustrated Newspaper, published in Prague, 1935

Tasks

1. **Propaganda**
    a) Describe the poster (M1).
    b) Express its message and the effect it should have on the German people.
2. **An "Economic Miracle"?**
    a) Transform the tables M4 and M5 into bar charts. Transform M6 into a line graph. Use different colours.
    b) List the measures the Nazi government took to fight unemployment (text).
    c) Study Hitler's memo (M3) and assess the statement that the economic development in Germany can be regarded as an "economic miracle".
3. **A Critical View**
    a) List keywords to describe the condition and mood of industrial workers in Nazi Germany (M7).
    b) Interpret the collage (M8) and relate it to the report (M7).
4. **Discussion**
    a) Work in groups and discuss Hitler's economic policy. Also compare it to today's measures of fighting unemployment.
    b) When (right-wing) people today talk about Hitler some often praise him because of the "Autobahn". How would you respond in such a discussion?

Vocabulary

to affirm: to state firmly or publicly

honourable: morally correct and deserving respect

withdrawal: the act of moving or taking sth. away or back

outrage: a strong feeling of shock and anger

domestic: inside a particular country; not foreign or international

to register: to make your opinion known officially or publicly

belligerent: unfriendly and aggressive

legitimate: for which there is a fair and acceptable reason

to pacify: to make sb. who is angry or upset become calm and quiet

Hitler's Foreign Policy – road to disaster

From the beginning the aim of Nazi foreign policy was expansion. In "Mein Kampf" (1925) Hitler had already *affirmed* that his goal would not be the re-establishment of Germany's pre-1914 borders but the conquest of living space in eastern Europe. Germany was to become a world power or cease to exist.

But in the first few years, the German public as well as statesmen abroad believed that Hitler was merely continuing the efforts of governments of the Weimar Republic to achieve a revision of the Versailles Treaty. Hitler needed time to prepare for war and the European Powers allowed themselves to be deceived as to Hitler's true intention. The German Chancellor acted cautiously. In peace speeches he stressed his desire to settle disputes peacefully and the signing of the non-aggression pact with Poland in January 1934 seemed to prove his *honourable* intentions.

Revision – cooperation and confrontation 1933 – 1938

But Hitler did not lose much time to achieve his true programme. The revision of the treaty of Versailles was not his main goal but an important pre-condition and a good cover to prepare for future expansion. Already in 1933 Germany announced its *withdrawal* from the League of Nations on the grounds that Germany would not be treated on equal terms in the question of disarmament. In 1935 the Saar region rejoined the Reich after a referendum in which 90 per cent of voters opted for Germany. The same year, in March, compulsory military service was introduced and Hitler claimed that Germany was no longer bound by the military clauses of the Versailles Treaty. This step caused public *outrage* in western Europe and the governments of Italy, France and Britain protested against it, but they did not take any action. On the contrary, in June 1935 an Anglo-German naval agreement was

M1 The Third Reich and Europe 1935-1939

signed which ignored the Treaty of Versailles and allowed the German navy to increase its fleet. In 1936 the German army marched into the demilitarized Rhineland. Hitler's next aim was to reunite with Austria, which was also forbidden by the Peace Treaty of 1919. Interfering in *domestic* political affairs in Austria, the Nazis provoked an uprising and finally the German army crossed the border to "restore order". On 13 March 1938, Hitler announced the "Anschluss", or union, of the two countries in "Greater Germany". In April the dictator ordered a plebiscite on the issue of Austrian independence and 99.7 per cent of Austrians favoured the union of their country with Germany.

Appeasement

For a long time Great Britain and France did little to counter the German violations of the international order established at Versailles. Their governments *registered* diplomatic protests but seemed impotent or unwilling to stand up to Hitler. The British Prime Minister Neville Chamberlain stated in 1938 that "nothing could have arrested this action by Germany unless we and others with us had been prepared to use force to prevent it". But neither France nor Britain were prepared to wage war for territory that was considered German anyway. Very few people in Britain realized how aggressive and *belligerent* Hitler's plans really were. Until 1938 Hitler had always claimed merely to execute the right for self-determination of the German people and many western politicians thought that the wish to reunite all Germans in one state was a *legitimate* aim. Many politicians felt that the Versailles treaty was too harsh on Germany and, having the Great War of 1914–18 still in vivid memory, took every step to avoid another military conflict. In addition to that the western armies were not in a condition to act offensively and needed time to modernize and prepare for war.

Consequently France and Britain pursued a policy of **appeasement**, which meant that they gave in to Hitler's demands in order to *pacify* the dictator and prevent a military conflict. This policy was and still is controversial. Did it sharpen Hitler's appetite for further conquest? Was it a policy lacking courage? Was there an alternative with a nation and an army not ready for war?

The crisis over Czechoslovakia became the climax of western "appeasement policy". Claiming that the principle of national self-determination was denied to the German majority in the Sudetenland, Hitler demanded this region be

Historical Terms

appeasement:
Beschwichtigung

M 2   Invasion of Czechoslovakia
Photograph, 15 March 1939

Vocabulary

to incorporate: to include sth. so that it forms a part of sth. else

concession: sth. you give or allow to sb. in order to reach an agreement

to resent: to feel bitter or angry about sth. you feel is unfair

to seal: to make sth. definite, so that it cannot be changed

inevitable: sth. you cannot avoid or prevent

incorporated into the Reich. Chamberlain believed that the crisis could be solved by negotiations and at the Munich Conference in September 1938 the matter was settled peacefully. Excluding the Czech government, the governments of Germany, France, Britain and Italy agreed to transfer the Sudetenland to Germany, while guaranteeing the remaining Czech frontiers. Prague only had the chance to comply or fight alone, which was impossible. On his return to London, Chamberlain told the British people, "I believe it is peace for our time".

Expansion – the road to war 1939

The revisionist phase of Nazi foreign policy included diplomatic pressure, aggression and the threat of military force. Through the annexation of Austria and the Sudetenland, Germany gained valuable additional resources of manpower, raw materials, industry and foreign exchange. It was also strategically better placed to pursue Hitler's basic aim – the conquest of territory in the east.

When German troops marched into Czechoslovakia on 15 March 1939, a breach of the Munich Agreement Hitler himself had signed, the phase of violent expansion began. The Slovaks demanded greater autonomy from the Czechs and asked Hitler for help, who finally sent troops to occupy the country and to "restore order". Bohemia and Moravia became a "protectorate" of Germany, Slovakia independent. Public opinion in France and Britain was outraged and after Hitler seized the Memel territory both powers gave a guarantee of support to Poland in the event of an attack on it. All hopes that Hitler could be appeased by *concession* were finally crushed. In May 1939 Germany signed a Pact of Steel with Italy stengthening the "axis" between the two countries. Later Japan joined the alliance making up the third member of the Axis Powers.

Then Hitler turned against Poland. For many Germans, and certainly for Hitler, the most *resented* losses imposed on Germany at Versailles were the eastern German provinces passed to Poland. The Polish Corridor divided Germany in two and Hitler demanded the return of Danzig to Germany and a road and a railway to East Prussia. But in fact, the existence of entire Poland was intolerable to the German dictator and he ordered the army to prepare for an invasion. To make sure that the Soviet Union could not attack he surprised many people by signing a non-aggression pact with his ideological archenemy. Both countries agreed not to support any third power, if that power attacked either of them. The secret agreement to invade and divide Poland between the two powers and allow the Soviet Union to occupy the Baltic States – Latvia, Lithuania and Estonia, was not made public. When the German Foreign Minister von Ribbentrop returned from Moscow, Hitler hailed him as a "second Bismarck". Hitler was convinced that with a neutral Russia, Britain would not risk a military confrontation. Removing the fear of a war on two fronts, the Nazi-Soviet Pact finally *sealed* the fate of Poland and made the coming of war *inevitable*.

M 3   Great Britain's Military Spending 1933–39

Year	1933/34	34/35	35/36	36/37	37/38	38/39
in million ponds	108	114	124	186	266	391

Eberhard Aleff, Das Dritte Reich, Hannover: Verlag für Literatur u. Zeitgeschehen 1970, p. 148.

Revision and Appeasement 1933–38

M 4 "Peace"?

Adolf Hitler's First Radio Address as Chancellor (1 February 1933):

"[…] In foreign policy, the National Government will see its highest mission in the preservation of our people's right to an independent life and in the regaining thereby of their freedom. The determination of this Government to put an end to the chaotic conditions in Germany is a step towards the integration into the community of nations of a state having equal status and therefore equal rights with the rest. In so doing, the Government is aware of its great obligation to support, as the Government of a free and equal nation, that maintenance and consolidation of peace which the world needs today more than ever before. May all others understand our position and so help to ensure that this sincere desire for the welfare of Europe and of the whole world shall find fulfilment."

"Völkischer Beobachter", February 2, 1933; Transl. quoted from: Jeremy Noakes and Geoffrey Pridham (eds.), Nazism 1919–1945, Vol. 1, The Rise to Power 1919–1934. Exeter: University of Exeter Press, 1998, pp. 131–34. http://germanhistorydocs.ghi-dc.org/docpage.cfm?docpage_id=4868 [July 12, 2018].

M 5 Liebmann Memorandum

Hitler's Comments at a Dinner with the Chiefs of the Army and the Navy (3 February 1933). General Lieutenant Liebmann took the following notes.

"[…] 2. Foreign policy: Battle against Versailles. Equality of rights in Geneva; but useless if people do not have the will to fight. Concern for allies.
[…] 4. Building up of the armed forces: Most important prerequisite for achieving the goal of regaining political power. National Service must be reintroduced. […]
How should political power be used when it has been gained? That is impossible to say yet. Perhaps fighting for new export possibilities, perhaps — and probably better — the conquest of new living space in the east and its *ruthless* Germanization. […]"

Transl. quoted from: Jeremy Noakes and Geoffrey Pridham (eds.), Nazism, 1919–1945, Vol. 3: Foreign Policy, War and Racial Extermination. Exeter: Exeter University Press, 2001, pp. 20f. http://ghdi.ghi-dc.org/sub_document.cfm?document_id=1538 [July 12, 2018].

Vocabulary

ruthless: without any consideration of other people

M 6 "Stepping Stones to Glory?"

English Cartoon by David Low, Evening Standard, 8 July 1936

Vocabulary

Useful words

spine: backbone

to do the goose-step: a way of marching in which the legs are raised high and straight

thumb your nose at sb./sth.: show a lack of respect, make a fool of somebody

Vocabulary

ultimate goal

steps on the path: Rearmament, Rhineland, Danzig, Boss of the Universe

facial expression of sadness, pain and disappointment

Revision and Appeasement 1933–38

M 7 Munich Agreement

Speech by Winston Churchill in Parliament on the Munich Agreement, October 1938:

"I will begin by saying that everybody would like to ignore or forget but which must nevertheless be stated. We have experienced a total defeat. I have always held the view that the maintenance of peace depends upon the *accumulation of deterrents* against the aggressor, coupled with a sincere effort to *redress grievances*. […] After [Hitler's] seizure of Austria in March… I *ventured* to appeal to the Government […] to give a pledge that *in conjunction* with France and other Powers they would guarantee the security of Czechoslovakia while the Sudeten-Deutsch question was being examined either by a League of Nations Commission or some other *impartial* body, and I still believe that if that course had been followed events would not have fallen into this disastrous state. […] The government has neither prevented Germany from re-arming, nor did it re-arm ourselves in time. Thus they have left us without adequate national defence. […] and do not suppose this is the end. This is only the beginning."

Adapted from: https://winstonchurchill.org/resources/speeches/1930-1938-the-wilderness/the-munich-agreement/ [July 12, 2018].

M 8 "Peace for our Time"

British Prime Minister Neville Chamberlain on his return from the Munich Conference, 1 October 1938: "My good friends, for the second time in our history, a British Prime Minister has returned from Germany bringing peace with honour. I believe it is peace for our time […] Go home and get a nice quiet sleep."

M 9 Invasion of Czechoslovakia

Chamberlain defines his attitude towards Czechoslovakia. Excerpt from his diary, 20 March 1938.

"You only have to look at the map to see that nothing France or we could do could possibly save Czechoslovakia from being overrun by the Germans […]. The Austrian frontier is practically open; the great Skoda munitions works are within easy bombing distance of German *aerodromes*, the railways all pass through German territory, Russia is 100 miles away. Therefore we could not help Czechoslovakia – she would simply be a *pretext* for going to war with Germany. That we could not think of unless we had a reasonable prospect of being able to beat her to her knees in reasonable time, and of that I see no sign. I have therefore *abandoned* the idea of giving guarantees to Czechoslovakia, or the French in connection with her obligations to that country."

Quoted from: Keith Feiling, The life of Neville Chamberlain, London: Macmillan & Co. Ltd. 1946, pp. 347f.

Vocabulary

accumulation of deterrents: the fact (or: act) of increasing means to discourage an enemy from attacking

redress grievances: to correct sth. you think is unfair and that you protest about

to venture: to dare, to risk

in conjunction: together with

impartial: not supporting one person or group more than another, neutral

aerodromes: airports

pretext: a false reason that you give for doing sth.

to abandon: to leave, to give up

Tasks

1. **Hitler's Foreign Policy – deception and lies?**
   a) Study the map (M1). Which territories did Hitler gain between 1935 and 1939?
   b) Compare Hitler's speeches (M4 and M5) and explain the contradictions.
   c) List the main aims of Hitler's foreign policy.
2. **Appeasement – a failure?**
   a) Describe Low's cartoon (M6) and show how Hitler and the "leaders of democracy" are presented.
   b) Explain the message of the cartoon (M6).
   c) Analyse sources (M7 and M9) and list the motives of the appeasement policy.
   d) "Chamberlain's policy of appeasement was the right policy at the time". Use the sources (M3, M7 and M9) and your own knowledge to explain whether you agree or not with this view.

The Road to War 1939

M 10 Russian View on the Hitler-Stalin Pact

Nikita Khrushchev was the secretary of the Moscow Regional Committee in 1939. He, who was with Stalin when the Nazi-Soviet Pact was signed, wrote about these events in his autobiography "Khrushchev Remembers" (1971):

"I believe the Ribbentrop-Molotov Pact of 1939 was historically *inevitable*, given the circumstances of the time, and that in the final analysis it was profitable for the Soviet Union. It was like a *gambit* in chess: if we hadn't made that
5 move, the war would have started earlier, much to our disadvantage. It was very hard for us – as Communists, as anti-fascists – to accept the idea of joining forces with Germany. It was difficult enough for us to accept the paradox ourselves. For their part, the Germans too were
10 using the treaty as a maneuver to win time. Their idea was to divide and conquer the nations which had united against Germany in World War I and which might unite against Germany again. Hitler wanted to deal with his adversaries one at a time. He was convinced that Germany had been
15 defeated in World War I because she tried to fight on two fronts at once. The treaty he signed with us was his way of trying to limit the coming war to one front."

Nikita Sergejevich Khrushchev, Khrushchev Remembers. With an Introduction, Commentary and Notes by Edward Crankshaw, transl. by Strobe Talbott, Boston/Toronto: Little, Brown & Company 1971.

Vocabulary

inevitable: unavoidable
gambit: an opening in which a player seeks to obtain some advantage
calamity: disaster

M 11 "Now at War"

Prime Minister's (Mr. Chamberlain) Broadcast to the German People on 4 September 1939

"German people!
Your country and mine are now at war. Your Government has bombed and invaded the free and independent State of Poland, which this country is in honour bound to defend […] God knows this country has done everything possible to 5 prevent this *calamity*. But now that the invasion of Poland by Germany has taken place, it has become inevitable… Your Government had previously demanded that a Polish representative should be sent to Berlin within twenty-four hours to conclude an agreement. […] The Polish 10 representative was expected to arrive within a fixed time to sign an agreement which he had not even seen. This is not negotiation. This is a dictate… Negotiations on a free and equal basis might well have settled the matter in dispute… Why did we feel it necessary to pledge ourselves to defend 15 this Eastern Power? […]
The answer is – and I regret to have to say it – that nobody in this country any longer places any trust in your Leader's word.
He gave his word that he would respect the Locarno Treaty; 20 he broke it.
He gave his word that he neither wished nor intended to annex Austria; he broke it.
He declared that he would not incorporate the Czechs in the Reich; he did so. 25
He gave his word after Munich that he had no further territorial demands in Europe; he broke it. He gave his word that he wanted no Polish provinces; he broke it.
He has sworn to you for years that he was the mortal enemy of Bolshevism ; he is now its ally. 30
Can you wonder his word is, for us, not worth the paper it is written on?"

Adapted from: The Prime Minister's broadcast talk to the German people on September 4, 1939, in: The British War Bluebook. Documents concerning German-Polish relations and the outbreak of hostilities between Great Britain an Germany on September 3, 1939, New York: Farrar & Rinehard 1939, pp. 249f. (No. 144). https://archive.org/details/british-warbluebo002673mbp [July 12, 2018].

Tasks

1. **The Hitler-Stalin Pact – "a paradox"?**
   Study Khrushchev's text (M10) and explain the reasons Hitler and Stalin had to conclude a pact with the ideological archenemy.

2. **The Outbreak of War – who is to blame?**
   a) Analyse Chamberlain's broadcast (M11).
   b) Write a newspaper article for the London Times about the outbreak of war.

The Second World War

Vocabulary
to retreat: to move away from a place or an enemy because of danger or defeat
campaign: a series of attacks and battles to achieve a military aim during a war
air raid: an attack by planes dropping bombs on a place
to safeguard: to protect
supply: an amount of sth. that is available to be used
to deprive: to take away, to prevent sb. from having or doing sth.
postponement: arrangement for an event to take place at a later time
to shatter: to destroy
annihilation: complete destruction
extermination: the killing of a group of people or animals
deployment: use

When German troops invaded Poland on 1 September 1939, its only allies were Italy and Japan which also sought to expand their spheres of influence by the use of military force. The three formed the **Axis Powers**. Britain and France declared war on Germany on 3 September and were later joined by the Soviet Union and the USA. They are referred to as the Allies.

The role Germany played in the Second World War can be divided into three phases. The first runs from the invasion of Poland to the invasion of Yugoslavia in April 1941. It was a period of uninterrupted German successes, during which Hitler's armies overran much of Europe. In the second phase from December 1941, the war became a global conflict and the German armies were forced to *retreat*. In the final phase – 1944/45 – the Allies reached the German borders and occupied the country.

Initial Victories – the "Blitzkrieg" (1939–1941)

In the Polish *campaign*, Hitler achieved his first "Blitzkrieg" or **"lightning war"** victory. Fast moving tank divisions, supported by *air raids*, raced across Poland and defeated the Polish army within a few weeks. Then, in April 1940, Hitler turned against Denmark and Norway *to safeguard* the *supply* of iron ore, which was needed to produce weapons. Violating the neutrality of the Benelux states, German forces conquered France in June 1940. France was occupied in the north by the Germans while the pro-German Vichy government ruled southern France. Hitler's next target was Britain. Despite the German air raids on English cities like London and Coventry, which caused tens of thousands of civilian casualties, the new Prime Minister Winston Churchill resolved to continue the fight. The German air force was defeated in the Battle of Britain. This *deprived* the German invasion fleet of

M 1

The Second World War in Europe 1939-1942

Axis Powers
- 1939
- Allies 1941
- occupied territories to November 1942
- Eastern front, Dec. 1941

Allies
- territory of Allies in Nov. 1942

- neutral countries
- state borders at the beginning of war 1.9.1939

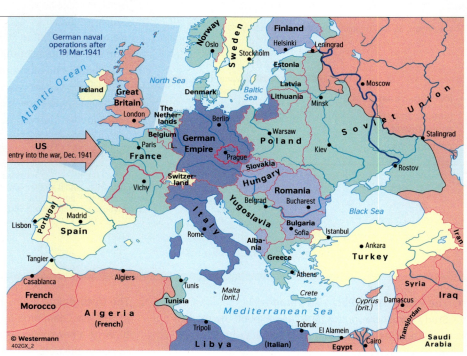

M 2 War in Poland
German soldiers shooting Polish civilians, September 1939

vital air cover, forcing Hitler to cancel the campaign. He decided to switch the military focus, and to start preparing for the invasion of the Soviet Union even before Britain had been defeated.

In April 1941 Hitler had to order the invasion of Yugoslavia and Greece in order to help Italian forces which had failed in their attempt to get control of the Balkan region and to secure the oil-fields in Romania, a source of German oil. Italy proved to be a weak ally also in North Africa. To prevent Italian defeat by the British, Hitler had to transfer troops to a region he did not consider important. All these events led to a *postponement* of the invasion of the Soviet Union.

"Crusade against Bolshevism" and the Turning of the Tide (1941–1943)

When Hitler turned against the USSR he argued with the grain and oil resources essential to the war effort or with the belief that Russia's defeat would force Britain out of the war, but actually he pursued his ultimate goal: win "Lebensraum", living space for the German people, in the east and at the same time fight Bolshevism/Communism.

On 22 June 1941 Hitler broke the Nazi-Soviet non-aggression pact. Three million German troops, supported by Finnish, Romanian and Italian divisions, crossed a border that stretched 1500 miles from the Arctic Ocean to the Black Sea. But this war turned out to be very different from the lightning war in the west. Although German troops advanced quickly to Leningrad and Moscow, the beginning of winter with temperatures dropping to –40° Celsius and the stubborn resistance of Soviet troops *shattered* the illusion of a swift victory in December 1941. Also, the character of war was not the same. Nazi ideology foresaw military conquest but also *annihilation* and racial *extermination*. During the "Crusade against Bolshevism" Communist leaders and millions of civilians, among them most of the Jewish population, were shot, starved to death or reduced to slave labour. The country's industrial and agricultural base was destroyed. At the end of the war the Soviet Union had suffered casualties of about 20 million people.

Historical Terms

Axis Powers: Achsenmächte
"lightning war": "Blitzkrieg"

The Third Reich

M 3 House-to-house Fighting
Russian soldier in the ruins of Stalingrad, 1942

Vocabulary

self-delusion: the act of believing sth. that is not true

Historical Terms

unconditional surrender: bedingungslose Kapitulation

The Japanese attack on Pearl Harbor (Hawaii) on 6 December 1941 turned the European war into a World War. Although the alliance with Japan did not oblige Hitler to do so, he declared war on the USA, the most advanced industrial nation in the world. The Soviet Union, Britain and the USA formed an "anti-Hitler coalition" and agreed to fight Germany until its **unconditional surrender**. America's enormous military and economic strength combined with Soviet manpower finally led to Allied superiority and German defeat. In 1942/43 the Germans suffered significant setbacks. Their troops were driven out of Africa and lost the battle of Stalingrad. The loss of about 250,000 troops was a disaster for Hitler and a major turning point of the war. From 1943 on German strategy was defensive, its armies retreated.

Towards Defeat in Europe and the Pacific (1944–1945)

By 1943 German troops were fighting on four fronts: in Italy, in the east, in the Atlantic and in the air over Germany. In June 1944 the landings by the Western Allies in Normandy added another front and Germany's military situation grew still more desperate. The final phase of the war began.

In September British and American troops reached the Rhine; in October Soviet troops were on the German border to East Prussia. Hitler's counter-offensive in the Ardennes in winter 1944/45 failed and cost the last reserves of troops. The final useless effort to defend Germany with the "Volkssturm", a badly trained and equipped army made up of men over 60 and boys, some younger than 16, only increased the number of senseless casualties.

The war was lost, a fact which should have been realized as early as 1942. German resources and economic power had been stretched too far and could not keep up with the Allies' huge industrial power. The American economy alone produced more steel, oil and motor vehicles in 1941 than the rest of the world put

M 4 The Second World War in Europe 1942–1945

together. The USSR had vast resources of raw materials and human manpower. However, the fight on several fronts with long supply lines and limited manpower continued. Hitler had lost touch with reality and lived in a world of *self-delusion*. After his suicide the German forces surrendered unconditionally on 8 May 1945. The war in Europe finally came to an end and left the continent in ruins.

The war in the Pacific took some more months. In June 1942, a decisive aircraft carrier battle near Midway Island marked the end of Japanese expansion and the United States took the initiative and began an "island-hopping" campaign to drive back the Japanese. One island after the other was captured with heavy casualties on both sides. In April 1945 the Americans assaulted Okinawa, on the most southern island of Japan. The Japanese launched the greatest Kamikaze raids of the war, but although they caused tremendous damage and high losses of American lives, they could not prevent the American landing. A massive invasion in the Tokyo area was scheduled for 1 March 1946 if Japanese resistance continued. Fearing that the invasion of Japan would cost the lives of countless US soldiers, President Truman ordered the atomic bombings of Hiroshima and Nagasaki on 6 and 9 August. The two bombs killed over 200,000 people, including many who died months later from the effects of radiation. Together with the Soviet declaration of war on 8 August Japanese leaders were forced to recognize the inevitable. Emperor Hirohito announced Japan's surrender and with V-J Day on 2 September 1945 the greatest conflict in human history came to an end. The Second World War was the bloodiest and most devastating conflict in the history of mankind. The number of casualties amounted to about 55 million people.

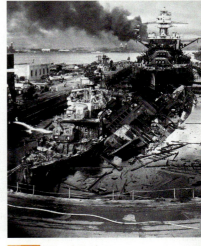

M 5   Pearl Harbor
After the Japanese attack on Pearl Harbor, 7 December 1941

M 6   Mushroom Cloud
The US bomber "Enola Gay" was the first aircraft to drop an atomic bomb. It exploded over Hiroshima and cost the lives of hundreds of thousands of people. Photograph, 6 August 1945.

M 7   Hiroshima After the Attack
Photograph, August 1945

War in the Pacific – dropping the bomb

M 8 **Harry S. Truman**
Photograph, 1947

M 9 **Reflections on the Atomic Bombings**

a) In a letter to history professor James L. Cate, President Harry Truman wrote (1953):

"[…] When the message came to Potsdam that a successful atomic explosion had taken place in New Mexico, there was much excitement and conversation about the effect on the war then in progress with Japan. The next day I told the Prime Minister of Great Britain and Generalissimo Stalin that the explosion had been a success. The British Prime Minister understood and appreciated what I'd told him. Premier Stalin smiled and thanked me for reporting the explosion to him, but I'm sure he did not understand its significance. […]

I asked General Marshall what it would cost in lives to land on the Tokyo plain and other places in Japan. It was his opinion that such an invasion would cost at a minimum one quarter of a million casualties, and might cost as much as a million, on the American side alone, with an equal number of the enemy. The other military and naval men present agreed. I asked Secretary (of War) Stimson which sites in Japan were devoted to war production. He promptly named Hiroshima and Nagasaki, among others. We sent an ultimatum to Japan. It was rejected.

I ordered atomic bombs dropped on the two cities named on the way back from Potsdam, when we were in the middle of the Atlantic Ocean. […] Dropping the bombs ended the war, saved lives, and gave the free nations a chance to face the facts. When it looked as if Japan would quit, Russia hurried into the *fray* less than a week before the surrender, so as to be in at the settlement. No military contribution was made by the Russians toward victory over Japan. … (but) Manchuria was occupied by the Soviets, as was Korea, North of the 38th parallel."

Adapted from: www.atomicarchive.com/Docs/Hiroshima/Truman.shtml [July 12, 2018].

b) The following is an excerpt from President Obama's speech in Hiroshima, Japan, 2015

"Seventy-one years ago, on a bright cloudless morning, death fell from the sky and the world was changed. A flash of light and a wall of fire destroyed a city and demonstrated that mankind possessed the means to destroy itself. Why do we come to this place, to Hiroshima? We come to ponder a terrible force *unleashed* in a not-so-distant past. We come to mourn the dead, including over 100,000 Japanese men, women and children, thousands of Koreans, a dozen Americans held prisoner.

Their souls speak to us. They ask us to look inward, to *take stock* of who we are and what we might become […] The world war that reached its brutal end in Hiroshima and Nagasaki was fought among the wealthiest and most powerful of nations. Their civilizations had given the world great cities and magnificent art. Their thinkers had advanced ideas of justice and harmony and truth. And yet the war grew out of the same base instinct for domination or conquest that had caused conflicts among the simplest tribes, an old pattern *amplified* by new capabilities and without new constraints.

In the span of a few years, some 60 million people would die. Men, women, children, no different than us. […] Yet in the image of a mushroom cloud that rose into these skies, we are most starkly reminded of humanity's core contradiction. How the very spark that marks us as a species, our thoughts, our imagination, our language, our toolmaking, our ability to set ourselves apart from nature and bend it to our will — those very things also give us the capacity for unmatched destruction.

[…] The wars of the modern age teach us this truth. Hiroshima teaches this truth. Technological progress without an equivalent progress in human institutions can *doom* us. The scientific revolution that led to the splitting

---

Vocabulary

fray: fight, competition
unleashed: free, let loose
to take stock: to stop and think carefully about the way in which a particular situation is developing in order to decide what to do next
to amplify: to make larger or more powerful, increase

of an atom requires a moral revolution as well... we have a shared responsibility to look directly into the eye of history and ask what we must do differently *to curb* such suffering again.

Some day, the voices of the *hibakusha* will no longer be with us to bear witness. But the memory of the morning of Aug. 6, 1945, must never fade. That memory allows us to fight *complacency*. It fuels our moral imagination. It allows us to change.

And since that fateful day, we have made choices that give us hope. The United States and Japan have forged not only an alliance but a friendship that has won far more for our people than we could ever claim through war. The nations of Europe built a union that replaced battlefields with bonds of commerce and democracy. Oppressed people and nations won liberation. An international community established institutions and treaties that work to avoid war and aspire to restrict and roll back and ultimately eliminate the existence of nuclear weapons. [...] And yet that is not enough. For we see around the world today how even the crudest rifles and barrel bombs can serve up violence on a terrible scale. We must change our mind-set about war itself. To prevent conflict through diplomacy and strive to end conflicts after they've begun. To see our growing *interdependence* as a cause for peaceful cooperation and not violent competition. To define our nations not by our capacity to destroy but by what we build. And perhaps, above all, we must reimagine our connection to one another as members of one human race.

For this, too, is what makes our species unique. We're not bound by genetic code to repeat the mistakes of the past. We can learn. We can choose. We can tell our children a different story, one that describes a common humanity, one that makes war less likely and cruelty less easily accepted. [...]

M 10 **Barack Obama**
Photograph, 2014

The world was forever changed here, but today the children of this city will go through their day in peace. What a precious thing that is. It is worth protecting, and then extending to every child. That is a future we can choose, a future in which Hiroshima and Nagasaki are known not as the *dawn* of atomic warfare but as the start of our own moral awakening.

Adapted from: The White House Office of the Press Secretary.

Vocabulary

to doom: to destine or condemn to death or a terrible fate
to curb: to control or limit sth., especially sth. bad
hibakusha: the Japanese word for the surviving victims of the 1945 atomic bombings of Hiroshima and Nagasaki
complacency: self-satisfaction especially when accompanied by unawareness of actual dangers
interdependence: the fact of depending on each other
dawn: sunrise

Tasks

1. **War in Europe**
   a) Study the maps (M1, M4) and list the countries Germany attacked in a chronological order (text).
   b) Explain the problems German warfare faced in 1942 (M1, text).
   d) Explain why Germany lost the war (M1, M4, text).
2. **War in the Pacific – dropping the bomb**
   a) Assess President Truman's decision to use the atomic bombs (M9a).
   b) Discuss in class whether the use of the atomic bomb against Japan was necessary.
   c) What does, according to Obama (M9b), Hiroshima tell us today, 72 years after the dropping of the atomic bomb?
   e) Discuss Obama's statements with a partner and then in class (M9b).

Societies at War

Historical Terms

military intelligence: militärischer Nachrichtendienst

scorched earth policy: Politik der verbrannten Erde

The two world wars of the 20th century were total wars that involved the whole nation, and the "home front" became an important part of the war effort. Although it was the men who went off to fight the war, the people left behind at home also had a part to play in the war. The Home Front refers to the effect of the war on people's everyday lives.

All countries at war censured the press and selected the news which the public should be given. Public morale should not suffer, but – with the help of propaganda campaigns – be boosted. Mobilizing economic output was a major factor in supporting combat operations so every government took measures to increase production. Working hours were extended and women called upon to take over the jobs traditionally done by men. Rationing food, clothing, petrol, leather and other items was another action taken which affected life significantly.

Britain and France

Vocabulary

malnutrition: a poor condition of health caused by a lack of food

military intelligence: to provide timely, relevant and accurate information about the enemy

crusade: historically the wars fought in Palestine by European Christian countries against the Muslims in the Middle Ages

expulsion: forcing somebody to leave a house or land

to resettle: to move people to another area

In September 1940 the German Air Force began air raids on London known as "the blitz". It caused considerable damage and over 40,000 civilian casualties. Already in September 1939 the British government had ordered the evacuation of high-risk cities. Children were sent to Canada, the USA, Australia or evacuated to safer areas in the countryside. When German submarines attacked British shipping lanes in the Atlantic, imported supplies were reduced and rationing was introduced. The British people, however, were adequately fed during the war, which was not the case in occupied Europe where rationing was severe and *malnutrition* common.

M 1 Debris of the Cathedral of Coventry
After a German air raid, 1940

After the quick German victory in June 1940, France surrendered. The north was occupied and the south, with its capital in Vichy, became an informal ally of the Germans. The Germans captured about two million French soldiers, and kept them in prisoner of war camps inside Germany. Most Frenchmen in the occupied north and west tried to live their normal lives without attracting attention from the Germans, some co-operated and others resisted. The Vichy French government cooperated closely with the Germans, sending food, machinery and workers to Germany. Several hundred thousand Frenchmen and women were forced to work in German factories, or volunteered to do so, as the French economy was in a poor state. The Vichy government also actively collaborated in the extermination of the European Jews opening concentration camps in France where it interned Jews, Gypsies, homosexuals or political opponents. In some cases French police assisted the Gestapo and some thousand French volunteers fought against the Soviet Union on the eastern front. On the other hand there was a strong resistance movement, which, especially after the Anglo-American invasion in 1944, helped to fight the German armies. The resistance provided **military intelligence**, executed acts of sabotage or helped Allied soldiers trapped behind enemy lines.

M 2 Church in Oradour after the Massacre

On 10 June 1944, 642 of the inhabitants of the village, including women and children, were locked in the church, shot and burnt alive by a German Waffen-SS company. Photo, 1944

Poland and the Soviet Union

As mentioned above, the war in the east was a different one. It was an ideological, racial *crusade* for living space. It opposed the "inferior" Slavic people and Communism. Consequently, the east European population had to suffer most. Germany's occupation of Poland is one of the darkest chapters of World War II. Some 6 million people, almost 18 percent of the Polish population, were killed during the Nazi reign of terror that saw mass executions, forced *expulsions* and enslavement. Starvation was used as a weapon when the Germans started a system of food controls, including severe punishments for black marketing. By 1941, the German minority in Poland received over 2000 calories per day, while Poles received about a third and Jews in the ghetto only about 200. The Jewish and Polish rations did not in the least meet the daily needs. In late 1942, police officers began brutally evacuating more than 100,000 Polish farmers to make way for 20,000 ethnic Germans. Those fit for work were sent to Germany, old people and children were *resettled*, while anyone considered "inferior" or "unreliable" was deported to concentration camps. Many Poles fled the police, hiding in the forests, and forming resistance groups. They attacked trains and blew up railways and bridges. The Warsaw Ghetto Uprising of 1943 was the largest single revolt by Jews during the war, but it failed. So did the Warsaw Uprising by the Polish underground resistance in summer 1944. The attempt to liberate the Polish capital from German occupation was not supported by the approaching Soviet Red Army. It was finally crushed after 63 days of fighting. However, it was the single largest military effort taken by any European resistance movement during World War II.

World War II was also devastating to citizens of the USSR because it was fought on Soviet territory and caused massive destruction. During the rapid German advances in 1941 and 1942 factories were evacuated or destroyed. The harvest was not brought in and led to malnutrition. In Leningrad, under German siege, over a million people died of starvation and disease. In many other Russian districts the government started a **scorched earth policy** in order to deny the invaders access to electrical, telecommunications, rail, and industrial resources. Parts of the telegraph network were destroyed, some railways and bridges were blown up and

M 3 Inhabitants of Murmansk

carrying their luggage through the destroyed city. Photograph, 1942

many power stations were sabotaged. The process was repeated later in the war by the German forces, which stole crops, destroyed farms, and burned villages and towns during several military operations. Of course, it was the civilian population that suffered most, paying for the war with millions of lives. There was also organized resistance in the German occupied areas. As early as 1941 Stalin ordered the formation of partisan units, which attacked German troops and by destroying communication and supply lines significantly disrupted their operations in the region.

Germany

The war also had a dramatic impact on Germans at home. The economy was not prepared for a long-lasting, major war. As a result the government had to introduce the rationing of food, clothing and basics like shoes, soap, or sweets. When it started, Germany was able to make up some shortages by taking goods from the countries it conquered. But civilian hardship intensified after 1943, as the heavy bombing of German cities like Cologne, Hamburg or Dresden led to destruction and killed hundreds of thousands of civilians. About four million homes were destroyed, factories and infrastructure damaged. The German government organized evacuation programmes for children ("Kinderlandverschickung"), introduced ration cards for food and clothes and obliged members of the Hitler Youth to support the war effort. They helped the fire services, collected metals, distributed food and coal or acted as anti-aircraft auxiliaries ("Flakhelfer"). The total mobilization of all forces also included women. Although Nazi ideology claimed the traditional domestic role of women, the need for workers in factories and agricultural industries had become more important. Women were called to duty to show their patriotism and fill the void left by men. Together with millions of foreign workers and prisoners-of-war women worked on the fields or in the armament industry. Some of them also voluntarily served in auxiliary units ("Nachrichtenhelferinnen") or as Air-Raid Wardens ("Luftschutzwachen"). The war put great pressure on women, especially in big cities where the Allied bombing placed them in the line of fire with little to no protection. Worried about their husbands at the front they had to bring up hungry children and organize life in damaged homes.

M 4 **Bomb Victims in Mannheim**
Photograph, 1943

M 5 **Hamburg After the Firestorm**
1943

Societies at War – propaganda posters

M 6 "Women of Britain – come into the factories"
British Poster, after 1940

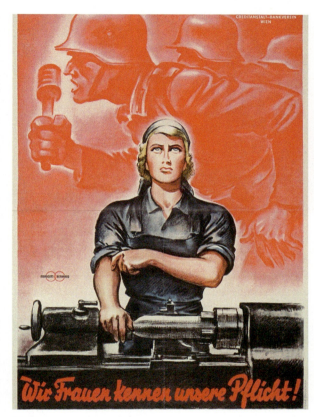

M 7 "We Women Know Our Duty"
German Poster, 1939/1940

M 8 "The Bad Days are Over! Dad Earns Money in Germany"
German Poster in occupied France to attract French workers for factories in Germany, Paris, 1942.

Tasks

1. Societies at War – propaganda posters
   a) Analyse the propaganda posters (M6–M8).
   b) Explain the effect they should have on the observer.

Societies at War – the war in the east

M 9 A Burning Russian Village
Photograph, taken in 1944

M 10 Policy of Starvation

Alfred Rosenberg, Reich Minister for the Occupied Eastern Territories, justifying a policy of starvation, 19 June 1941:

"The job of feeding the German people stands at the top of the list [...] We see absolutely no reason for any obligation on our part to feed also the Russian people with the products of their surplus territory. We know that this is a
5 harsh necessity, bare of any feelings [...]."

Quoted from: William L. Shirer, The Rise and Fall of the Third Reich, p. 833, New York: Simon & Schuster 1960, p. 833.

M 11 Nazi Warfare

German Field Marshal von Reichenau instructs the German Sixth Army on its role in the Soviet Union:

"Army HQ, 10 October 1941
Subject: *Conduct* of Troops in Eastern Territories.
Regarding the conduct of troops towards the Bolshevistic system, vague ideas are still *prevalent* in many cases. The
5 most essential aim of war against the Jewish-Bolshevistic system is a complete destruction of their means of power and the *elimination* of Asiatic influence from the European culture. In this connection the troops are facing tasks which exceed the one-sided routine of soldiering. The soldier in the Eastern territories is not merely a fighter according to 10 the rules of the art of war but also a bearer of ruthless national ideology and the *avenger* of bestialities which have been inflicted upon German and racially related nations.
Therefore the soldier must have full understanding for the 15 necessity of a severe but just revenge on subhuman Jewry. The Army has to aim at another purpose, i.e. the annihilation of revolts in *hinterland*, which, as experience proves, have always been caused by Jews."

Quoted from: Hitler's Army: Soldiers, Nazis, and War in the Third Reich, New York: Oxford University Press 1991), pp. 129f.

Vocabulary

conduct: behaviour
prevalent: widespread
elimination: removal
avenger: sb. who takes revenge
hinterland: (here) area behind the front lines

M 12 Execution of Hostages

US-President Franklin D. Roosevelt on the execution of hostages by the Nazis, 25. October 1941:

"The practice of executing [...] innocent *hostages* in *reprisal* for isolated attacks on Germans in countries temporarily under the Nazi heel revolts a world already *inured* to suffering and brutality. Civilized peoples long ago adopted
5 the basic principle that no man should be punished for the deed of another. Unable to *apprehend* the persons involved in these attacks the Nazis characteristically slaughter fifty or a hundred innocent persons [...] The Nazis might have learned from the last war the impossibility of breaking
10 men's spirits by terrorism [...] It only sows the seeds of hatred which will one day bring fearful *retribution*."

Department of State Bulletin, October 25, 1941, quoted from: http://www.ibiblio.org/pha/policy/1941/411025a.html [July 12, 2018].

Vocabulary

hostage: sb. taken as prisoner so that the other side will do what the enemy demands
reprisal: sth. unpleasant done to punish an enemy as kind of revenge
inured: familiar with an unpleasant experience
to apprehend: to arrest sb.
retribution: severe punishment for sth. seriously wrong that sb. has done

M 13 A Public Hanging of Alleged Partisans
Photograph, taken in 1942

Tasks

1. **Bombs to Undermine Morale on the Home Front?**
   Find out about air raids in your region and the effects they had (M1, M2).

2. **War Behind the Front Line**
   Analyse in groups sources M3, M9–M13 and describe the peculiarity of the war on the eastern front.

3. **Societies at War**
   Find keywords for the consequences of war on societies and arrange them in a diagram.

A Controversy in England About the Right Way to Remember

M 1 **"RAF Bomber Command deserves to be remembered – with honesty"**

The Guardian, 22 June 2012:

"There is a case to recognise the sacrifice of 55,573 air crew, and to hold to account those who ordered them to kill so many:
"After almost 70 years, the 55,573 dead of RAF (= Royal Air Force) Bomber Command are to be honoured in a prominent memorial at the western end of London's Piccadilly. This is no straightforward act of remembrance. Fighter Command has been *acknowledged* in a variety of ways, stretching back to the window and chapel in Westminster Abbey installed more than 60 years ago. Bomber Command veterans were given no campaign medal, despite the *scale* of losses, and Air Chief Marshal Harris was passed over when others got their *peerage*.

M 2 **Memorial near Buckingham Pallace**
to commemorate the more than 55,000 crew members of the Royal Air Force Bomber Command killed in action, opened in 2012.

The problem with remembering Bomber Command has always been the profound *ambivalence* felt in British postwar society about the ethics of wartime bombing. Opinion polls made during the blitz found people divided evenly on the question of bombing enemy civilians – 46% for, 46% against. After the publicity given to the bombing of Dresden, and the less well-known, but more deadly, bombing of Hamburg, postwar opinion found it hard to *reconcile* Britain's image of a just war on behalf of shared liberal values with the killing of half a million enemy civilians.

During the war these doubts were covered over by repeated *assurances* in parliament and from RAF spokesmen that only military targets were ever attacked [...]. Once it was clear that this had not been the case, and indeed that the central residential areas of cities were the intended target, it became more difficult for the bombing to be absorbed into the popular memory of the war [...]. Seventy years later, the gulf still exists between those who see British bombing as an unfortunate *lapse* from an otherwise morally secure war effort, and those who think that bombing was entirely ethically justified as a response to the blitz and the need to end the war by any means against an evil and dangerous enemy.

The argument is not, of course, as simple as that. The aircrew who are to be honoured with the new memorial did not volunteer to bomb city centres and kill civilians [...]. At every briefing they were told about the industrial and military targets that lay within the area they were told to bomb. No doubt many, perhaps most, knew that their bombs would not just hit the designated objectives, but also shatter the city that housed them.

Yet *recollections* by surviving crew make it clear that, in this, one of the most dangerous environments of the war, exposed to continuous danger not once, but 30 times if they survived (and most did not), their moral reference points were their immediate comrades on board and the other flyers around them, not whatever might be happening, invisibly, on the ground.

There is a real sense in which the crew of Bomber Command were victims too, sent out often in poor weather, against distant targets, cold, fearful and aware of the hungry presence of death, by commanders who knew that survival rates were poor and that the military-industrial targets were a mere *front* for a *deliberate* policy of killing civilians and destroying the civilian milieu, a policy first developed during the course of 1941. This was a policy shielded from the public and from the crews, because it raised *awkward* questions. Among those in the know, it was felt that the greater moral failing would be *to abstain from using* every means to end the war and preserve British lives.

No one needs to be Socrates to work out that two wrongs do not make a right. If German bombing of civilians was wrong, so too was British. Those who made policy understood this. Yet it was possible for the RAF chief of staff, Charles Portal, to suggest to Churchill, Roosevelt and the assembled combined military commanders at Quebec in August 1943 that the RAF hoped to kill 900,000 German civilians without raising any *demur* among western leaders except over its *feasibility*. [...] Somehow bombing created a moral blind spot that allowed airmen to do to the enemy population what soldiers could not.

The opening of the Bomber Command monument is perhaps a moment to try to find some common ground over this unresolved element of Britain's wartime *legacy*. There is a good case for recognising the sacrifice of the 55,000-plus who died, just as we remember the wasted dead at the *Somme or Passchendaele*. But it is surely time that the ethical *subterfuge* performed all through the war, in pretending that city areas were militarily justifiable targets, was confronted honestly.

The result is a paradox. While allowing the dead of Bomber Command at last to share in the common status of wartime victims, the responsibility of those who shaped and approved of British bombing strategy and urged it on to ever higher levels of destruction cannot be sidestepped. The military will do whatever they are ordered or permitted to do according to the strategic directives they have been given; it is those who give the permission who need to be held to account."

Richard Overy, on: https://www.theguardian.com/commentisfree/2012/jun/22/raf-bomber-command-remembered-with-honesty [July 12, 2018].

Vocabulary

acknowledge: to accept that is true
scale: size or extent of something
peerage: members of the nobility
ambivalence: the fact of having or showing both good and bad feelings about something
to reconcile: to find an acceptable way of dealing with two or more ideas opposed to each other
assurance: a statement that something will certainly be true or will certainly happen
lapse: a small mistake
recollections: memories
front: behaviour that is not genuine, done in order to hide your true feelings or opinions
deliberate: done on purpose
awkward : making you feel embarrassed
to abstain from using: to not use
demur: protest
feasibility: quality of being possible and likely to be achieved
legacy: sth. that is the result of events in the past
Somme or Passchendaele: bloody battles of WW I in France and Belgium
subterfuge: a secret, usually dishonest, way of behaving

Tasks

1. **A Controversy in England About the Right Way to Remember**
   a) Analyse the text and list the facts and arguments of the controversy (M1).
   b) Discuss them with your partner and find a position.
   c) Give your opinion in a class discussion.

From Loss of Rights to Mass Murder

The Treatment of Minorities

Hitler's determination to achieve a national community of genetically healthy, socially efficient and politically loyal Aryans was the heart of Nazi ideology. From 1933 on measures were adopted to mark social outcasts and they finally ended in extermination during the war.

After Hitler's seizure of power political opponents and "*asocials*" like tramps or beggars were arrested and forced to do compulsory work. More harshly treated were groups or individuals who were considered racially impure or posing a threat to the purity of the "Aryan race". Apart from the Jews, minorities like Gypsies (Roma and Sinti) or homosexuals were discriminated against, persecuted and finally sent to concentration camps. There they faced forced labour, beatings, sterilization and finally extermination.

The Nazi program to eliminate "life unworthy of life" focused on the mentally and physically handicapped. On the basis of a questionnaire medical experts decided whether a disabled child or adult was allowed to live. **Euthanasia** ("good death" in Ancient Greek) refers to ending a life in a painless manner, but during the Third Reich "mercy killings" took place without consent of patients or relatives. The ruthless murder of thousands of patients by means of injection or carbon monoxide gas was ordered only because they were considered of no value. Religious protest especially by Catholic priests like Bishop von Galen caused Hitler to order the official cancellation of the programme in 1941.

Discrimination and Persecution of Jews

From the start Jewish people were the main target of Nazi persecution. Hitler's obsession with the threat of a Jewish-Bolshevist "world-conspiracy" led to radical and brutal measures against the Jewish population in Germany and then in occupied Europe.

Nazi policy against Jews, who numbered about 500,000 in Germany, also *proceeded by stages*. Hitler exploited the *latent hostility* of broad sections of German society towards the Jews. Anti-Semitism had a long tradition in Europe and was still strong in Germany in the twentieth century. Jews were blamed for the defeat in the First World War and in times of economic crisis prejudice increased against a group that was viewed as privileged. These *resentments* partly explain why the Nazis' aggressive programme of *stigmatizing* and excluding Jews from the national community was carried out without public protest.

A boycott of Jewish shops, doctors and lawyers in March 1933 was followed by a number of laws which banned Jews from public service and *the professions*. The Nuremberg Laws of 1935 barred Jews from citizenship and imposed a ban on marriages and "*extramarital* relations" between Aryans and Jews.

In the following years Jews were excluded from German social life by further bans from public pools, parks, cafés, theatres and transportation. On the **"Night of Broken Glass"** of 9–10 November 1938 the Nazi regime launched a shocking persecution of the Jewish community. The assassination of a German diplomat in Paris by a Jew two days earlier gave the Nazis the excuse for **pogroms** throughout Germany during which Jewish homes and shops were destroyed, *synagogues* burned down, over 90 Jews killed and thousands of Jewish men arrested and imprisoned in **concentration camps**. This outburst of violence, carried out by

M 1 **Boycott of Jewish Shops**
1 April 1933

M 2 **Public Humiliation Cuxhaven**
July 1933

Historical Terms

Euthanasia: Euthanasie

"Night of Broken Glass": "(Reichs-)Kristallnacht"

pogroms: Pogrome

concentration camp: Konzentrationslager

genocide: Genozid, Völkermord

"Final Solution of the Jewish Problem": "Endlösung", Ermordung der europäischen Juden

M 3   A Burning Synagogue in Bielefeld
9 November 1938

party activists, not only upset people abroad but also many Germans. However, most of them remained silent and did little to help their Jewish neighbours.

The position of Jews *deteriorated* more rapidly after 1938 as decrees expelled Jewish pupils from schools and transferred remaining businesses to non-Jewish owners ("aryanization"). The social isolation and economic exclusion of the Jewish minority in Germany was complete.

The Holocaust

As for the Jewish community itself, Nazi persecution did lead to the emigration of nearly 150,000 people (nearly 30% of the 1933 Jewish population) between 1933 and 1938. But as many Western countries were not prepared to take Jewish *refugees*, many took the risk and stayed in Germany.

The outbreak of war transformed Nazi racial policy into a policy of extermination. Hitler's threat in January 1939 that a future war would lead to "the destruction of the Jewish race in Europe" became reality as military victories brought millions of European Jews under Nazi control. In 1940 the Jewish population in Poland was isolated in ghettos and forced to wear a yellow Star of David. Ghetto conditions were appalling; diseases spread and hundreds of thousands of Jews died of starvation. The first mass killings of Jews were undertaken by special SS units ("Einsatzgruppen") after the invasion of the Soviet Union in June 1941. Jews were *rounded up* and taken out to forests where they had to dig their own graves, were lined up naked, and were then shot into the graves. It soon became clear to the regime that this method of killing was unable to cope with the large numbers of people who the Nazis deemed "sub-human".

In January 1942 leading Nazis met in the Berlin district of Wannsee to organize the systematic **genocide** of the Jews. Reinhard Heydrich, chief of the SS Secret Service SD and the Gestapo, presented the ultimate aim of the **"Final Solution of the Jewish Problem"** to exterminate all 11 million Jews in Europe either by

Vocabulary

asocials: (here) people unable or unwilling to conform to Nazi standards of social behaviour

to proceed: to go on

latent: existing, but not yet very noticeable

hostility: unfriendly or aggressive feelings

resentment: a feeling of anger or unhappiness about sth. considered unfair

to be stigmatized: to be treated by society as if you should be ashamed of yourself

the professions: jobs that need a high level of education and training, such as doctors, professors

extramarital: outside marriage

synagogues: Jewish houses of worship

to deteriorate: to become worse

refugee: a person who has been forced to flee from his country or home

to round up: to arrest

M 4   Jews Arrested in Warsaw
They are rounded up to be taken to the extermination camps in 1943. The boy in the foreground managed to survive the war.

Vocabulary

inconceivable: impossible to imagine or believe

working them to death or by execution. With almost *inconceivable* technical perfection the genocide of European Jews (called the "Holocaust" today) was planned and carried out.

Extermination camps like Auschwitz, Belzec or Treblinka were built in remote areas in Poland. Jews from Germany and German-occupied Europe were deported there by rail in freight or cattle cars. When they arrived, they were immediately divided into those fit for slave labour and those – usually children, the sick and the elderly – who were sent to the gas chambers. Jewish workers were tatooed on the arm with a number and sent to work in factories or mines. Their life expectancy was three months. The prisoners died of disease, exhaustion or lack of food. If they were too weak to work they were shot.

The death camps continued to operate with constantly increasing capacity until late 1944, shortly before they were liberated by Soviet troops. It is estimated that about six million Jews died in the Holocaust, a horrible crime and unspeakable tragedy in the history of mankind.

Secret or Public Knowledge?

Many Germans could not believe that their own government would commit such atrocities. At the same time the SS tried to keep the extermination programme secret and Germans were told that Jews were being resettled in the east. But many Germans had witnessed the methods of their arrest and transportation, had heard rumours about the killings in the east and hundreds of thousands of Germans even co-operated or were directly involved in the genocide. So many Germans knew, but most of them did not want to know. They preferred to ignore or disbelieve what did not concern them directly and which was unthinkable. The fate of the Jews was also known by the British, American and Soviet governments but they did not intervene and instead concentrated on the military defeat of Germany in war.

M 5 "The Last Cry"
Painting by Adolf Frankl, former prisoner in Auschwitz

M 6 Heinrich Himmler

Biography

Heinrich Himmler (1900 – 1945)

Heinrich Himmler was one of the most powerful men in Nazi Germany and mainly responsible for the concentration camps (KZ) and the Holocaust. He was born as the son of a teacher in Munich on 7 October 1900. During World War I he joined the army but did not fight at the front. After the war he studied agriculture and in 1923 he joined the Nazi Party (NSDAP). In 1929 he was appointed commander of the Schutzstaffel (SS). In the following years he expanded the SS. In 1934 he took command of the Gestapo, Germany's secret police, and in 1936 of all German police. He set up and controlled the concentration camps in Germany and when war broke out Hitler extended Himmler's authority for both security and settlement operations to occupied Poland and later the Soviet Union. SS mobile killing units (Einsatzgruppen) and other police units executed the mass murder of Jews, Soviet officials, Roma (Gypsies), and other victim groups. After 1942 extermination camps were built in Poland, run by Himmler's SS, killing millions of Jews. When Germany's defeat came near in 1944/45, Himmler made attempts to negotiate with the Allies. Hitler was furious and dismissed him from all his offices. Following Germany's surrender, Himmler tried to escape under a false identity but was captured by the British. On 23 May 1945 he committed suicide.

The Holocaust

M 7 Selection at the Ramp of Auschwitz
Photograph, June 1944

M 8 The Killing Process

A Report by SS Sturmbannführer Gricksch, Auschwitz, 1943:

"The unfit go to cellars in a large house which are entered from outside. They go down five or six steps into a fairly long, well-constructed and well-ventilated cellar area, which is lined with benches to the left and right. It is brightly lit, and the benches are numbered. The prisoners are told that they are to be cleansed and disinfected for their new assignments. They must therefore completely undress to be bathed. To avoid panic and to prevent *disturbances* of any kind, they are instructed to arrange their clothing neatly under their respective numbers, so that they will be able to find their things again after their bath. Everything proceeds in a perfectly orderly fashion. Then they pass through a small corridor and enter a large cellar room which resembles a shower bath […]. When three- to four-hundred people have been herded into this room, the doors are shut, and containers filled with the substances (poison gas Zyklon B) are dropped down […] that put the people to sleep in one minute. A few minutes later, the door opens on the other side, where the elevator is located. The hair of the corpses is cut off, and their gold-filled teeth are extracted by Jewish specialists. It has been discovered that Jews were hiding pieces of jewelry, gold, platinum etc., in *hollow* teeth. Then the corpses are loaded into elevators and brought up to the first floor, where ten large crematoria are located. (Because fresh corpses burn particularly well, only 50–100 lbs. of coke are needed for the whole process.) The job itself is performed by Jewish prisoners, who never step outside this camp again. The results of this "resettlement action" to date: 500,000 Jews. Current capacity of the "resettlement action" ovens: 10,000 in 24 hours."

Quoted from: Gerald Fleming, Hitler and the Final Solution, Berkeley: University of California Press 1984, pp. 142f.

Vocabulary

disturbance: trouble, disorder
hollow: having a hole or empty space inside

The Holocaust

M 9 Furnaces of the Concentration Camp Majdanek
Photograph of 27 July 1944, after the liberation by the Red Army

M 10 Arrival at Treblinka

A Report by a Jewish Survivor:

"When the train arrived in Treblinka I can remember seeing great piles of clothing. Now we feared that the rumours really had been true. I remember saying to my wife more or less: this is the end […] I can remember the terrible confusion when the train doors were pulled open. The Germans and Ukrainians shouted "get out, out" […] The people who had arrived began to scream and complain. I can remember that whips were used on us. Then we were told: "Men to the right, women to the left and get undressed". My little daughter who was with me then ran to her mother when we were separated. I never saw her again and could not even say goodbye. Then, while I was undressing I was selected by a German to be a so-called work-Jew."

Quoted from: Jeremy Noakes and Geoffrey Pridham (eds.), Nazism 1919–1945. Volume 3: Foreign Policy, War and Racial Extermination: A Documentary Reader (Exeter Studies in History), Exeter: University of Exeter Press 1988, pp. 1154f.

M 11 Two Reports from *Perpetrators*: Weaklings or Willing Executioners?

a) SS Guard Hans Stark in the Auschwitz Trial at Frankfurt 1963–1965. Hans Stark, born in 1921, was convicted for joint murders and sentenced to a term of ten years imprisonment:

"As I have already mentioned, I used to receive my orders to take the newly arrived prisoners to the shooting room by telephone from Grabner (SS officer). Sometimes he would come and tell me in person. I never attempted to avoid carrying out such an order. It never entered my head. I had been a member of the SS for a long time and my whole *outlook* was coloured by the training I had received during this period. I certainly felt that these orders were an injustice and also tried repeatedly to volunteer for service at the front; however, I was only able to leave Auschwitz when my request to continue my studies was finally approved."

Quoted from: Ernst Klee, Willi Dressen and Volker Riess (eds.), The Good Old Days. The Holocaust as Seen by Its Perpetrators and Bystanders, New York: The Free Press 1991, pp. 252–55.

b) A Soldier of the Reserve Police Battalion 101 Carrying out Executions in June 1942:

"It was in no way the case that those who did not want to or could not carry out the shootings of human beings with their own hands could not keep themselves out of this task. No strict control was being carried out. I therefore remained by the arriving trucks and kept myself busy […] It could not be avoided that one or another of my comrades noticed that I was not going to the executions […] They showered me with remarks such as "shithead" and "weakling" to express their disgust. But I suffered no consequences for my actions. I must mention here that I was not the only one who kept himself out of participating in the executions."

Quoted from: Christopher Browning, Ordinary Men: Reserve Police Battalion 101 and the Final Solution in Poland, New York: Harper Collins 1992, pp. 65f.

Vocabulary

perpetrator: sb. who does sth. illegal
outlook: the attitude to life and the world

M 12 Mass Execution
Photo, Ukraine, 1942

M 13 The Lessons to be Learned

Speech by British Prime Minister Tony Blair on the Holocaust, 28 January 2001:

"Each step of human progress is a struggle between good and evil. The Holocaust was the greatest act of collective evil in history. It is to *reaffirm* the triumph of good over evil that we remember it. What are its lessons then?
First, that we are capable of such evil. That it happened in my father's lifetime under the Nazis. That it was repeated in Cambodia and Rwanda in my own lifetime. And again in the Balkans in the lifetime of my children.
Second, that racism must be fought against from the moment it appears. That what permits racial genocide is as much the *indifference* [...] as the acts of violence [...]
Third, that the origins of racism can lie in something we all seek. A sense of *belonging*. We want to belong. Our family. Our community. Our country. Our religion. We value this. And rightly. But we must never let our desire to belong be a reason to *exclude*. I remember talking to people in Kosovo, who would tell me how for years they had lived next door to each other – Albanians and Serbs – their children played together; their families ate their evening meal together. But when the soldiers came, the same family pointed them out and helped the murder of their young men and the *rape* of their women [...]
Fourth, that we can hope. Fascism was defeated. Europe has been at peace for over half a century. Good can win if we want it to do so [...]
Fifth, that we must teach our children about the Holocaust, racism and genocide; that if we do not forget history we are less likely to repeat it.
Let not one life sacrificed in the Holocaust be in vain. Let each death stay in our minds and those of our children as a monument to our capacity to do evil but our desire to do good [...]
And in remembering the Holocaust and its victims, we *commit* ourselves to the kind of society that we all believe in.
A democratic, just and tolerant society.
A society where everyone's worth is respected, regardless of their race or religion or skin colour.
A society where each of us demonstrates, by our words and actions, our commitment to values of humanity and compassion.
A society that has the courage to confront prejudice and persecution.
This is our hope. And that is why the Holocaust deserves this permanent place in our collective memory."

http://webarchive.nationalarchives.gov.uk/20080909020148/http://www.number10.gov.uk/Page7446 [July 12, 2018].

Vocabulary

to reaffirm: to state sth. again in order to emphasize that it is still true

indifference: a lack of interest, feeling or reaction towards sb./sth.

belonging: feeling comfortable and happy with a particular group of people

to exclude: opposite of include

rape: the crime of forcing sb. to have sex with you

commit: to promise sincerely that you will definitely do sth.

Tasks

1. **How did Nazi Anti-Semitism change over time?**
   a) Put the different phases of the Nazi policy against Jews into order and explain them. The following terms can help you: genocide, loss of rights, discrimination, physical threats and exclusion from society and economic life.
   b) Find out about the events of 9 November 1938 in your town. Use sources in libraries or city archives.
2. **The "Final Solution" in Practice**
   a) Find out about the historical background of the photo (M4).
   b) Show what the pictures and reports (M7–M11) tell us about the terrible situation of the victims in extermination camps.
   c) Anne Frank (1929–45) was a Jewish girl from Frankfurt am Main. Her diary has become famous. Find out about her fate with the help of an encyclopedia or the Internet.
3. **Special Action Groups – who is to blame?**
   a) The question how such a crime was possible is still difficult to answer. Analyse M11 and discuss in a group the reasons to participate in the Holocaust and alternative options.
   b) Discuss the question of guilt and assess the following statement: "Hitler is responsible for the crimes against the Jews between 1933 and 1945."
4. **How to remember**
   a) Analyse M13 and comment on the statement: "Now it's time to draw a line under this matter. Other nations have incurred guilt."

M 1   Julius Leber
(1891–1945)

M 2   Bischof Graf von Galen
(1878–1946)

M 3   Dietrich Bonhoeffer
(1906–1945)

Opposition and Resistance in Germany

Definition and Obstacles

Defining the terms "opposition" and "resistance" is still controversial, but most historians use the term "opposition" to describe all acts of public *defiance* such as listening to the BBC, refusing to join the Hitler Youth or helping victims of persecution. The term "resistance" is usually reserved for the smaller group of people who made an organized attempt to *undermine* or even *overthrow* the Nazi regime by force.

Many Germans accepted National Socialism and this did not change until the end of the war. It was not destroyed by a popular uprising from within Germany but by the military effort of the Allies. Nevertheless, there were some courageous groups and individuals who made attempts to oppose Hitler and end his rule. They came from all walks of life, represented different classes of German society, but hardly worked together. Different political attitudes and ideas of a future Germany hampered the development of a unified resistance movement. However, all opponents shared one common conviction: They advocated human dignity as the highest political principle and *contested* the right of the state to rule over the lives and consciences of its citizens.

Opposition against a regime of terror required courage and strong determination. The risk of imprisonment or even death was always present. Most Germans, blinded by Hitler's political successes, regarded opponents as traitors and refused to support them. On the contrary, many "loyal" Germans even helped the Gestapo track down opponents. This lack of popular backing and the *repressive* nature of Nazi rule made it extremely difficult to organize co-ordinated resistance. To make matters worse, the Allies were unwilling to recognize that there was any opposition to the Nazis. They demanded "unconditional surrender" from Germany and were not prepared to help or even *negotiate* with members of the German opposition.

Opposition Groups

Many Communists and Social Democrats went underground after 1933. Despite persecution, regional party contacts were organized, *leaflets* were secretly distributed, and brochures were smuggled into Germany from abroad. The Communist group "Red Orchestra" ("Rote Kapelle") supplied the Soviets with *intelligence* and carried out acts of sabotage. Former labour unionists like Wilhelm Leuschner or the Socialist Julius Leber joined a group called the "Kreisau Circle", who wrote a plan for a constitution of a democratic post-war Germany.

Also individual representatives of Protestant and Catholic churches expressed opposition to the regime and its inhumane policies. Churchmen like Bishop von Galen, Reverend Martin Niemöller, Dietrich Bonhoeffer and Alfred Delp considered Christianity incompatible with National Socialism, spoke out against it in public or became active members of the resistance.

Apart from non-conformist youth groups like the "Swing Kids" or the "Edelweiss Pirates" another example of young people who organized themselves against the Nazis was a group of students in Munich. They became known as the "White Rose" and were led by Hans and Sophie Scholl. They printed and distributed leaflets urging people to resist Hitler while criticizing the lawlessness of the regime and the *futile*, criminal war. They also painted slogans and crossed-out *swastikas* on walls. However, their attempts to rouse public opposition and connect with other resistance groups to weaken the regime were not successful. In February 1943, they were seen dropping leaflets in the university building and arrested by the Gestapo. A few days later they were sentenced to death.

Another resistance group consisted of people who had once been prepared to tolerate the Nazis but who had become disillusioned with Hitler's policies, above all with the war. Members of the conservative elites – diplomats, civil servants and army officers – formed a complex network of conspirators determined to overthrow the Nazi regime. Ludwig Beck, a former general, and Carl Friedrich Goerdeler, former mayor of Leipzig, became the leading figures. They wanted Hitler replaced not by a parliamentary democracy but by an authoritarian regime based on tolerance and the rule of law. Their opposition to the Nazis started in 1938, but it took several years of military setbacks and the murder of millions before the group finally set up a detailed plan for military and political action to overthrow Hitler's regime and kill the dictator.

M 4 Hans (1918–1943) and Sophie Scholl (1921–1943)

Assassination Attempt on Hitler's Life

There were many attempts to kill Hitler, but he escaped from them all, either because of his extraordinary good fortune or technical failures. Few people ever came into contact with Hitler, who hardly appeared in public after 1939, but stayed in the Chancellery in Berlin, in his heavily guarded mountain residence in Berchtesgaden or in his remote military headquarters, the "Wolf's Lair" ("Wolfschanze"), in East Prussia. Since the highest-ranking German generals refused to participate in a *plot* against Hitler, 37-year-old Colonel Claus Schenk Graf von Stauffenberg was left to take the decisive step. On 20 July 1944 he attended a meeting with Hitler at his headquarters in East Prussia.

Had Stauffenberg been successful, the final phase of the war would certainly have gone differently. A German surrender in summer 1944 would have saved many lives and many cities from destruction. The fact remains that more people died between the July assassination attempt and the end of the war than in the prior four and a-half years.

Info

20 July 1944

Despite great difficulties, Stauffenberg planted an armed bomb under a table near Hitler, left the room without being noticed and observed the detonation from a safe distance. Unfortunate circumstances prevented the attempt from succeeding, and Hitler survived with minor injuries. Still, Stauffenberg was convinced that his assassination attempt had been successful, but in the confusion that followed in Berlin the plotters did not carry out their plans quickly enough. The radio announcement of Hitler's survival put an end to the conspiracy. Von Stauffenberg was arrested and executed the same night. Gestapo investigations exposed most of the others involved in the plot. They were brought to trial before the People's Court, sentenced to death, and executed. Only a few succeeded in going underground or hiding their relations with the conspirators. The total number of arrests and death sentences remains unknown to this day.

Vocabulary

defiance: open refusal to obey

to undermine: to make sth., especially sb.'s confidence or authority, gradually weaker or less effective

to overthrow: to remove a leader or a government from a position of power by force

to contest: to state formally that you do not agree with sth.

repressive: controlling people by force and restricting their freedom

to negotiate: to try to reach an agreement by formal discussion

leaflet: a printed sheet of paper, usually folded and provided free

intelligence: (here) secret information

futile: unsuccessful or useless

plot: a secret plan made by a group of people to do sth. wrong or illegal

circumstances: conditions and facts that affect a situation, an event or action

plotter: a person who makes a secret plan to harm sb.

conspiracy: s. plot

Opposition and Resistance in Germany

M 5   A White Rose Leaflet

Munich, February 1943:

"Fellow Fighters in the Resistance!
Shaken and broken, our people *behold* the loss of the men of Stalingrad. Three hundred and thirty thousand German men have been senselessly and irresponsibly driven to death and destruction by the inspired strategy of our World War I Private First Class. Fuhrer, we thank you! […]
Do we want to sacrifice the rest of German youth to the ambitions of a Party clique? No, never! The day of *reckoning* has come – the reckoning of German youth with the most *loathsome* tyrant our people have ever been forced to endure. In the name of German youth we demand […] our personal freedom, the most precious treasure we have …
We grew up in a state in which all free expression of opinion is unscrupulously suppressed […]
For us there is but one slogan: fight against the party! Get out of the party organizations, which are used to keep our mouths *sealed* and hold us in political *bondage*! Get out of the lecture rooms of the SS corporals and sergeants and the party bootlickers! We want genuine learning and real freedom of opinion. No threat can terrorize us, not even the shutting down of the institutions of higher learning. This is the struggle of each and every one of us for our future, our freedom, and our honor under a regime conscious of its moral responsibility […]

The frightful bloodbath has opened the eyes of even the stupidest German – it is a slaughter which they arranged in the name of "freedom and honor of the German nation" throughout Europe, and which they daily start anew.
The name of Germany is dishonored for all time if German youth does not finally rise, take revenge, and *atone*, smash its *tormentor*s, and set up a new Europe of the spirit. Students! The German people look to us […] Our people stand ready to rebel against the National Socialist enslavement of Europe in a *fervent* new breakthrough of freedom and honor."

Transl. by Hermann Feuer on: http://www.holocaustresearchproject.org/revolt/wrleaflets.html [July 12, 2018] Courtesy of the Holocaust Education & Archive Research Team www.HolocaustResearchProject.org.

Vocabulary

to behold: to look at
reckoning: time when sb.'s actions will be judged to be right or wrong and he may be punished
loathsome: extremely unpleasant
sealed: closed
bondage: the state of being a slave or prisoner
to atone: to show that you are sorry for doing sth. wrong in the past
tormentor: a person who causes sb. to suffer
fervent: having or showing very strong and sincere feelings about sth.

M 6   Colonel Claus Schenk Graf von Stauffenberg
(far left) meeting Hitler at his headquarters in East Prussia in July 1944

M 7   The Conference Room at the "Wolfschanze" ("The Wolf's Lair")
After the Assassination Attempt on 20 July 1944

M 8 "A Traitor?"

Claus Graf von Stauffenberg in July 1944:

"It is time for something to be done. Yet he who dares to do something must be aware that he is likely to go down in German history as a traitor. If he failed to do the deed, however, he would be a traitor to his own conscience."

Quoted from: German Resistance Memorial Center and the Foundation 20th July 1944 (eds.), Claus Schenk Graf von Stauffenberg and the Attempted Coup of July 20, 1944. Exhibition catalogue. Translated by Katy Derbyshire, 2nd edition 2008, p. 5. https://www.gdw-berlin.de/fileadmin/bilder/publikationen/sonderpublikationen/PDFs_fuer_Download/Stauffenberg_Katalog_Deu_Eng_2._Aufl._2008.pdf.

M 9 "The Decisive Step"

General Henning von Tresckow in July 1944:

"The assassination must be attempted at any cost. Even should it fail, the attempt to seize power in the capital must be undertaken. We must prove to the world and to future generations that the men of the German Resistance Movement dared to take the decisive step and to risk their lives upon it. Compared with this object, nothing else matters."

Quoted from: William L. Shirer, The Rise and Fall of the Third Reich, p. 833, New York: Simon & Schuster 1960, p. 1043.

M 10 "Reign of Terror"

Extracts from a planned Statement by General Beck to the German People:

"Monstrous things have taken place under our eyes in the years past. Against the advice of all his experts, Hitler has unscrupulously sacrificed whole armies to his desire for glory […] to maintain his power, he has established an *unbridled* reign of terror, destroying justice, banishing *decency* […] and destroying the happiness of millions. We must not continue on that course! Having examined our conscience before God, we have assumed executive power […] Without hatred, we will attempt the act of domestic *conciliation*. With dignity, we will attempt that of foreign conciliation."

Quoted from: Stephen Lee, Weimar and Nazi Germany, Oxford: Heinemann 1996, p. 90.

M 11 "I was silent …"

Pastor Martin Niemöller in a Conversation after 1945:

"First they came for the Socialists, and I did not speak out — Because I was not a Socialist.
Then they came for the Trade Unionists, and I did not speak out — Because I was not a Trade Unionist.
Then they came for the Jews, and I did not speak out — Because I was not a Jew.
Then they came for me — and there was no one left to speak for me."

Translation quoted from: https://www.ushmm.org/wlc/en/article.php?ModuleId=10007392 [July 12, 2018]

Vocabulary

unbridled: uncontrolled
decency: honest, polite behaviour that follows accepted moral standards and shows respect for others
conciliation: peace, harmony

Tasks

1. **The Obstacles of Opposing a Dictatorship**
   a) Why was there no large-scale opposition to Hitler in Germany?
   b) Choose one of the persons mentioned in the author's text and give a short presentation on his life.

2. **Forms of Resistance**
   a) Analyse the poem (M11) and explain Pastor Niemöller's thinking.
   b) Show the criticism and the aims of the White Rose (M5) and discuss whether their appeal to the Germans was naïve.
   c) Analyse sources M6 – M10 and comment on Hitler's statement in a radio message to the German people on 21 July: "… A very small clique of ambitious, irresponsible and, at the same time, senseless and stupid officers has carried out a plot to eliminate me…"
   d) Work in groups and create a wallpaper that shows the different aspects of the resistance against Hitler in Germany. Include forms of opposition, groups, leading figures, motives etc.

3. **Keeping the Memory Alive**
   a) Try to find out how your city or region commemorates the members of the German Resistance (names of schools or streets, memorials, etc.).
   b) The City Council wants to name a street after a member of the German resistance against Hitler. Write a letter in which you suggest a name and explain your choice.

4. **Opposition Today**
   Discuss in class which forms of protest or opposition you could make use of in today's Germany to influence political decisions.

HISTORICAL WORKSHOP — The Third Reich

Vocabulary

to commemorate: to remind people of an important person or event from the past
atrocious: terrible
incomprehensible: impossible to understand
to access: to enter
distress: a feeling of great worry or unhappiness
dread: a feeling of great fear
indefinable: difficult or impossible to explain
ignominy: public shame and loss of honour
regrettable: used to show that you are sorry that sth. happened you wish had not happened
admittedly: accepting that sth. is true

Today's Germany and the Third Reich

Memorials play an important role in national consciousness and international politics. They tell us about the conception of history at the time of their construction and their architectural design can become extremely controversial. In 1989 the idea to build a Holocaust memorial in Berlin was raised.

After a long debate, the German Bundestag decided in 1999 to dedicate a memorial to the murdered Jews of Europe. The aim was to acknowledge the uniqueness of this crime and the historic responsibility of the Federal Republic of Germany. In 2005, 15 years after the fall of the Berlin Wall and the reunification of Germany, the memorial was opened to the public. It also includes an underground information centre with exhibition rooms recording the names of all known Jewish Holocaust victims, seminar rooms and a bookshop. It is located in the centre of Berlin not far from Hitler's former chancellery and bunker and covers five and a half acres (19,073 m²). The costs amounted to Euro 27,6 million.

A study of the memorial and the controversy it caused can give deep insights into the present conception of the Holocaust in Germany.

M 1 The Holocaust Memorial, designed by the American architect Peter Eisenman, is a vast grid of 2,711 concrete pillars or stelae. Visitors can move through the stones – each one unique in shape and size – from and into any direction. There are no plaques, inscriptions or symbols along the way. Standing on an uneven piece of land, the stelae almost fall into the centre of the site, rising up again towards the edge, thus forming uneven stone corridors. Walking down one of these passages is disorientating, and frightening; you can't see who is approaching you, nor who is behind. The lack of view offers some slight idea of the Jewish experience from WWII: your past stolen, your present situation unbearable and your future insecure, little hope of escape. Some people say that the memorial resembles a vast field of nameless tombstones and captures the horror of the Nazi death camps. Photograph, 2005.

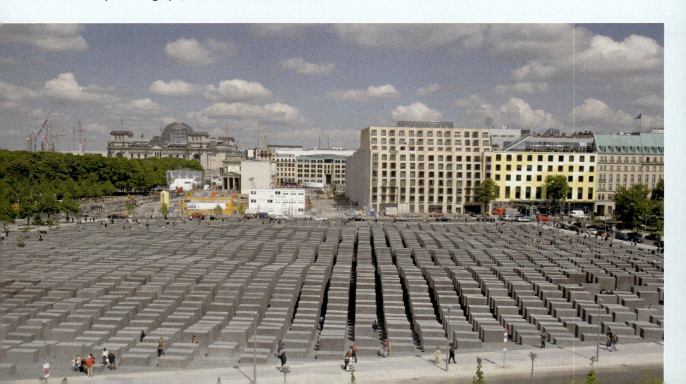

M 2 "An Open Work of Art"

Wolfgang Thierse, President of the German Parliament at the Public Opening of the Memorial, 10 May 2005:

"Today we are opening a memorial that *commemorates* the worst, the most *atrocious* of the crimes committed by Nazi Germany, the attempt to destroy a whole people [...]. The Holocaust [...] touches the limits of our understanding. This monument operates at those limits. It expresses the difficulty of finding any adequate artistic form at all for the *incomprehensible*, for the monstrosity of Nazi crimes, for the genocide of the European Jews [...]. This memorial – together with the information centre – can help those of us alive today and future generations to confront the incomprehensible with both heads and hearts [...] The Memorial to the Murdered Jews of Europe is a sculpture that visitors can enter and walk through to experience what, I feel, is its immense emotional power [...]. It is, in the true sense of the word, an open work of art. It is open to the city and the surrounding area into which it merges. And it is open to its many different individual uses: this is not a memorial which can be *accessed* collectively; it singularizes. It generates an emotional conception of isolation, *distress*, *dread*. It forces nothing.

I hope that people, particularly young people, will feel this, will sense the memorial's *indefinable* power of expression, will be touched and moved by it and will seek out the information center with their questions. This is where the victims are given names, faces and fates – and who could be left unmoved by this? And I hope the visitors will then return to the field of stelae and remember the victims."

Transl. by Thomas Dunlap at: http://germanhistorydocs.ghi-dc.org/pdf/eng/Chapter5_doc14-English.pdf [July 12, 2018].

M 3 No Memorial to the Holocaust

The German novelist Martin Walser in accepting the Frankfurt Book Fair Peace Prize in October 1998:

"It will be obvious later what kind of harm was done by those who, in the discussion about the Holocaust memorial, felt responsible for the conscience of others. To concrete the center of a capital with the football field-sized nightmare! To monumentalize the *ignominy*! [...] Take all towns in the world. Check whether in any of these towns there is a memorial of national ignominy. I have never seen such. The Holocaust is not an appropriate subject of a memorial and such memorials should not be constructed [...]."

Transl. quoted from: www.pbs.org/wgbh/pages/frontline/shows/germans/germans/controversy.html [July 12, 2018].

M 4 Confusion

Julius Schoeps, Director of the Moses Mendelsohn Centre for European Jewish Studies in Potsdam, "Tageszeitung", 6 May 2005:

"[Other memorials] stand in the landscape but people don't even know what they remind us of anymore. I'm afraid this will also happen with the Holocaust memorial. [...]
I especially regret the memorial's unclear message. Who is being remembered at this location? The Jews? Or maybe the fallen German soldiers? It's all not really clear. [...] The memorial will certainly become a tourist attraction. But is that what is intended? As a teacher, I would rather take young people to the authentic places, that is, where the crimes were committed. That would be relatively easy to do. Camps like Sachsenhausen, Ravensbrück, and others are all around Berlin. In part, however, they are in poor condition."

"Tageszeitung", 6 May 2005, transl. by Deanna Nebert.

Historical Workshop

Analysing Monuments

1. Description
a. Describe the memorial.
b. List the basic facts (name, year, place, costs, material, size).

2. Analysis
a. Assess the importance of its location.
b. Explain why the idea to build such a memorial in Berlin arose in the late 1990s.
c. In which respect does this memorial differ from other forms of public dealing with the Holocaust (concentration camps, documentaries on TV, etc.)?
d. Work with a partner and study either sources M2, M3 or M4. Take notes on the given arguments and their persuasiveness.
e. Inform your classmates about your results and discuss the importance of the memorial.

3. Assessment
a. Discuss in groups the design of a Holocaust memorial you consider appropriate.
b. Write an essay in which you formulate what the memorial and the controversy tell us about the present conception of the Holocaust in Germany and your point of view.

100 SUMMARY — The Third Reich

1926 — 1928 — 1930 — 1932 — 1934

1929: The Great Depression

1933/34: Nazi "seizure of power"

1935: Nuremberg Race Laws

The Extermination of the Jews in Europe (the "Final Solution") 1939–1944

- Greater Germany
- General Government
- German allies
- occupied territories
- Germany's enemies
- ■ extermination camps
- ■ Jewish ghettos
- ✡ 65 numbers of Jews murdered (in thousands)

The Third Reich – the historical map

1938: "Night of Broken Glass"

1939: German invasion of Poland

1942: Wannsee Conference

1939–1945: Second World War

1945: Hitler's suicide and end of war

DATES

30 January 1933: Adolf Hitler's appointment to Chancellor
28 February 1933: emergency decree
23 March 1933: "Enabling Act"
1 September 1939: German troops invade Poland
1939–1945: Second World War
9–10 November 1938: "Night of Broken Glass"
8–9 May 1945: German forces surrender

HISTORICAL TERMS

National Socialist German Workers' Party
"leadership principle"
"people's community"
"Enabling Act"
"seizure of power"
Germany's secret police
War Crimes Tribunal
appeasement
Axis Powers
lightning war
unconditional surrender
military intelligence
scorched-earth policy
"Night of Broken Glass"
Euthanasia
concentration camp
genocide
"Final Solution of the Jewish Problem"

PERSONS

Joseph Goebbels
Heinrich Himmler
Sophie und Hans Scholl
Dietrich Bonhoeffer

HISTORY WORKSHOP

Analysing Monuments

Summary

When Hitler became Chancellor on 30 January 1933 he brought an end to parliamentary democracy. Within a few months he suspended constitutional civil rights, enacted laws without the involvement of the Reichstag and established a system of totalitarian control over all aspects of society. With the help of a policy of "coordination" ("Gleichschaltung") – the alignment of individuals and institutions with Nazi goals – the culture, economy, education, churches all came under Nazi control. Nazi mass organizations like the German Labour Front or the Hitler Youth controlled political and social life in Germany and had to help building a "people's community". Socialists, Jews or disabled people, however, were excluded, discriminated against and persecuted.

According to the "leadership principle," Hitler stood outside the legal state, demanded unquestioning obedience and determined matters of policy himself.

A police state was established which suppressed all forms of criticism and sent opponents to the regime into concentration camps. Although Hitler's government was popular with most Germans there was some German opposition to the Nazi state, ranging from nonconformity to the attempt to kill Hitler on 20 July 1944.

In the field of the economy extensive public investments were made to prepare Germany for war and fight unemployment at the same time. It worked, but the level of public debt reached new heights.

Extensive propaganda was used to spread the regime's goals and ideals. Nazi foreign policy first seemed to continue the revisionist policy of Weimar governments, but actually it was guided by the racist belief that Germany was biologically destined to expand eastward by military force and that an enlarged, racially superior German population should establish permanent rule in Eastern Europe and the Soviet Union. Within this framework, "racially inferior" peoples, such as Jews and Gypsies, would be eliminated.

Hitler started World War II in 1939 and aimed from the beginning to wage a war of annihilation against the Soviet Union. In the context of this ideological war, the Nazis planned and implemented the Holocaust, the mass murder of the Jews.

In 1945, after years of unprecedented killing and destruction, war came to an end. The Allies had defeated Nazi Germany and Japan and the world had become a different one.

M 1 US and Soviet Soldiers Meeting at Torgau on the Elbe Photograph, 25 April 1945

M 2 Churchill, Truman and Stalin in Potsdam Photograph, July 1945

M 3 "Making Progress with the Marshall Plan" West German poster, about 1949

M 4 "Out" East German poster, about 1949

03 THE COLD WAR AND GERMAN DIVISION
1945 – 49

When World War II ended in Europe on 8 May 1945, the Allies had to deal with a never before seen degree of destruction. They had partly agreed on how to administer Germany and Austria before the war ended, but the real conditions they found were severe. Shelter and food were scarce; the currency was worthless. Millions of Germans expelled from Eastern Europe had to find housing. Other millions of foreigners in Germany, such as concentration camp prisoners, prisoners of war, and forced labourers, needed to get back to their home countries. The Allies had cooperated with each other as long as they were fighting the war. When it was over, their different goals for Germany led to disagreement.

The Potsdam Conference on the Allied occupation in Germany took place in July and August 1945. The agreement from the conference outlined the Allied goals for Germany. Nevertheless, their cooperation ended with a new Cold War.

The different interests of the Four Powers in Germany changed as time went on. The situation was dangerous, because military conflict among them could have begun quickly. At the same time, Germans used opportunities they could not have found if the Allies had been more united.

Berlin was a special problem. The city was divided into four sectors which depended on Allied cooperation. But Berlin was located inside the Soviet zone, isolated from the three Western zones. If the USSR did not cooperate, it would be difficult for the Western Allies to get supplies to the city. The Berlin Blockade in 1948 – 49 was an extreme test for the Allies and for Germany.

The one last principle on which the Four Powers still agreed was that Nazi war criminals should be tried. All the other Allied principles of occupation in Germany failed by 1949. The country was divided into two regions (the three Western zones in one, the Soviet zone in the other). The next logical step was to found two new countries, which meant that national unity no longer existed.

This chapter deals with many questions such as:
- Why did the Allies disagree after World War II?
- How did the Potsdam Agreement affect the Allies' administration of Germany?
- How were refugees treated in 1945 and afterwards?
- What is a suitable way to remember German refugees today?
- What changed in Allied policies after the Potsdam Agreement?
- What were the effects of the Berlin Blockade?
- How did the two new German states differ?
- What can popular films tell us about historical situations?

Vocabulary

coercion: the use of force to make sb. do sth.

booty: valuable things that a victorious army takes away somewhere

to plunder: to take sth. by force

Historical Terms

Cold War: Kalter Krieg

Allied Cooperation and Rivalry

Allied cooperation lasted as long as the Allies depended on each other to fight their common enemies. However, when the war ended, Allied rivalries became more important.

Allied Unity Falls Apart

World War II forced the governments of the Soviet Union, Great Britain and the United States to work together for one goal – the defeat of Nazi Germany. The alliance seemed stable, but the Allies did not trust each other because of the contradictions of their different social and political systems, communism and capitalism. Joseph Stalin, a fearsome dictator, led the Soviet Union. Voters elected the British Prime Minister Winston Churchill and the US President Franklin D. Roosevelt and held them responsible for their actions.

The Soviet Union feared the economic strength of the USA, which recovered from the war surprisingly quickly. The USA feared communist infiltration when the Soviet Union extended her political influence in Eastern Europe and in Asia after World War II. Both sides stabilized their positions through rearmament – a situation which led the world to the brink of atomic war several times. Fortunately, such a war was never fought, largely because both sides came to see how useless atomic warfare was. Instead, the superpowers used military *coercion* and economic pressure to force the opposing side to accept demands – a tactic called the **Cold War**.

M 1 "Now what? – Plan for a victory monument"

Cartoon in the "Schweizer Illustrierten Zeitung", 11 April 1945

M 2 "Stalin's Iron Curtain"
Cartoon by David Low, Britain, 1947

M 3 From War *Booty* to Essential Ally

Hope Harrison, an American historian, views the superpowers in Germany after 1945:

"Both superpowers initially treated their part of Germany as war booty to be *plundered* and kept weak, but as the cold war developed, they would each come to see their part of Germany as an essential ally whose needs were intertwined with their own. For political, military, economic, and ideological reasons, the superpowers engaged in a competition for allies to show that their side of the cold war was the stronger, more popular, more vibrant one. They also wanted to ensure that their German ally would not unite with the other against them. Beginning in the 1950s, the superpowers invested themselves, and their reputations, increasingly in their German allies, who were adept at taking advantage of this situation."

Hope M. Harrison, Driving the Soviets up the Wall: Soviet-East German Relations, 1953–1961 (Princeton Studies in International History and Politics), Princeton: Princeton University Press 2003, p. 1.

Tasks

1. **Allied Unity Falls Apart**
   a) Characterize the Allied relationship during World War II (text).
   b) Explain why the Allies had difficulty agreeing after World War II ended.

2. **Two Cartoons**
   Work as partners.
   a) Describe one of the cartoons (M1 or M2).
   b) Compare your cartoon with your partner's.
   c) Analyse the cartoonists' views on the situation of the Allies after 1945.

4. **From War Booty to Essential Ally**
   a) Summarize Harrison's text briefly (M3).
   b) Analyse how Germans could take advantage of the Allies in the 1950s.

M 1 German Refugees Flee from Soviet Troops on Foot and with Horsecarts
Photograph, February 1945

Flight and Expulsion from Eastern Europe

Even before World War II ended, millions of civilians were caught up in the moving military fronts. Some of these civilians were expelled from their homes, others fled in panic for their lives. The Allied agreements for Eastern Europe increased the numbers of refugees.

German Civilians Leave the Eastern Front

In the last months of World War II the eastern front collapsed. German civilians were not protected while the Soviet army advanced. Some civilians had tried to make plans to leave the eastern areas before the Soviet troops arrived, but the Nazi authorities forbade such measures as demoralizing and traitorous. They told the civilians that they were perfectly safe and that the war would still be won. Orders for civilians to leave the front area came too late.

When the Red Army began its advance into East Prussia on 12 January 1945, large numbers of civilians were completely unprepared. Nazi officials fled, leaving the civilians to fend for themselves. The winter of 1944–45 came early and was unusually cold. The consequences for the refugees from the eastern areas were disastrous. People had to go on foot or, at best, with horse and cart transportation. The advancing Soviet army fired on the treks or tanks simply mowed down whatever was still on the road when they passed. Those who had no warm or dry clothing (babies often had no dry diapers) froze to death. Many others died of hunger.

By 23 January the Red Army cut East Prussia off from the rest of Germany. Thousands of refugees tried to flee over frozen inlets of the Baltic Sea to reach harbours near Danzig. Heavy carts broke through the ice, horrifying those who saw the scenes of desperation. One incident stands out: The German troop transport ship "Wilhelm Gustloff" left Gdingen on 30 January with an estimated 10,000 refugees and wounded soldiers, but was torpedoed and quickly sank. Only 1,252 passengers could be saved from the icy waters. To this day the "Gustloff" holds the record of a single ship sinking with the largest loss of lives.

Ethnic Germans Expelled

Between 1939 and 1943, the German and Soviet governments together drove an estimated thirty million people in Eastern Europe from their homes. The retreat of the German army reversed this process. Whether they were new settlers or ethnic Germans who had lived in the area for generations, German civilians had to leave their homes and belongings and flee towards Germany as quickly as they could. The local population kept property the refugees left behind, which encouraged locals to drive Germans out. Also, the Nazi occupation had been harsh, so local people felt that all Germans, even civilians, deserved the treatment they got. Poles and Czechs, who had been forced to move by the Nazis, claimed German property early. When the Polish borders were moved farther west, two and one-half million Poles had to relocate. These Polish refugees took over German homes. Many refugees had to leave even before the Allies formally agreed on their relocation. These unofficial expulsions were especially difficult and dangerous.

After the **Conferences of Yalta** (February 1945) and **Potsdam** (July-August 1945) Allied plans to remove all ethnic Germans from Eastern Europe became more concrete. Although the Potsdam Conference explicitly stated that ethnic Germans should be relocated in "an orderly and humane manner", this high ideal was not met. Between twelve to fourteen million people moved in chaotic conditions. It is estimated today that more than two million German refugees died as a result.

Defenseless German civilians faced battle-hardened soldiers who had been fighting for more than five years. Anyone who resisted a demand could be abused and/or shot on the spot. Over twenty million Soviet soldiers and citizens were killed during the war. The hatred of Soviet soldiers showed in their mistreatment of the German population. German civilians who remained in East Prussia, Danzig, Pomerania, and Silesia became victims of a plundering, murdering, and raping Red Army which sought revenge for its own mistreated countrymen under the Nazis.

It was difficult for a Germany in ruins to integrate more than twelve million refugees in 1945 and the years afterwards.

M 2 Mother with her Children, Going West on Foot
Photograph, 1945

Historical Terms

Conference of Yalta:
Konferenz von Jalta; auch Krim-Konferenz

Conference of Potsdam:
Potsdamer Konferenz

Poles and Displaced Persons After 1945

The Soviet Union and Nazi Germany displaced, removed or expelled millions between 1939 and 1945. Poland lay directly in the path of both these powers. The percentage of deaths was higher in Poland than in any other country involved in the war – estimates range between 16% and 21.4% of the entire Polish population.

German forces invaded Poland in the west and, on 17 September 1939, Soviet forces in the east. The Soviet and Nazi occupation authorities treated Polish civilians harshly. Various measures kept the population under control, including arresting and imprisoning many as slave labourers, or killing military, intellectual or social leaders outright. At the end of the war the survivors needed to be sent back to their "homes". However, the Yalta and Potsdam agreements meant that millions could not go home because the Polish borders moved west.

Poles and citizens of other nations who were living outside their home countries were called "displaced persons", or DPs. There were an estimated eleven million DPs, not counting Germans, in Germany at war's end. A United Nations Relief and Rehabilitation Administration (UNRRA) was set up in New York in 1943 to deal with this refugee crisis; in 1951 there were 200,000 DPs still living in camps in Germany. The lives of millions were changed by a political and military catastrophe for which they were not personally responsible.

M 3 Search for Missing Persons
Photograph, after 1945

Flight and Expulsion from Eastern Europe

M 4 Refugees 1945

A British officer describes German refugees:

"*Flotsam* and *jetsam*! Women who had lost husbands and children, men who had lost their wives; men and women who had lost their homes and children; families who had lost vast farms and estates, shops, distilleries, factories,
5 flour-mills, mansions. There were also little children who were alone, carrying some small bundle, with a pathetic label attached to them. They had somehow got detached from their mothers, or their mothers had died and been buried by other displaced persons somewhere along the wayside."
10

Quoted from: Tony Judt, Postwar: A History of Europe Since 1945, New York: The Penguin Press 2005, p. 23.

Vocabulary

flotsam: bits of a wrecked ship floating on the sea
jetsam: bits of a wrecked ship washed on to land

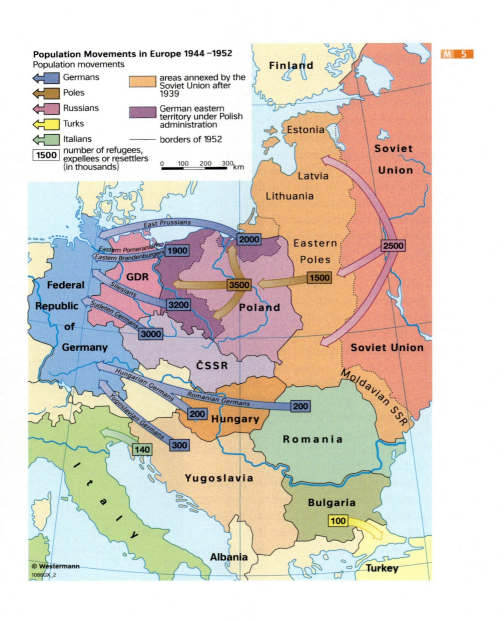

M 5 Population Movements in Europe 1944–1952

M 7 German Refugees at a Displaced Persons Camp
Photograph, Uelzen, 1949

M 6 "International Children for Repatriation"
Photograph, 1947

M 8 Displaced Persons
before their departure on the first DP emigration vessel in Bremen, 1948

Tasks

1. **German Civilians Leave the Eastern Front**
   a) Make a timeline of the events (text).
   b) Assess who was responsible for the poor treatment of the civilians fleeing the front.
2. **Ethnic Germans Expelled**
   a) Show how local people treated Germans who were expelled (text).
   b) Explain why both groups acted as they did.
3. **Poles and Displaced Persons After 1945**
   a) Show how Poles were treated before and after 1945 (text).
   b) Describe what happened to the Polish borders in Yalta and Potsdam.
   c) Discuss how Poles and Germans might try to overcome their difficult historic legacy.
4. **Using the Photographs**
   Work with a partner or in small groups.
   a) Describe each photograph briefly (M1–M3, M6–M8).
   b) Discuss the problems the people in the photographs have.
   c) Choose the photograph you find most interesting, giving reasons for your choice.
5. **Population Movements in Europe 1944–52**
   a) Add up the numbers of German, Polish, or Soviet refugees and list where they came from (M5).
   b) Assess the hardships each group had to deal with in relocation.
6. **Refugees**
   a) Sum up the text briefly (M4).
   b) Compare the text with the photograph in M3.
   c) Comment on the ten difficulties refugees faced then and today.

Culture of Remembrance

Vocabulary
revanchist: sb. who wants to get back territory lost in war

Remembering the Past: Germans Expelled After World War II

Over sixty years after World War II, expellees and refugees will be remembered in an official setting. The new **Foundation Flight, Expulsion, Reconciliation** will operate from a German government building in Berlin.

Millions of Germans in Eastern Europe were expelled from their homes following World War II. They had to survive the flight in difficult conditions and then integrate into new environments when they arrived in Germany. In 2005 two members of the West German parliament, Erika Steinbach (CDU) and Peter Glotz (SPD), suggested a museum to remember these expellees. Steinbach at the time was the President of the **League of Expellees**. She sometimes had controversial views. For example, she supported claims for compensation for Germans and German firms which had been forced to leave Poland. She also refused in the Bundestag to recognize the Oder-Neiße border between Germany and Poland in 1991. Poles criticized the suggestion to build a museum to remember the German expellees harshly.

The CDU/CSU/SPD government agreed in 2005 to establish a "visible sign" against expulsion. In 2007 Polish Prime Minister Donald Tusk suggested an alternative – a Museum of World War II dealing with many subjects including (but not limited to) expulsion, could be built in Gdansk. Instead, in 2008 the Bundestag passed a law to set up the Foundation Flight, Expulsion, Reconciliation in Berlin. The foundation should prepare permanent and temporary exhibitions, a document and information centre on expulsions and reconciliation. Poles and others fear that the project expresses empathy for victims and perpetrators evenly.

The foundation's board has six members from the League of Expellees and has been involved in several public disputes. A member of the foundation's board of trustees said that forced labourers in World War II should not be paid compensation by the German government. Another claimed that Poland and Great Britain were responsible for the start of World War II. Both had to resign when other trustees complained about their *revanchist* views. A committee of historians asked for revisions to the concept of the foundation in 2012. The foundation replaced its director in 2016. The building housing its permanent exhibition and document centre is scheduled to open in 2019.

M 1 The Former Deutschlandhaus Will Become the Location of the Foundation Flight, Expulsion, Reconciliation in Berlin

Photograph, 2014

M 2 Foundation Flight, Expulsion, Reconciliation

The Foundation Flight, Expulsion, Reconciliation States Its Concept, 2012:

"Unique in Germany and with an overall European perspective, the Foundation Flight, Expulsion, Reconciliation is intended to be an internationally visible place of learning and remembrance for the history of forced migration in the 20th century. It rests on two pillars: The permanent exhibition is intended for a general audience and will present the causes, course and consequences of ethnic cleansing in Europe, with a primary focus on the flight, expulsion and integration of Germans. The documentation and information centre will offer opportunities for further study and research and will serve as a specialized institution for disseminating research on forced migration in Germany, Europe and the rest of the world.

The exhibition, documentation and information centre will be housed in the Deutschlandhaus building in Berlin. Due to its geographical location, historical context, role as the capital of unified Germany and home to numerous memorial sites, Berlin is uniquely suited as the location for the Foundation. The Deutschlandhaus building is across the street from the ruins of the Anhalter Bahnhof train station, where Berlin Jews were loaded into transports to Theresienstadt starting in 1942. The headquarters of the Gestapo, SS and Reich Security Main Office (Reichssicherheitshauptamt) were located nearby, at the site now occupied by the Topography of Terror Documentation Centre. The Deutschlandhaus building itself was used for several decades starting in 1960 as a meeting place for expellee organizations in West Berlin. The exhibition will also examine the history of the building in presenting aspects of the integration of expellees.

The Foundation's exhibitions will be targeted at a general audience and will offer information about the flight, expulsion and integration of Germans during and after World War II and about other forced migrations, primarily in 20th-century Europe. The target audience includes expellees and their descendants, Berlin residents and tourists from the rest of Germany and abroad. Many tourists come from countries where the subject of forced migration receives as much attention as it does in Germany. Exhibits will be described in multiple languages, and the permanent exhibition will have additional offerings (audio guides, special guided tours, etc.) for foreign visitors, especially those from north-eastern, central, south-eastern and eastern Europe."

Conceptual framework for the Foundation (pp. 12f.), transl. by Gretchen Wiesehan, http://www.sfvv.de/sites/default/files/downloads/conceptual_framework_2012_sfvv_0.pdf [July 12, 2018].

Historical Terms

Foundation Flight, Expulsion, Reconciliation: Stiftung Flucht, Vertreibung, Versöhnung
League of Expellees: Bund der Vertriebenen

Tasks

1. Remembering the Past: Germans Expelled After World War II
   a) Look up the foundation's website at www.sfvv.de.
   b) Ask whether members of your family had to flee from their homes at the end of the war. Make a report for your class.
   c) Assess the website and its intentions.
   d) Agree or disagree with the statement: "Your story – keeps memory alive." Give reasons for your opinion.

M 1 The "Big Three" at the Conference of Potsdam
Churchill, Truman and Stalin in July 1945

Historical Terms

unconditional surrender: bedingungslose Kapitulation
Control Council: Kontrollrat

Planning the Post-war World

Several Allied agreements dealt with Germany before the war ended. The first post-war conference on how to occupy Germany was held in Potsdam.

Allied Cooperation Before 1945

While World War II still was being fought, the Allies discussed their post-war plans for Germany several times. On 14 August 1941 British Prime Minister Churchill and US President Roosevelt met and agreed on a charter of human rights. In 1943 at Casablanca they agreed that the German surrender must be unconditional, so that the defeat was clear to all – unlike in 1918. Later in 1943 the Big Three – Stalin, Roosevelt, and Churchill – coordinated military strategy at Tehran. In February 1945 at Yalta, the three Allied leaders agreed to disarm Germany, to divide the country into zones of occupation (including a new zone for France), and to bring war criminals to trial. Stalin wanted to set the total amount of reparations from Germany at twenty billion dollars (50 per cent should go to the Soviet Union), but the question of reparations was postponed.

The Allies cooperated while the war with Germany continued, but this cooperation had its limits. After the **unconditional surrender** was signed (several times at different places, so that each Ally could technically claim responsibility for the signing) on 8 May 1945, the weaknesses in these wartime agreements became clear.

The Potsdam Conference

The conference in Potsdam was held from 17 July to 2 August 1945. Soviet Premier Joseph Stalin was the only leader who had attended the earlier conferences in Tehran and Yalta. US President Roosevelt had died in April 1945 and Harry Truman took his place. Potsdam was Truman's first diplomatic experience. Prime Minister Winston Churchill arrived for the beginning of the conference, but Clement Attlee replaced him when the British general election results were announced on 26 July. France, although an occupying power, did not have a functioning government to participate in the conference in 1945.

As agreed at Yalta, the German eastern border was moved west to make room for new Polish borders which would become permanent after a later peace conference. The Allies divided Germany into four zones of occupation and Berlin into four sectors. Each power was to administer its zone and sector separately, but Germans were to be treated the same throughout the country. Germany should stay a single economic unit. A **Control Council**, agreed on in 1944 in London, was in charge of affairs which affected Germany as a whole. The country was to be disarmed, Nazism and Nazi organizations rooted out and destroyed.

Reparations were a difficult topic. The Western Allies feared Soviet demands would weaken German recovery. They hoped Germany would soon become self-sufficient. The final agreement was for each Ally to take reparations from its own zone of occupation. Also, the Western zones would give part of their reparations to the Soviet zone. This made it impossible for the German economy to remain one unit, as the protocol stated. The Allies agreed that Nazis and war criminals should be put on trial.

Info

There is a map showing the Cold War and German Division 1945–49 on page 128.

Info

Important Results of the Potsdam Agreement

1. demilitarization
2. denazification
3. *dismantling*
4. democratization
5. *decartelization*
6. All military organizations are disbanded, the armaments industry stopped, all weapons confiscated.
7. All Nazi organizations are dissolved, Nazi laws repealed, prominent Nazis arrested; main war criminals are put on trial.
8. Germany must pay the victorious powers to repair destruction caused by the war. The occupying powers can dismantle industrial plant and remove it to their own countries.
9. Political life is to return to the basic principles of democracy, but no central German government is foreseen for the time being.
10. Large industrial conglomerations are to be broken up.
11. Germany will be treated as a single economic unit.

Vocabulary

dismantling: taking sth. apart, put it into pieces
decartelization: breaking up of big business companies

M 2 "Confused and Unreal Discussions"

US diplomat George Kennan on his criticism of the Potsdam Conference in 1945:

"I viewed the labours of the Potsdam Conference with unmitigated skepticism and despair. I cannot recall any political document the reading of which filled me with a greater sense of depression than the communiqué to which President Truman set his name at the conclusion of these confused and unreal discussions. It was not just the knowledge that the principles of joint quadripartite control, which were now supposed to form the basis for the administration of Germany, were unreal and unworkable. The use in an agreement with the Russians of general language – such words as "democratic", "peaceful", and "justice" – went directly counter to everything I had learned, in seventeen years of experience with Russian affairs, about the technique of dealing with the Soviet government. The assertion, for example, that we and the Russians were going to cooperate in reorganizing German education on the basis of "democratic ideas" carried inferences wholly unjustifiable in the light of everything we knew about the mental world of the Soviet leadership and about the state of education in Russia at that time. […]
Anyone in Moscow could have told our negotiators what it was that the Soviet leaders had in mind when they used the term "democratic parties". Not even the greatest naiveté could excuse the confusion [created] by the use of this term in a document signed by Stalin as well as by […] Truman and Attlee."

George F. Kennan, Memoirs 1925–1950, Boston/Toronto: Little, Brown & Company 1967, pp. 258f.

Tasks

1. **Allied Cooperation Before 1945**
   a) Make a list of the important Allied agreements before the end of World War II (text).
   b) Point out what the Allies could not agree on before the end of the war.
2. **The Potsdam Conference**
   a) List the Allied leaders at the conference (text).
   b) Choose three results from the Potsdam Agreement (Infobox) which you think are the most important.
   c) Discuss your choice in class.
3. **Map of Occupying Powers 1945–49**
   a) Point out the different Allied zones on the map (page 128).
   b) Show why Berlin was a source of problems.
   c) Assess the Allied occupation from a territorial point of view.
4. **"Confused and Unreal Discussions"**
   a) Sum up Kennan's attitude to the Potsdam Conference briefly (M2).
   b) Discuss the Russian meaning of the term "democracy", according to Kennan.
   c) Comment on Kennan's criticism, giving reasons for your arguments.

Vocabulary

containment: the US policy after World War II of stopping the political and territorial expansion of the USSR

The Four Powers in Germany 1946–48

The Allied powers had different goals in their occupation of Germany after 1945. These differences led to disagreement and disputes among them.

Different Goals for the Allies

- **The USSR:** The main Soviet goal was to force Germany to pay reparations for the great destruction caused by the war in the Soviet Union. Soviet dismantling began immediately and continued longer than in any of the western zones, where it slowly ended by 1951. In Marxist thinking economic factors determine politics. Therefore, the Soviet Union insisted that the German economy be dealt with as a unit. Political unity was certain to follow. Soviet intentions in Germany remain uncertain even today. At least three explanations are possible. One, the occupation may have been part of a Soviet strategy for both Poland and Germany. Two, the occupation in eastern Germany may have been part of a plan to sovietize western Germany later and then all of Europe. Three, the Soviet zone may have been seen as an opening for later negotiations with the Western Allies. Historians may find answers to these questions now that archives in the former USSR have been opened.

- **The USA:** The American government began its occupation to punish Germany by dismantling industry and dividing the country politically. In April 1945 American troops in Germany were warned to treat German civilians firmly, but to keep them at a distance; Germans had to realize that the country had been destroyed as a result of their own actions. Roosevelt had a concept of "One World" and he hoped to assure peace through the United Nations. He was willing to compromise with the Soviet Union to win cooperation. In addition, he wanted to win Soviet support in the war against Japan. However,

M 1 Truman Addresses the Joint Session of Congress
Photograph, 12 March 1947

M 2 The Private American Charity CARE Collected Funds to Send Food and Supplies to Germany
Photograph, 1946

M 3 German Children Receive Allied Food Supplies at School
Photograph, Hamburg, 1947

as costs of occupation increased and Soviet influence in Europe expanded, American plans changed. If Germany were only punished and not rebuilt, Americans would have to help Germans fight Soviet aggression for a long time. Therefore, the USA revised its course and started to rebuild Germany. This change in US policy in the western zones showed in the idea of *containment* of the Soviet Union, the creation of the Bizone (later Trizone), the introduction of Marshall Plan aid, and currency reform.

- **Great Britain:** The British government supported dismantling and political decentralization at first. But Britain revised the policy when the Soviet Union seemed as dangerous as Nazi Germany had been. In 1946 former Prime Minister Churchill already referred to the "Iron Curtain" which divided the free world from the Communist sphere in Europe. In British policy Germany became a bulwark against Soviet expansion. Also, because Britain depended on American financial support after 1945, she followed American ideas on Germany more and more. Like the USA, Great Britain hoped to renew its markets in Germany when the country recovered economically.

- **France:** France had not signed the Potsdam agreement and opposed any decision that conflicted with French policy. France had fought Germany three times since 1871. Therefore, France concentrated on weakening the country and seeking revenge. Long-standing French interests in western Germany (in the Ruhr and Saar areas) were clear from the start of occupation. The French feared that a central German government might fall under Soviet influence. That could lead to a German restoration. To avoid this French policy supported regional rather than central solutions.

These conflicting interests led to Allied disagreement on how to administer Germany. By 1948 cooperation among the Four Powers ceased.

The Four Powers in Germany 1946–48

M 4 "Tired of Babying the Soviets"

US President Truman in a note to Secretary of State Byrnes, 5 January 1946:

"At Potsdam we were faced with an accomplished fact and were by circumstances almost forced to agree to Russian occupation of Eastern Poland and the occupation of that part of Germany east of the Oder River by Poland. It was high-handed *outrage*.
At the time we were anxious for Russian entry into the Japanese War. Of course we found later that we didn't need Russia there and that the Russians have been a headache to us ever since. [...]
Unless Russia is faced with an iron fist and strong language another war is in the making. Only one language do they understand: 'How many divisions have you?' [...] I'm tired of babying the Soviets."

Quoted from: John Traynor, Europe 1890–1990, Walton-on-Thames, Surrey: Nelson 1992, p. 330.

M 5 The Four Zones and German Economy

US Secretary of State Byrnes Restates American Policy in Germany, 1946:

"The conditions which now exist in Germany make it impossible for industrial production to reach the levels which the occupying powers agreed were essential for a minimum German peacetime economy. Obviously, if the agreed levels of industry are to be reached, we cannot continue to restrict the free exchange of *commodities*, persons, and ideas throughout Germany. The barriers between the four zones of Germany are far more difficult to surmount than those between normal independent states.
The time has come when the zonal boundaries should be regarded as defining only the areas to be occupied for security purposes by the armed forces of the occupying powers and not as self-contained economic or political units. [...]
[T]he American Government [...] has formally announced that it is its intention to unify the economy of its own zone with any or all of the other zones willing to participate in the unification.
So far only the British Government has agreed to let its zone participate. We deeply appreciate their cooperation. Of course, this policy of unification is not intended to exclude the governments not now willing to join. The unification will be open to them at any time they wish to join. [...]"

James F. Byrnes, speech in Stuttgart, September 5, 1946, quoted from: http://germanhistorydocs.ghi-dc.org/docpage.cfm?docpage_id=2990 [July 13, 2018].

M 6 The Truman Doctrine

President Truman addresses a joint session of Congress, 12 March 1947:

"I believe that it must be the policy of the United States to support free peoples who are resisting attempted subjugation by armed minorities or by outside pressures.
I believe that we must assist free peoples to work out their own destinies in their own way.
I believe that our help should be primarily through economic and financial aid which is essential to economic stability and orderly political processes. [...] The seeds of totalitarian regimes are nurtured by misery and want. They spread and grow in the evil soil of poverty and strife. They reach their full growth when the hope of a people for a better life has died. We must keep that hope alive.
The free peoples of the world look to us for support in maintaining their freedoms. If we *falter* in our leadership, we may endanger the peace of the world – and we shall surely endanger the welfare of our own nation."

Harry S. Truman address before a joint session of Congress, March 12, 1947; quoted from: www.fordham.edu/halsall/mod/1947TRUMAN.html [July 13, 2018].

M 7 Harry S. Truman

The US President at the lectern, 1947

M 8 The Marshall Plan

US Secretary of State Marshall addresses the graduating class at Harvard University, 5 June 1947:

"The truth of the matter is that Europe's requirements for the next three or four years of foreign food and other essential products – principally from America – are so much greater than her present ability to pay that she must
5 have substantial additional help or face economic, social, and political deterioration of a very grave character. [...] It is logical that the United States should do whatever it is able to do to assist in the return of normal economic health in the world, without which there can be no political
10 stability and no assured peace. Our policy is directed not against any country or doctrine but against hunger, poverty, desperation, and chaos. Its purpose should be the revival of a working economy in the world so as to permit the emergence of political and social conditions in which free
15 institutions can exist. Such assistance, I am convinced, must not be on a piecemeal basis as various crises develop. Any assistance that this Government may render in the future should provide a cure rather than a mere palliative. Any government that is willing to assist in the task of
20 recovery will find full cooperation, I am sure, on the part of the United States Government. Any government which maneuvers to block the recovery of other countries cannot expect help from us. [...] It would be neither fitting nor *efficacious* for this Government to undertake to draw up unilaterally a program designed to place Europe on its feet 25 economically. This is the business of the Europeans. The initiative, I think, must come from Europe. [...] The program should be a joint one, agreed to by a number, if not all, European nations."

George C. Marshall at Harvard University on June 5, 1947; quoted from: www.fordham.edu/halsall/mod/1947marshallplan1.html [July 13, 2018].

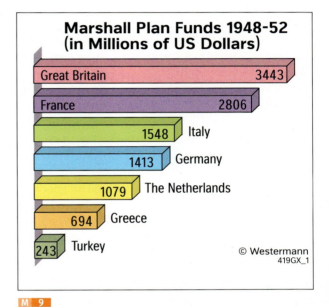

M 9

Vocabulary
outrage: a feeling of great anger and shock
commodities: goods
to falter: to weaken
efficacious: efficient, useful

Tasks

1. **Differences Among the Allies**
   a) Make a table of the different interests of the Allies (text).
   b) Add the changes in Allied policies which came later.
   c) Assess the effects of these policy changes for Germans.
2. **Dealing with Photographs**
   a) Describe one of the photographs briefly (M2 or M3).
   b) Explain the changed Allied policies in Germany, according to the evidence in the photograph.
   c) Look up CARE on the Internet and report on how the charity functions to your class.
3. **US President Truman and the Truman Doctrine**
   a) Explain why Truman changed his mind about the Soviet Union (M4).
   b) Summarize Byrnes's arguments briefly (M5).
   c) Define the "Truman Doctrine" briefly (M6).
   d) Discuss the changed US and British policies, using evidence from the texts to prove your arguments.
4. **The Marshall Plan**
   a) Summarize US Secretary of State Marshall's speech, 1947 (M8).
   b) Compare and contrast the aid given to different European countries through the Marshall Plan (M9).
   c) Find out from the Internet how the Marshall Plan worked and why it was especially effective in Germany.

Berlin Blockade and Allied Confrontation 1948/49

As Allied disagreement on Germany increased, the danger of military conflict grew. A major confrontation developed over Berlin, which had far-reaching political and diplomatic consequences.

Disagreement Among the Four Powers

It slowly became clear that the Four Powers could not administer Germany together. As financial and ideological problems grew, the Western powers agreed that German unity was not as important as *self-sufficiency* in the Western zones. They looked for alternatives to the Potsdam Agreement. In early 1948 the Western Allies, together with the directly affected Benelux countries, held a six power conference in London to discuss the fate of the three Western zones. They set up an international commission excluding the Soviet Union to control coal and steel production in the Ruhr. The Soviet Union protested on 20 March 1948 and left its seat in the Control Council empty. Because Berlin was surrounded by the Soviet zone, the Western sectors of the city became easy targets in any Allied confrontation.

Currency Reform in the Western Zones

During the 1930s and especially during the war, the Nazis used wage and price controls and rationing to keep inflation in check. After 1945 German currency was completely worthless. *Bartering* was common and black markets appeared. People even paid for goods in cigarette butts. The six power decision in London to reform currency in the Western zones provided a solution, but the Soviet Union bitterly opposed it. When the new German mark was introduced on 20 June 1948, the Soviet Union quickly introduced its own currency on 23 June and demanded that the new Western currency not be used in Berlin. To back up this demand, the Soviets closed roads and waterways to West Berlin, saying the measures were "for repairs". It seemed clear that the Soviet Union would only reopen land routes to the city if all of Berlin fell under Soviet authority.

Confrontation: The Berlin Blockade and Airlift

The Berlin Blockade lasted from 24 June 1948 until 12 May 1949. It was the first dramatic confrontation among the Four Powers after 1945 and very nearly led to war. At first the Western Allies were uncertain about how to react to the blockade,

M 1 Mayor Ernst Reuter Calls on World Opinion to Support West Berlin
9 September 1948

Ernst Reuter (1889–1953)

Reuter was born in Apenrade (later Denmark). During World War I, he helped to organize the Volga German Autonomous Soviet Republic and became active in the Communist Party of Germany (KPD) after the war. Later he joined the SPD, worked as a journalist, and was elected mayor of Magdeburg in 1931. After his arrest and removal from office in 1933, he emigrated to Turkey and taught urban planning at the University in Ankara. Reuter returned to Berlin and rebuilt the public transport system there in 1946. He was elected mayor in 1947 and became a spokesman and leader of "Free Berlin" during the Berlin Blockade. On 9 September 1948 in front of the ruins of the Reichstag, Reuter addressed the "people of this world ... look upon this city and see that you should not, cannot abandon this city and this people". Reuter was elected Governing Mayor in West Berlin in 1951. He died in office in 1953.

but the use of the three air corridors which had been agreed to in writing in November 1945 seemed the least dangerous. American and British commanders were uncertain, however, that it would be possible to supply the population of West Berlin with enough food and goods to ensure its survival for more than a few months. Not only did food have to be flown into the city, everything essential for daily life had to be transported by air – coal for heat and generating electricity, medication, clothing, even building materials. It was estimated that 4000 tons of goods needed to flow into Berlin every day. The airlift was a logistical exercise in transport never before attempted on such a scale. The record of transported goods was reached on 11 April 1949, when 1,383 flights moved 12,899 tons of goods within twenty-four hours.

The Soviet Union did not expect the airlift to succeed, either. When it did, the Soviets opened up the land routes to the city once again.

The long-term effect of the blockade surprised the Western Allies, too. During the airlift German attitudes toward the Allies changed. Instead of occupiers, the Western Allies became friends and supporters. The Soviet Union, on the other hand, came to be seen as a threatening bully. More than any other single event after 1945, the blockade and the airlift meant a serious loss in prestige for the Soviet Union, and a gain for the Western Allies. French resistance to more cooperation with the British and Americans was overcome – by April the Bizone expanded to the Trizone. West Berlin emerged as a symbol of freedom and resistance to oppression. The final blow was given to the idea of Four Power cooperation. West Germans willingly turned to the Western Allies to seek help and advice, a tendency which certainly helped Konrad Adenauer in his efforts to align West Germany more closely with the West.

Vocabulary

self-sufficiency: ability to provide all you need by yourself or: ability not to need the help of other people

bartering: trading for goods or services instead of using money to buy them

M 2   Airlift Planes Kept West Berlin Alive During the Blockade
During the airlift 101 people were killed, including 39 British and 31 American airmen

Berlin Blockade and Allied Confrontation 1948/49

M 3 Western Allied Considerations in Berlin

a) American General Lucius Clay in a telegram to his superiors, June 13, 1948:

"There is no practicability in maintaining our position in Berlin and it must not be evaluated on that basis. [...] We are convinced that our remaining in Berlin is essential to our prestige in Germany and in Europe. Whether for good or bad, it has become a symbol of the American intent."

Jean Edward Smith (ed.), The Papers of General Lucius D. Clay: Germany 1945–1949 Vol. 2, Bloomington/Indiana: Indiana Unviersity Press 1974, p. 677.

b) French declaration to US General Clay regarding the Berlin airlift, June 1948:

"The French Government is obliged to dissociate itself from all responsibility with regard to these consequences." [In spite of its doubts, the French government cooperated with Britain and the US during the Berlin crisis of 1948–49.]

Jean Edward Smith (ed.), The Papers of General Lucius D. Clay: Germany 1945–1949 Vol. 2, Bloomington/Indiana: Indiana Unviersity Press 1974, p. 692.

Vocabulary

rubble: broken pieces of stone or wall
dungarees: trousers

M 4 Positive Results of the Blockade

From an article in The Manchester Guardian, 7 July 1949:

"The face of Berlin has changed almost beyond recognition in a few short weeks. Immeasurably tidier streets – one of the few positive results of the blockade, when a great deal of clearing up of *rubble* took the place of normal industrial production – are crowded with sightseers. Sightseers in packed street cafés watch the new, fashionably and differently dressed crowds on the pavements; and, conversely, the casual strollers have come out to stare into cafés and shop-windows, inquisitive to probe the new, apparently astonishing prosperity which has rolled into Western Berlin like a tidal wave. One Berliner to whom I spoke was almost lyrical about it: the face of Berlin, he thought, was once the face of the middle-aged, weather-beaten woman in patched *dungarees* who stacked bricks along the edges of the city's shattered streets; now it is the face of a young girl, eager, excited – a young girl in fresh, summery frock and sandals."

„Berlin after the blockade", The Manchester Guardian July 7, 1949; quoted from: https://www.cvce.eu/content/publication/2002/9/23/8890f956-541f-41ed-84cd-939c80dd62a4/publishable_en.pdf [July 13, 2018].

Tasks

1. **Disagreement Among the Four Powers**
   a) State the disagreements among the Four Powers briefly (text).
   b) Assess the decision of the Western Allies to meet in London without the USSR.
2. **Currency Reform in the Western Zones**
   a) Explain why currency reform was necessary (text).
   b) Comment on the Soviet decision to close land routes to Berlin "for repairs".
   c) Analyse reasons for the USSR to oppose the new Western currency in Berlin.
3. **Confrontation: The Berlin Blockade and Airlift**
   a) Explain why neither side in the confrontation expected the airlift to be successful (text).
   b) Sum up the American and French positions on Berlin (M3).
   c) Comment on the Manchester Guardian's view on the Berlin Blockade in 1949 (M4).
4. **Biography: Ernst Reuter**
   a) List three aspects of Reuter's life which you think are important.
   b) Explain why Reuter's appeal to the "people of the world" was effective.
   c) Assess the importance of the Berlin Blockade in consolidating support for the Western Allies among Germans.
5. **Tempelhof Airfield**
   a) Explain why M2 is the most popular photo of the airlift.
   b) Estimate the dangers in running an airlift from Tempelhof in 1948. (Note also the deaths mentioned in the caption to M2.)
   c) Look up the controversy about Tempelhof on the Internet.
   d) State your opinion on what should be done with the airfield today.

M 1 Flag of the Federal Republic of Germany
Photograph

M 2 Flag of the German Democratic Republic, 1959–1990
Until 1959 the East German flag had the same design as the West German flag.

Founding Two German States 1949

The Berlin Blockade and the airlift made it clear that Germany could no longer be administered according to provisional rules. Both the Soviet and Western Allies needed permanent structures instead.

Founding the Federal Republic of Germany in the West

Currency reform in the Western zones was part of a strategy to found a West German state. The Western Foreign Ministers made further plans (called the London Documents in English, but the Frankfurt Documents in German) at the London Conference in June 1948. The eleven minister-presidents in the Western zones saw these plans for the first time when they met on 1 July 1948. The documents called for a constituent assembly to work out a constitution and rearrange provincial borders. The Western Allies promised to formulate a new Statute of Occupation to give the occupation of West Germany a legal basis if the minister-presidents agreed to the suggestions.

The minister-presidents met again in Koblenz on 10 July. They were uncomfortable with the proposals. They wanted to redefine several terms, such as "constituent assembly", "constitution", and "referendum". They feared that creating a West German state would divide Germany permanently and end all hope of national unity. The British, American, and French governments compromised on the wording of the documents. A constituent assembly, called the **Parliamentary Council**, wrote a constitution called the **Basic Law**. There was no referendum on the final draft of the Basic Law; instead the provincial parliaments ratified it.

The Parliamentary Council had sixty-five members, many of whom had been members of parliament in the Weimar Republic. They tried to make certain that problems which had led to the failure of Weimar were avoided in the new Federal Republic:

- Human and civil rights play a prominent role in the Basic Law as the first twenty articles. These rights are legally binding and cannot be changed in their content.
- The functions of the Federal President are limited; the office has far fewer powers than the President of the Weimar Republic.

Historical Terms

Parliamentary Council: Parlamentarischer Rat
Basic Law: Grundgesetz

M 3 Proclamation of the Basic Law
Photograph, 23 May 1949

The Cold War and German Division 1945–49

Biography

Konrad Adenauer (1876–1967)
Adenauer was born in Cologne and studied law. He joined the Centre Party and started his political career in Cologne. In September 1917 he was elected mayor. In 1933 the Nazis dissolved the Cologne city council and dismissed him as mayor. He was imprisoned briefly in 1934 and in 1944. US forces appointed him mayor of Cologne after the war ended, but British authorities dismissed him in December 1945. He then started a new political party, the Christian Democratic Union (CDU). His leadership of the CDU in the British zone led to his seat and then the presidency of the Parliamentary Council, which wrote the West German Basic Law in 1948–49. Adenauer was elected the first Chancellor of West Germany. He served as Chancellor until 1963. His political nickname was "the oldster" ("der Alte") after 1945.

M 4 **Konrad Adenauer (CDU)**
Photograph, 1947

Vocabulary

émigrés: (fr.) emigrants, people forced to leave their country for political reasons

- Parties and political groups who oppose democracy or democratic institutions can be forbidden by law.
- The federal structure of the government is guaranteed constitutionally. The provinces are relatively independent of the national government and have an independent role in the legislative process through the **Federal Council**.
- A Chancellor can only be removed from office through a **constructive vote of no confidence**. The Bundestag may not withdraw support for a Chancellor without electing a successor to the office.
- The voting system combines both majority and proportional representation.

First elections to the Bundestag were held on 14 August 1949. Sixteen different political parties stood for election, but two factions attracted the most votes: the Christian Democratic Union (CDU) together with its Bavarian sister the Christian Social Union (CSU) won 139 seats, while the Social Democratic Party of Germany (SPD) won 131. Theodor Heuss, a member of the smaller Free Democratic Party (FDP), was elected the first Federal President. The 73-year-old Konrad Adenauer (CDU), who had also been the President of the Parliamentary Council, was elected Federal Chancellor by a majority of only one vote. Bonn became the provisional capital of the new Federal Republic of Germany ("Bundesrepublik Deutschland", BRD), officially founded on 23 May 1949.

Founding the German Democratic Republic in the East

A group of German communist *émigrés* ("the Ulbricht group") who returned to the country before the war had ended in 1945, organized the Soviet zone politically. They immediately set up plans to create a Stalinist state. Although dismantling made daily life in the zone difficult, the Soviets were the first of the Four Powers to allow political parties. However, the German Communist Party, which had political priority from the beginning, watched the other parties closely. After communist parties in Hungary and Austria lost elections in the fall of 1945, German Communists united their party with its larger and more successful political rival, the Social Democratic Party, in 1946. The new **Socialist Unity Party** ("Sozialistische Einheitspartei Deutschlands", SED) kept an iron grip on East German political life.

As a Marxist party, the Unity Socialists reformed the country to get rid of its class structure. They divided large estates and gave parcels of land to small farmers (which made it easy to collectivize farms later), nationalized the banks, often

Historical Terms

Federal Council: Bundesrat
constructive vote of no confidence: konstruktives Mißtrauensvotum
Socialist Unity Party: Sozialistische Einheitspartei Deutschland, SED

Biography

Walter Ulbricht (1893–1973)

Ulbricht was born in Leipzig and learned a trade as a carpenter. In 1917 he joined the Independent Social Democratic Party (USPD) and a soldiers' soviet. Ulbricht joined the KPD in 1920, became a member of the Central Committee, and was elected to the Reichstag from 1928 to 1933. After 1933, he went into exile in Paris and Prague. He worked as a representative of the Comintern in Spain and lived in the USSR from 1937 to 1945. Ulbricht returned to Germany on 30 April 1945 as part of the "Ulbricht Group". He rebuilt the German Communist party according to Stalinist principles and played a key role in uniting the SPD and the KPD into the Socialist Unity Party of Germany (SED) in the Soviet zone. Ulbricht became Deputy Chairman of the Council of Ministers after the founding of the DDR in 1949. In 1950 he became General Secretary of the SED Central Committee. He secured his position in East Germany after Stalin's death and the uprising of 17 June 1953. Ulbricht stopped the flow of refugees to the West with the Berlin Wall in 1961. The SED leadership (with Soviet agreement) forced him to resign his official functions "due to reasons of poor health" in 1971. He kept the office of Chairman of the State Council and an honorary position as Chairman of the SED until he died in 1973.

M 5   Walter Ulbricht
Photograph, about 1955

expropriated and nationalized factories, chose judges and teachers "of the people" to staff courts and schools. Comprehensive schools and health care were free of charge. Just as other satellite states within the Soviet sphere of influence adopted the principles of "sovietization", the Soviet zone became a police state supervised by the party.

Parallel with the efforts to form a Western state out of the Trizone, the Soviet zone moved in a similar direction. While criticizing the West for destroying German political unity, the Eastern zone moved to found its own state. Peoples' Congresses assembled and agreed on the principles. After the third such congress in March 1949, a constitution was written. On 7 October 1949 the Soviet military newspaper announced the new country. Wilhelm Pieck became the first President of the **German Democratic Republic** (GDR, "Deutsche Demokratische Republik"). Real power, however, lay in the hands of the Secretary-General of the Socialist Unity Party and Chairman of the State Council, Walter Ulbricht. No matter what the structural details were, the constitution of East Germany never introduced constitutional democracy to the country. The Constitution of 1949 did not separate the legislative, executive, or judicial powers. Unity party lists for elections chose candidates according to pre-determined factors (proportions for mass organizations, women, etc). The unity list had to be accepted in full, it was not possible to choose candidates individually. Some called the voting procedure "folding the ballot", as it was not necessary to mark it at all. The **State Security Service** grew and kept people under control by spying on them. The Stasi's large role in running the country did not become clear until East Germany collapsed in 1989.

German Unity – an impossible goal?

Although two German states existed side by side in 1949, both constitutions set German national unity as a goal. However, as the superpowers continued to disagree during the Cold War, German unity seemed to be unreachable. The East German constitution of 1968 dropped the goal of German unity, the Basic Law of West Germany continued to state this goal up to actual unification in 1990.

Historical Terms

German Democratic Republic, GDR: Deutsche Demokratische Republik, DDR

State Security Service: Staatssicherheitsdienst, also SSD, or Stasi

M 6   Founding of the GDR
The Provisional People's Chamber proclaims the founding of the GDR, 7 October 1949

Founding Two German States 1949

M 7 Excerpt from the East German Constitution

7 October 1949:

The German People, *imbued* with the desire to safeguard human liberty and rights, to reshape collective and economic life in accordance with the principles of social justice, to serve social progress, and to promote a secure peace and amity with all peoples, have adopted this Constitution.
Article 1: Germany is an indivisible democratic republic [...] There is only one German nationality.

Transl. quoted from: © United States-Department of State. Documents on Germany 1944–1985. Washington: Department of State, [s.d.]. 1421 p. (Department of State Publication 9446). p. 278–306. http://www.cvce.eu/obj/constitution_of_the_german_democratic_republic_7_october_1949-en-33cc8de2-3cff-4102-b524-c1648172a838.html [July 8, 2018]. This document is available at www.cvce.eu.

M 8 National Anthem of the GDR

After about 1972, the anthem was played, but the text was no longer sung in public:

From the ruins risen newly,
to the future turned, we stand.
Let us serve your good will truly,
Germany, our fatherland.
Triumph over bygone sorrow,
can in unity be won.
For we shall attain a morrow,
when over our Germany,
there is radiant sun,
there is radiant sun.

Transl. quoted from: http://www.nationalanthems.info/ddr.htm [July 12, 2018].

Vocabulary

to imbue: to fill or inspire with emotion

M 9 Election Results in East Germany, 1949–1986

election date	voter turnout	votes in favour	invalid votes
1st legislative period: 15 October 1950	98.53	99.72	0.28
1st legislative period: 15 October 1950	98.51	99.46	0.54
3rd legislative period: 16 November 1958	98.9	99.87	0.13
4th legislative period: 20 October 1963	99.25	99.95	0.05
5th legislative period: 2 July 1967	99.82	99.93	0.07
6th legislative period: 14 November 1971	98.48	99.85	0.15
7th legislative period: 17 October 1976	98.58	99.86	0.14
8th legislative period: 14 June 1981	99.21	99.86	0.14
9th legislative period: 8 June 1986	99.74	99.94	0.06

https://de.wikipedia.org/wiki/Volkskammer

Tasks

1. **Founding the Federal Republic of Germany in the West**
   a) Describe the Western Allies' plans for founding a West German state (text).
   b) Explain the reactions of the Western minister-presidents to the Allied plans (text).
   c) Outline the features of the Basic Law which were adopted to avoid the problems of the Weimar Republic (text, M12).

2. **Founding the German Democratic Republic in the East**
   a) Describe the developments in the Soviet zone in the years 1945–49 (text).
   b) Point out the role the Socialist Unity Party (SED) played in the GDR (text).
   c) Comment on how the unity party voting list worked (text).
   d) Assess the election results briefly (M9).
   e) Analyse the function of the Stasi in East Germany.

M 10 Excerpt from the West German Basic Law

23 May 1949:

Conscious of its responsibility before God and mankind, filled with the resolve to preserve its national and political unity and to serve world peace as an equal partner in a united Europe, the German people in [list of the West
5 German provinces] has, by virtue of its constituent power, enacted this Basic Law of the Federal Republic of Germany to give a new order to political life for a transitional period. It acted also on behalf of those Germans to whom participation was denied.

Transl. quoted from: Archives Nationales du Luxembourg, Luxembourg. Deuxième Guerre mondiale. Question allemande. Loi fondamentale de l'Allemagne 1949, AE 4191, p. 2. https://www.cvce.eu/obj/the_basic_law_of_the_frg_23_may_1949-en-7fa618bb-604e-4980-b667-76bf0cd0dd9b.html [July 13, 2018]. This document is available at www.cvce.eu.

M 11 National Anthem of the FRG

Unity and right and freedom
For the German fatherland!
Let us all pursue this purpose
Fraternally with heart and hand!
5 Unity and right and freedom
Are the pledge of happiness;
|:Flourish in this blessing's glory,
Flourish, German fatherland!:|

Transl. quoted from: https://www.bundestag.de/en/parliament/symbols/anthem [July 13, 2018].

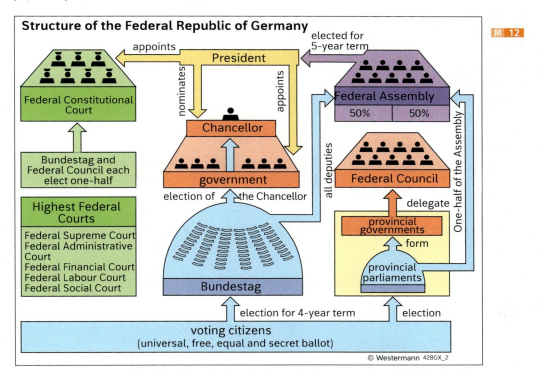

M 12

Tasks

1. **Two Constitutions**
   a) Point out the role national unity plays in both German constitutions (M7, M10).
   b) Explain why two different German states were founded in spite of the importance of national unity.

2. **National Symbols**
   a) Compare and contrast the flags of West and East Germany (M1, M2).
   b) Compare and contrast the national anthems (M8, M11).
   c) Assess the effect of not singing the East German national anthem in public (M8).

Film Analysis: "One, Two, Three"

M 1 Lilo Pulver (Ingeborg), James Cagney (MacNamara), Hanns Lothar (Schlemmer)

M 2 **Selections from the *screenplay***

1) on the difference between US and Soviet soldiers:

MacNamara: Have any trouble getting out of East Berlin?
Schlemmer: No – but I had a little trouble in West Berlin – I was picked up by an American soldier in a jeep – he was very fresh – wanted to take my picture for something called Playboy.

2) on National Socialism after 1945:

MacNamara: Just between us, Schlemmer – what did you do during the war?
Schlemmer: I was in the Untergrund – the underground.
MacNamara: Resistance fighter?
Schlemmer: No. Motorman. In the underground – you know, the subway.
MacNamara: And of course you were anti-Nazi – and you never liked Adolf –
Schlemmer: Adolf who? You see, down where I was, I didn't know what was going on up there. Nobody ever told me anything.

3) on the heritage of the US Civil War:

[Scarlett has inflated the balloon enough so that MacNamara can read the lettering on it.]

MacNamara: Yankee Go Home?!
Scarlett: They come in all colors – green and yellow and blue –
MacNamara: You've been helping this guy spread anti-American propaganda?
Scarlett: It's not anti-American – it's anti-Yankee. And where I come from, everybody's against the Yankees.

4) on raising children in the USSR:

Otto: At the age of six months, the baby will be enrolled in the people's nursery school. Naturally, we will have visiting rights every other Sunday.
Scarlett: Every other Sunday?
MacNamara: You can bring him some *pablum* with a *file* in it.
Otto: (to MacNamara) Imperialist *stooge*! (to Scarlett) And of course, we'll see him on May Day – he'll be marching in the parade – we can wave to him.
MacNamara: You can also wave to him on Lenin's birthday, and on *Yuri Gagarin*'s birthday – that kid'll be parading all the time.
Scarlett: Well, at least it'll keep him off the streets.

Billy Wilder, I. A. L. Diamond, "One, Two, Three" Screenplay, Hollywood/Ca.: Script City 1988.

Opinions about the film

Billy Wilder: "A great miscalculation, as people were being shot trying to climb the Wall."
Horst Buchholz: "In Germany, people thought [the film] was about the Wall, which, of course, it wasn't. It took generations of people who had lived with the Wall to make it, years later, a success. In cinemas, here in Germany, they are still showing 'One, Two, Three', and of course it's on television."

Vocabulary

screenplay: the script of a film
pablum: soft, plain baby food
file: (here) a tool for cutting through prison bars
stooge: stupid person
Yuri Gagarin: first man to orbit the Earth (1961)
newsreel: short documentary film of current events
blockbuster: an expensive film, intended to be very popular
fast-paced: moving at a fast speed

History Workshop: Analysing Films

Many different types of film are used in studying history. There are documentary films, usually *newsreels* (for television or movie theatres) or films made to show an event at the time that it happened. Another type of factual film shows events recreated in films, especially in cases where no camera recorded the event. Other films fictionalize historical events as entertainment – these films are often Hollywood *blockbusters*, which may or may not be historically accurate. Sometimes scenes from entertainment films become historically interesting later, when a setting is suddenly changed by events. One example of such a film is "One, Two, Three", a comedy made in Berlin in 1961 just before the Berlin Wall was built.

Billy Wilder originally admired the Marx Brothers' film "Duck Soup", an utterly crazy comedy. He had also seen the 1929 Berlin stage production of Ferenc Molnár's farce "Eins, Zwei, Drei" and wanted to adapt it to film. He decided to take the Marx Brothers' approach to make fun of the entire East-West conflict during the Cold War and chose Berlin as his setting. During the shooting of the film the Berlin Wall was suddenly built. For years the film was one of few entertainment films which showed the Brandenburg Gate and some of the wartime destruction in East Berlin before the Wall was built.

The film makes fun of Americans, Germans, Russians, capitalists and communists. The dialogue is *fast-paced*, so it is often difficult to catch the jokes. The shots of West and East Berlin in 1961 show many aspects of the two parts of the city quite clearly. Beyond the silly plot, the film reflects typical attitudes of the time. A careful study of it can show how many people in both the East and the West felt about themselves and their ideological opponents during the Cold War.

A word of caution in analysing films is necessary, however. Pictures can overpower historical facts, leaving a vision in the viewer's mind of things as they never were.

Historical Workshop

Film Analysis Worksheet

1. Describing the film
a. List the title, author(s), director(s), main actors and other important people who worked on the film.
b. List three ideas and characters appearing in the film.
c. Note the setting and any unusual features it has.
d. Summarize the plot briefly.

2. Finding information
a. Determine the type of the film (documentary, training, newsreel, entertainment, private, other).
b. Note any effects which influence the viewer (special effects, music, narration, colour, dramatization, background noise, live action, animation, other).
c. Assess the tone of the film created by the effects.
d. Choose one character or theme and show how it is developed during the film.

3. Interpreting the film
a. State the main message(s) of the film.
b. Point out whether the film appeals to reason or to emotion, giving reasons for your choice.
c. Give two examples of the film's use of exaggeration.
d. Explain the impression the film makes on you.
e. Mention specific information the film shows about life in Berlin, the US or the USSR at this time which is new to you.

SUMMARY: The Cold War and German Division 1945–49

1942 | 1943 | 1944 | 1945 | 1946

World War II.

German surrender 08/09 May 1945

Potsdam Agreement

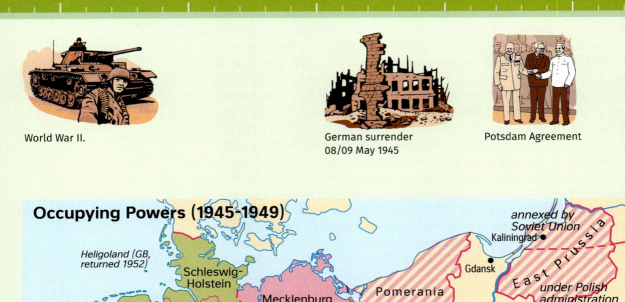

The Cold War and German Division 1945–49 – the historical map

Marshall Plan

Berlin Blockade

West Germany founded
East Germany founded

Konrad Adenauer

Summary

The Allies had different goals in their occupation of Germany. One major problem was the question of reparations. The Soviet Union depended on reparations to recover after World War II, but the Potsdam Agreement did not name a concrete sum. The Soviet government was disappointed when its claims for higher reparations were not met. The Western Allies, who had planned to occupy Germany only until the country recovered enough to sustain herself, worried that Soviet reparations would prevent or slow down German recovery. Their concern about Soviet expansion in Eastern Europe also grew. When the Allies had such different interests, their plan to keep Germany as one economic unit and to administer the zones of occupation separately failed.

The early post-war period in Germany was grim. Living conditions were poor; destruction was wide-spread. It was difficult to integrate millions of German expellees from Eastern Europe into the country under such circumstances. For many years the fate of expellees was not a primary consideration. Even today the expellees' displacement seems less important compared to the millions of others who were killed, harmed or dispossessed by the National Socialists. The new Foundation Flight, Expulsion, and Reconciliation will deal with this historical legacy in future.

The Western Allies gradually changed their approach to the German occupation. First the USA, then Great Britain, and finally France decided that the Soviet Union was a greater threat to peace than Germany. The Truman Doctrine and the Marshall Plan offered help and support to the Western zones of Germany, reversing a policy of punishment. Naturally, the USSR found these changes in agreed policy disturbing.

The most dramatic Allied dispute in the years 1945-49 was over Berlin. When the USSR blocked land routes, US and British forces (later joined by France) decided to risk an airlift to bring supplies to the isolated city. The fact that the Western Allies invested such effort to support West Berlin changed some German thinking about the Allied occupation. After the Berlin Blockade, Germans saw at least some of the occupiers as friends rather than enemies. However, the city continued to be a dangerous flashpoint among the Four Powers for many years.

Lasting improvement in post-war German life was impossible unless the Western and Eastern zones were stabilized. Therefore, two German states were founded in 1949: The Federal Republic of [West] Germany and The Social Democratic Republic of [East] Germany. Their leaders, Konrad Adenauer in the West and Walter Ulbricht in the East, had large tasks ahead of them.

DATES

2 August 1945:
Potsdam Agreement

1948 – 1952:
Marshall Plan

1948 – 1949:
Berlin Blockade

23 May 1949:
West Germany founded

7 October 1949:
East Germany founded

HISTORICAL TERMS

Cold War
Conference of Yalta
Conference of Potsdam
Foundation Flight, Expulsion, Reconciliation
League of Expellees
unconditional surrender
Control Council
Parliamentary Council
Basic Law
Federal Republic of Germany
Federal Council
constructive vote of no confidence
Socialist Unity Party
German Democratic Republic
State Security Service

PERSONS

Winston Churchill
Franklin D. Roosevelt
Joseph Stalin
Harry S. Truman
Konrad Adenauer
Walter Ulbricht

HISTORY WORKSHOP

Analysing Films

The Two Germanies within Europe

M 1 "The Month of German-Soviet Friendship"
Poster, East Germany, 1952

M 2 Soviet Tanks in the Streets
Photograph, East Berlin, 17 June 1953

M 3 Election Poster of the CDU
West Germany, 1957

M 4 Building a Wall
Photograph, Berlin, 13 August 1961

M 5 "In the Country Cottage"
Photograph, East Germany, 1980s

M 6 Chancellor Brandt in Warsaw
Photograph, 7 December 1970

M 7 Berlin, 10 November 1989
Photograph

04 THE TWO GERMANIES WITHIN EUROPE

1949–1990

A chapter like this needs a theme. A structure has to be found that helps learners to understand a story. In the case of the two German states and their history since 1949, the structure must be that of parallels.

In 1949, two German states were founded in postwar Germany. For forty years, "the German Question" was unanswered. What was "the German Question"? An answer was very difficult to find, because the "question" varied: Why were there two states? How did both states manage to live next to each other as parts of two opposing military blocs and two opposing ideologies? Did both states still contain one nation? Was reunification possible?

This chapter then will tell a story of two states facing each other, two states which cannot be understood without the other. After 40 years, in 1989, the story of East Germany ended: In the end, the East Germans lost faith in their state. And because the other state, West Germany, had always been present as the more successful example, a peaceful revolution led to a quick reunification.

But this reunification did not end the question of how united Germany is: A last outlook will therefore provide material to discuss the way the consequences of 40 divided years shaped our present.

This chapter deals with many questions such as:
- What did both states do to recover from the consequences of the Second World War?
- How did both states find their places in two opposing blocs?
- What was the role of the younger generations?
- How did various West German governments try to solve the German question?
- Is it possible to live with a dictatorship?
- How did the East Germans try to start revolutions?

The Two Germanies within Europe

Western and Eastern Integration?

The newly-formed two German states had their roots in the developing Cold War. But how could the two half-states find their places in relation to these two opposing sides?

Political Developments in West Germany

The first general elections in the Federal Republic of Germany, FRG ("Bundesrepublik Deutschland", BRD) were won by a centre-right coalition of the newly formed Christian Democratic Union/Christian Social Union (CDU/CSU), the Free Democratic Party (FDP) and the German Party ("Deutsche Partei", DP). By only a one-vote majority Konrad Adenauer was elected the first Chancellor on 15 September 1949. Three days later the popular and unconventional leader of the FDP, Theodor Heuss, became the first President. The opposition leader, Kurt Schumacher (SPD), favoured Germany's reunification and was willing to accept German neutrality if that led to a united country.

M 1   Konrad Adenauer (CDU, 1876 – 1967)
Photograph, about 1960

Adenauer's policies

But Adenauer had different ideas about Germany's future. Even though he insisted that he also wanted **reunification**, his first goals were national sovereignty and the solution of the economic and social problems in the country after World War II. Adenauer's first aim was making West Germany secure from Soviet domination. For him, that was more important than reunification. Winning the support of the three Western Allies would increase West German stability and independence and lead to a position of strength. Reunification would then follow later. He accepted West German rearmament as early as March 1949.

	1st step	2nd step	Price to be paid
"Adenauer's policy"	Stability and prosperity; position of strength/national sovereignty	Reunification	A divided country for some time

M 2   Kurt Schumacher (SPD, 1895 – 1952)
Photograph, about 1950

After the outbreak of the Korean War in 1950, the Western Allies increased their support of this goal. In addition to rearmament, the second important project was the integration of West European economies into a common market.

Adenauer pursued the integration of West Germany into the Western Alliance on an equal footing with the other states. The opposition fiercely criticized him as "Chancellor of the Allies" for this policy, but he held his course. The more the Cold War took shape and improvements within West Germany became visible, the more voters supported Adenauer. He won a large majority in the 1953 general elections.

Info

Steps towards integration into the West
1949 FRG joins the International Authority for the Ruhr
1951 European Coal and Steel Community
1955 FRG becomes sovereign, joins NATO, Bundeswehr founded
1957 Treaty of Rome: Common Market, Euratom

M 3   Theodor Heuss (FDP, 1884 – 1963)
Photograph, 1952

Developments in East Germany

In East Berlin the government was led by the experienced Communists Wilhelm Pieck and Walter Ulbricht. Their power rested on the presence of the Soviet Army and their legitimacy was based on *rigged* elections to maintain the influence of the SED. Other parties existed, but had to follow the rules made by the SED. A single list system for elections included not only the political parties but also mass organizations like the Free German Trade Union Federation ("FDGB") and the Free German Youth ("FDJ"), which were all dominated by the SED. The people could not choose between parties or candidates, and the "elections" were open: Everybody could see the ballot paper. So the "results" were no surprise. This system guaranteed the party's success.

Building of Socialism

The Second Party Congress in July 1952 proclaimed the "building of socialism" within the framework of a **planned economy**. Following land reform after 1945, **collectivization** of farming, fundamental changes in property ownership and the two-year plan of 1949, the direction of government policy was clear. The state was increasingly modelled on the Soviet Union. People who disagreed were *harassed*. The GDR adopted a Soviet-style system of government, social order and planned economy. From 1950 on, the SED maintained its power through the surveillance of its citizens, aided by the **Ministry of State Security**, known as the "Stasi". In the mid-50s, the GDR began border fortifications on the inner-German border: fences were put up, some villages were destroyed and the villagers were resettled further inland to create a special control zone along the border.

Both sides were theoretically interested in German unity. For all practical purposes, however, the two Germanies were drifting apart, integrating into their respective bloc systems.

The Soviet Note

To the surprise of many in the East and in the West, Soviet leader Josef Stalin proposed reunification in 1952. What kind of offer was that?

Stalin proposed a draft treaty for a peace conference to the Western Allies, offering German unity in exchange for neutrality. Stalin even wanted to grant Germany the right to maintain an army to defend itself. As the Korean War was still being fought, the Western Allies and Adenauer considered Stalin's offer an attempt to stop the process of Western integration. The key issue for this offer was the question of free elections. Stalin wanted the SED government to negotiate, the West wanted free elections in the GDR before any sort of negotiation. In the end, Stalin's offer was not accepted. Both German states became part of their respective systems.

Info

Steps towards a greater orientation towards the USSR
1951 First 5-Year-Plan
1952 collectivization of farms following the soviet model
1954 USSR declares GDR a sovereign state
1955 Treaty of Friendship GDR-USSR
1955 GDR joins Warsaw Pact

Vocabulary

to rig: to manipulate
to harass: to mistreat

M 4 "Learning from the Soviet Union is a Lesson in Victory"
Poster, about 1951

Historical Terms

reunification: Wiedervereinigung

planned economy: Planwirtschaft

collectivization: Kollektivierung

Ministry of State Security: Ministerium für Staatssicherheit ("Stasi")

The Soviet Note (1952) – source material

Info

The Soviet Note
The terms on offer:
- Germany is GDR+FRG, but not the lost Eastern provinces
- all foreign troops leave Germany
- Allied control ends
- Germany can have a small army for self-defence
- Germany must not join any military pact: It must remain neutral
- the changes to economy and society in the GDR must not be reversed

Vocabulary

inclined: here: tend to
creed: belief
to constrain: to control, to hinder
to forsake: to give up

M 5 German Reactions to the "Stalin Note"

Telegram by U.S. High Commissioner John McCloy to Secretary of State Dean Acheson on German reactions to the "Stalin Note" (29 March 1952):

"I. Not (repeat not) without good reason Germans are strongly *inclined* to view Soviet note of March 10 as addressed to them rather than to the Allies. They therefore tend to examine it as a serious offer of unity rather than as a propaganda move.

It is particularly difficult to judge German public opinion as soon after exchange of notes but we tend to believe that Germans' experiences of Russia as occupiers, prisoners of war and occupied make them skeptical of any Soviet offer and that they are therefore not (repeat not) as yet greatly impressed by it. This negative reaction is, however, not (repeat not) static and may be reversed by the politicians particularly if West Powers appear to oppose unification.

Among those politicians who have carefully studied implications of note and our reply there are basically two schools of thought. Adenauer whose entire political *creed* is based on Western integration considers note chiefly an effort to disrupt his policy. [...]

Adenauer however is *constrained* by fact that flat rejection gives appearance of *forsaking* Germany's own national interests in interests of Western Europe or as one Cabinet member put it of being more American than the Americans."

Quoted from: Rolf Steininger, The German Question. The Stalin Note of 1952 and the Problem of Reunification, New York: Columbia University Press 1990, pp. 151–55.

M 6 "Come on, let me neutralize you!"
Cartoon by Mirko Szewczuk, 1952

M 7 "The Fallen Oak"
Cartoon by Felix Mussil, West Germany, 1955

1945

1955

Tasks

1. **Personal Careers in Interesting Times**
   Find out about the personal careers of influential politicians in the first years of postwar Germany: Konrad Adenauer, Kurt Schumacher, Theodor Heuss, Walter Ulbricht, Wilhelm Pieck, Otto Grotewohl.
   Show how their personal backgrounds influenced their political lives (Internet).

2. **Adenauer's Position**
   a) Explain Adenauer's reasoning as seen in M5.
   b) Discuss which phrases show that this telegram is a secret telegram not meant for the public.
   c) "Two schools of thought" are mentioned – what might the other be? Write a statement for the other side contrary to Adenauer.

3. **"Come on, let me neutralize you!"**
   a) Analyse the cartoon M6.
   b) Explain the cartoon by referring to events.
   c) Comment on the cartoon: Is it fair to draw the cartoon like this?

4. **"The Fallen Oak"**
   a) Analyse cartoon M7.
   b) Comment on the cartoon.

Vocabulary

reconciliation: the end of disagreement and the start of good relations

surge: sudden increase of a strong feeling

The Adenauer Years

Even though he had only a small majority in parliament at first, Konrad Adenauer was such a successful Chancellor that his government won majorities in the 1953 and 1957 elections. Why did he become so successful that a whole era was named after him?

Rebuilding Germany

Not only did Adenauer maintain complex coalitions and execute foreign policy skilfully, his management of the office under the new Basic Law established what became known as "Kanzlerdemokratie": the person of the Chancellor became the most important political figure. Gradually West Germany proved a reliable partner in international politics and acted more autonomously. After being admitted to NATO (1955), West Germany became one of the founding members of the Common Market or European Economic Community (EEC, "Europäische Wirtschaftsgemeinschaft", EWG) in 1957. Adenauer's friendly relations with French President Charles de Gaulle led to the German-French Friendship Treaty 1963 (Élysée Treaty) and to the founding of the Franco-German Youth Association to promote mutual understanding and friendship among the young people of the former historic enemies. In addition, Adenauer established diplomatic relations with the Soviet Union (1955) and sought *reconciliation* with Israel (1952).

Adenauer's foreign policy followed the principles of the **Hallstein Doctrine**, which claimed the Federal Republic was the only representative of Germany, simply because the people in East Germany could not vote freely and thus had no democratic government. According to the doctrine, West Germany might break off its relations with foreign countries which recognized East Germany diplomatically.

West Germans faced enormous problems in 1949. Millions of refugees had to be integrated into a country that suffered from a lack of housing after World War II. Therefore, housing construction took on top priority. The form of compensation to be paid to refugees from the lost Eastern territories was regulated by a law passed in 1952. Another pressing problem was pension reform. Adenauer's government solved this by January 1957, which led to his winning an absolute majority in parliament in the next general election.

After a long political career, Adenauer resigned as Chancellor at the age of 87 in 1963.

M 1 "All the Roads of Marxism lead to Moscow"

Even though the Social Democrats (SPD) declared their party free from Marxism, the CDU used this poster in the 1953 general election. Poster, West Germany, 1953

Between Confidence and Americanization

Victory in the 1954 football World Cup marked a *surge* in West German confidence. Many felt that national honour had been recovered and that the future looked promising. Nevertheless, a German culture which had produced National Socialism and its destruction seemed so untrustworthy that some turned to the American way of life to find new values. Especially young people tried to break free of an environment they felt was too restrictive. American culture was available through the soldiers (and their radio stations) of the US military presence in West Germany as well as through the US companies which increasingly set up businesses in the country. Rock'n'roll, the new music of the 50s, took West German youth by storm.

On the other hand, many West Germans preferred more traditional ways of life and did not want too much change. The West German film industry met these desires and released a number of old-fashioned feel-good movies, many starring actors and actresses who had already been famous in Nazi Germany.

Economic recovery – the "economic miracle"

The Christian Democratic Union (CDU) won the 1949 elections with the slogan "**Social Market Economy** versus Socialist Planned Economy". Unlike a free market economy with no restrictions, the social market economy was relatively unrestricted, but accepted some limitations, such as employers' contributions to the social security system and acceptable, fair wages for employees. Ludwig Erhard, who popularized the term "social market economy", became Minister of Economics in Adenauer's government.

With the help of the Marshall Plan and favourable global conditions, the West German economy quickly recovered. An enormous economic boom with annual growth rates of around 10% lasted for fifteen years, making West Germany the third strongest industrial country in the world. One of the secrets behind this development was the high number of skilled East Germans who fled socialism and joined the West German workforce.

As the number of industrial workers grew, the number of trade union members also increased, because employers and unions negotiated wages directly. Trade unions aimed not only at employees sharing company profits with owners but also at improving working and living conditions. They successfully fought for fewer working hours and more holidays.

The structural economic developments also changed West German society. Before the boom there had been social divisions among the *self-employed*, the employees and the workers. The growing demand for industrial workers could no longer be filled by the end of the 1950s, leading to a campaign to find "**guest workers**" in southern Europe. At the same time, the number of workers and of self-employed persons in agriculture, trade and commerce decreased. Growing prosperity generated waves of mass consumption – first food and clothes, then housing and *household appliances* and finally cars, travelling and holidays abroad. Italy became the preferred destination for holidays. West Germany had become an *affluent* society with more free time to spend.

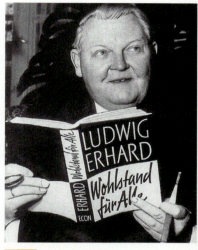

M 2 Ludwig Erhard
Minister of Economics.
Photograph, about 1959

Vocabulary

self-employed: when you own your business and work more or less alone

household appliances: washing machine, fridge, vacuum cleaner, etc

affluent: well-off, prosperous

M 3 The One Millionth Volkswagen Rolls off the Assembly Line
Photograph, Wolfsburg, West Germany, 1955

Historical Terms

Hallstein Doctrine:
Hallstein-Doktrin

social market economy:
Soziale Marktwirtschaft

guest workers: Gastarbeiter

Economic Recovery – the "economic miracle"

M 4 **Excerpt from a Speech given by Ludwig Erhard**

He speaks at a CDU congress in Frankfurt on 28 April 1960:

"No truly *sincere* person can deny, after the experiences of the past twelve years, that anything we have not so far achieved is in process of achievement, and that any further progress we make in the economic field will, in the first instance, benefit the broad mass of the people. To take only one example, the total of private incomes available for consumption and saving rose by 122% between 1950 and 1958. The net incomes of self-employed have increased by 71%, while the earnings of the mass of the people have gone up by 142%. In making these comparisons, however, we must bear in mind that invisible profits are not included and that the numbers of employed persons increased between 1949 and 1959 from 13.6 millions to 20.1 millions. But this in itself seems to me to be not the least of the achievements of our German economic policy, and it is also worth pointing out that the obvious success of a free economic and social system in Germany has produced a more and more *pronounced* trend towards market economy methods in other parts of the free world. One can, indeed, say that […] the basic pattern […] has so far proved itself as to be generally accepted today as the prototype of a worldwide system of free trading."

Ludwig Erhard, The economics of success, transl. by J. A. Arengo-Jones and D.J.S.Thomson, London: Thames and Hudson, 1963, p. 277.

Vocabulary

sincere: serious
pronounced: obvious, noticable

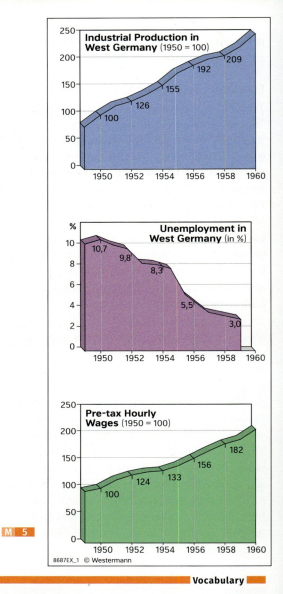

M 5

Vocabulary

Useful terms:
has risen / has been falling / increase / decrease / constantly / in waves / with ups and downs / since 1950 / for 10 years / during the 50s

---

Tasks

1. **Rebuilding and Reorientation**
   a) Describe the changes that took place in West Germany (text).
   b) List American products that became popular in West Germany after World War II.
   c) Find out about Elvis Presley and the impact he had on West German society (Internet).

2. **The "Economic Miracle"**
   a) Analyse Erhard's statement about his policy (M4). Explain the expression "economic miracle" based on this statement.
   b) Assess the way the economic development in West Germany is shown in M5.

"Guest Workers" in West Germany

M 6   "Guest Workers"

The magazine DER SPIEGEL reported in 1964:

"The Bavarian Ministry of Labor did not allow the Munich city utilities to hire women as tram drivers. It was argued that 'women did not meet the requirements of the Munich tram traffic' and suggested instead to recruit guest workers. Many women from the staff of Munich public transport had had expressed their interest by which the shortage of tram drivers could be compensated."

Der Spiegel 38/1964, 16.09.1964, http://www.spiegel.de/spiegel/print/d-46175384.html (transl. by Matthias Bode).

M 7   An Interview

In an interview for a book about "guest workers" in West Germany, a man from Turkey told about a day on a construction site in the 1960s:

"Once, as I was digging gravel, a man, dressed smartly, approached me, taking the shovel out of my hand and showing me how to do it: shoving the shovel deep under the pile, filling it up, and then unloading quickly. He returned my tool and left. I was astonished for a moment, and then I ran after him indignantly, waving my shovel in the air and shouting: Hey, who are you, actually, that you explain my job to me? Unfortunately, it turned out that the man was our boss. I could not sleep during the night: I was sure they would send me back to Turkey, we all thought that. What would I expect at home? Unemployment, poverty, anger, ridicule. I was desperate. When I came to work the next morning, I saw my boss from afar. He smiled at me. Oh, I was so relieved! He would not send me to Turkey. Apparently, he could laugh about it. It suddenly became clear to me: So that's the Europe everyone is talking about. Understanding and tolerant. Something like that would not have been possible in my homeland."

Quoted from: Jeanette Goddar und Dörthe Huneke (eds.), Auf Zeit. Für immer. Zuwanderer aus der Türkei erinnern sich (Schriftenreihe Band 1183), Bonn: Bundeszentrale für politische Bildung 2011, S. 49. (transl. by Matthias Bode).

	Total	Italy	Spain	Greece	Turkey
1954	72,900	6,500	400	500	–
1955	79,600	7,500	500	600	–
1956	98,800	18,600	700	1,000	–
1957	108,200	19,100	1,000	1,800	–
1958	136,300	31,500	1,500	2,900	–
1959	166,800	48,800	2,200	4,100	–
1960	279,400	121,700	9,500	13,000	2,500
1961	507,400	218,000	51,000	43,900	5,200
1962	655,500	266,000	87,300	69,100	15,300

From: Johannes-Dieter Steinert, Migration und Politik. Westdeutschland – Europa – Übersee 1945–1961, Osnabrück 1995, S. 281.

M 8   Guest Workers from Different Countries, 1954–1962

Tasks

1. **Migration from the South and the East**
   a) Analyse the table M8. Relate this table to the charts in M5.
   b) Between 1945 and 1961, about three million Germans had left the former Eastern provinces and the GDR and had settled in West Germany. Should the numbers of East Germans fleeing West be added in the table above? Refer to pages 144/145.
   c) Research the story of the "Empire Windrush". Compare to the German situation (Internet).

2. **German Image – and self-image**
   a) Adenauer's foreign policy concerns dealt with France, the USA, Israel and the Soviet Union. Discuss their order of importance for West Germany.
   b) Explain why West Germany winning the 1954 football world championship can be seen as the end of the immediate post war era.
   c) Comment on the Volkswagen ceremony in M3. Show the importance of that figure for West Germany.

The Early Ulbricht Era

Parallel to Adenauer, Walter Ulbricht was the most influential man in East Germany in the 50s and 60s. His policies shaped the way the GDR developed.

Rebuilding East Germany

He was the First Secretary of the SED and a member of the **People's Chamber**. In 1960 he became Chairman of the State Council and the National Defence Council, thus incorporating the leadership of the party and state. During his first years in office he was criticized by members of his party and also by intellectuals. In the end all his opponents either lost their positions in the party or their jobs.

Ulbricht launched a "national construction programme" based on communist ideology. Its aim was not only to build houses and flats but also to reconstruct whole towns and cities for the "new socialist man". Many old, traditional buildings were torn down, for example, the royal palace in Berlin.

M 1   Walter Ulbricht
Photograph, about 1960

Historical Terms

People's Chamber: Volkskammer

Free German Youth: Freie Deutsche Jugend, FDJ

The Economy

Collectivization in trade, industry and farming had already begun before the founding of the GDR and advanced with the five-year plans in the 1950s and 60s. The planned economy seemed to work well at first, as it led to better food supplies and more consumer goods in the shops of the state-owned trade organization ("Handelsorganisation", "HO-Läden"). The party insisted that East Germany would catch up with and overtake the West German economy by 1961. To show that, ambitious projects were launched: for example, new steel works were built in what later became Eisenhüttenstadt.

In agriculture, however, the SED government tried to impose a collectivization: small farmers were forced to become part of larger units, the so-called LPG (Landwirtschafliche Produktionsgenossenschaften), very often against the will of the people in the villages. These decisions to intensify in agriculture and to nationalize private businesses made many dissatisfied people think about the stories of the economic miracle in the West: In the end, many people left the country and moved to the West, especially skilled workers.

The planned economy proved to be slow and inflexible. Inefficient organization, poor quality of products and the lack of food imports from outside the socialist states caused discontent among people who often had to wait in long queues for goods.

The Youth Organization

To ensure that future generations became good socialists, the **Free German Youth (FGY)** was founded in 1946. It had three different goals: Organizing young people in factories, schools and living quarters, educating them in party ideology, and planning their spare time activities. Such activities included a kind of pre-military training. The youngest joined the Young Pioneers ("Jungpioniere"), older children the Thälmann Pioneers. Membership was about 40% in the 1950s, more than 70 % in the 1980s. Leaders of the Free German Youth were simultaneously members of the SED. The first secretary of the Free German Youth had a seat in the Politburo, the decisive political organ in the GDR. From 1963 on, 40 of the 500 members of the People's Chamber were officials in the youth organization. Membership in the FGY was crucial for the future career of young people. Students also had to be members. In addition, class background was important, as official policy favoured students

M 2   Mass Demonstration of the FGY, 1949
Photograph, Berlin, 11 November 1949

from the families of workers and farmers. It was difficult for young people from an academic or a religious family background to go to university.

The Free German Trade Union Federation

A number of mass organizations attracted members by offering them advantages. For example, the Free German Trade Union Federation ("Freier Deutscher Gewerkschaftsbund", FDGB) distributed places at *resorts* in the country for members to go on holiday. The federation also had a fixed number of seats in the People's Chamber, the GDR parliament.

17 June 1953 – a revolution?

After Stalin's death in March 1953 new hopes of reunification arose in the West. East Germans also hoped for economic and political improvements, which may have stopped the wave of refugees to the West for a time.

However, in May new *work norms* set longer working hours and higher production levels. Although East German leaders announced a "new course" to provide better supplies, cut prices and reduce pressure on 9 June, workers were not satisfied. On 17 June, strikes began and workers, especially in East Berlin, began spontaneous demonstrations which quickly spread to other parts of the GDR. Hundreds of thousands of demonstrators demanded not only economic reforms but also political changes such as free elections.

Troubles in East Berlin

Soviet tanks crushed the uprising and more than 100 people died. SED leader Walter Ulbricht, whose political authority had been disputed, returned to full power. On the other hand, it became clear that the GDR government did not have a full mass support. Obviously, the future of the GDR was in the hands of the Soviet Union. Especially working class people had participated in the protests, a serious blow for a party which saw itself as a "worker's party".

M 3 "FGY Shirt"
about 1970

Vocabulary

resort: holiday destination

work norms: for a certain wage, workers are expected to work a certain amount of time and to achieve a certain output. Higher work norms thus mean in effect lower wages for the same work or more work for the same wage.

M 4 Street Fighting
Detail of a photograph, East Berlin, 17 June 1953

The Early Ulbricht Era

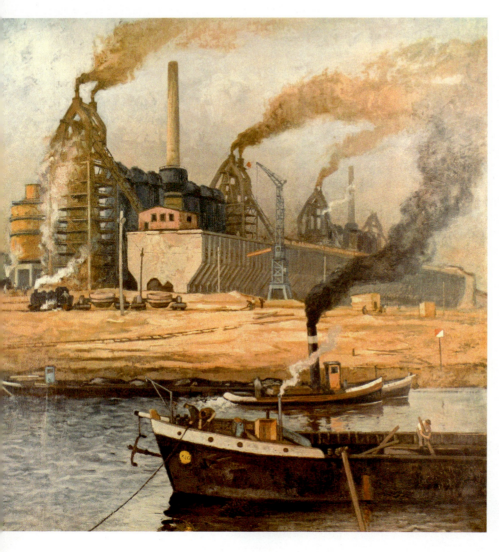

M 5 Eisenhütten Steel Works East
This steel factory was founded in 1951. It was considered a great socialist achievement and was meant to be the center of a new steel industry. About 20,000 steel workers used Soviet iron ore and Polish coal to produce steel. Next to this huge building "Stalinstadt" was built as housing for the workers. After Stalin's death, the town was renamed Eisenhüttenstadt. In 1953, it had 2,400 residents, by 1960 the number had reached 24,000. Painting by Herbert Aschmann, 1952.

1949	1950	1951	1952	1953	1954	1955	1956	1957	1958	1959	1960	1961
129,245	197,788	165,648	182,393	331,390	184,198	252,870	279,189	261,622	204,092	143,917	199,188	155,402

Total: 2,686,942

M 6 Refugees from East to West Germany by Year

Tasks

1. **Building a new state?**
    a) Describe the painting. Explain the "message" it is supposed to show (M5).
    b) Draw a chart to visualize the numbers (M6). Compare to M9 on page 139. Explain what these numbers tell us about the Ulbricht era.

17 June 1953 – a revolution?

M 7 Wilhelm Fiebelkorn: The workers were coming

These memories of the events of 17 June 1953 in Bitterfeld were written long after the events (excerpt):

"But then, it was about 9:30, a black wall was pushing furiously over the railway line close to our school: The workers were coming! My heart was throbbing with excitement [...]. Everyone was pushing and pulling. The feeling, the mass of people, made them strong and brave. [...] I was thrilled! First, I stood at the gate. Students ran out of the school. Windows were opened. Some teachers suddenly stood next to me. 'Are we going?' I asked them. They stood there, apparently completely surprised by the event, unable to speak. Maybe they were thinking further than I was at that moment. They remained passive.
I broke away from the crowd of teachers and students, walked up to the front of the march and called to the front row: 'I am also one of you! I think like you! I declare my solidarity with you! I want to march with you!'"

Quoted from: Stadtarchiv Bitterfeld, Wilhelm Fiebelkorn, Erinnerungen an die Vorgänge des 17. Juni 1953, STAB, Sign. 557; also in: Landesbeauftragte für die Stasi-Unterlagen in Sachsen-Anhalt, Materialerhebung zum 17. Juni 1953, Magdeburg 2003, zitiert nach: http://www.17juni53.de/karte/halle/fiebelkorn.html (transl. by Matthias Bode).

M 8 Workers on a Demonstration
Photograph, East Berlin, 16 June 1953

M 9 Telegram to Washington

In a telegram to Washington, a US officer informs the US government what the Allied commanders had told the mayor of West Berlin, 17 June 1953:

"Commandants then called in Acting Mayor [Walter] Conrad and Police President [Johannes] Stumm and French chairman informed them as follows:
1. Commandants consider their primary duty to maintain law and order in their sectors in Berlin. They appreciate sympathy of West Berliners for their fellow citizens in the East.
2. Commandants will not (repeat not) oppose orderly meeting or demonstrations of sympathy. However, they feel it their duty to warn West Berliners of grave consequences which might result were West Berliners to participate in *manifestations* in East sector. In this they are expecting the usual full cooperation of West Berlin police.
3. Commandants understand that West Berlin meeting is scheduled to take place at six this evening at Oranien Platz (SPD-sponsored sympathy rally). Commandants have no (repeat no) objection to such a meeting taking place, but feel that place chosen is too close to sector border and consequently might result in serious consequences. They, therefore, request that another meeting place be selected more removed from the sector borders.
4. Commandants scarcely feel it necessary to remind [West Berlin] Senat that status of Berlin is Allied responsibility and expect Senat to take no (repeat no) initiative to change it without consulting Allied Kommandatura."

Cecil Lyon, June 17, 1953 (NARA, RG 59, 762A.0221/6-1755, dok.), in: Christian F. Ostermann (ed.), Uprising in East Germany. The Cold War, the German Question and the First Major Upheaval Behind the Iron Curtain. National Security Archive Cold War Readers, New York: CEU Press 2001, Dokument Nr. 32, pp. 1194/95. http://www.17juni53.de/chronik/530617/17-06-53_0600_o.html [July 13, 2018].

Vocabulary

manifestations: (here) demonstrations

Tasks

1. **The Events of 17 June**
   a) Explain the problem for the GDR government that West German radio could be listened to all over the GDR.
   b) Summarize the events in June 1953 (text).
   c) Analyse the eyewitness report, explaining what Fiebelkorn means by "I was thrilled!" (M7).
   d) Explain the four points made by the Allied commanders (M9).
   e) Explain why the Western Allies and the FRG did not intervene.

2. **Assessing 17 June**
   a) Assess whether the events in June can be described as a failed revolution.
   b) Between 1954 and 1990, 17 June was a national holiday in West Germany. Today, there is hardly any public remembrance of 17 June. Discuss whether it should be more present in public memory.

Historical Terms

Berlin Wall: Die Mauer
Iron Curtain: Eiserner Vorhang

Vocabulary

barbed wire: spiky wire used in fences
to embarrass: to cause mental pain, to shame sb.

Building the Berlin Wall

The moment it was built, the **Berlin Wall** became the symbol of the Cold War. It showed in a drastic way that something was wrong in international politics and in the way the SED organized the GDR.

The Berlin Question

After World War II Berlin had been divided into four sectors. In 1949, when the Western zones merged into the FRG and the Soviet zone became the GDR, Berlin remained a divided city deep inside East Germany, but still occupied by the Allied forces. In the course of the Western "economic miracle", Berlin turned into a city of contrasts: Plentiful goods in the West, food and housing shortages in the East. Berliners crossed the borders of the sectors everyday to work, shop or visit relatives. But thousands of East Germans also fled their country via Berlin. Since 1952, the **Iron Curtain** dividing Germany had gradually been fortified with *barbed-wire* fencing, mine-fields and machine-gun posts by the East German government. Berlin provided the last gap in the dangerous border.

Taking Action 1961

By 1961 around three million people had fled East Germany, nearly one sixth of the entire population. Many who left were university graduates and skilled workers. Without them factories, hospitals, schools and offices would eventually come to a standstill. Moreover, the development *embarrassed* the Soviets deeply. The benefits of communism over capitalism were hard to believe when 10,000 people a week were leaving the country via Berlin in July 1961. On 12 August alone, there were 4000 refugees.

Since 1958 the Soviets had pressured the Western Allies to leave Berlin, but unsuccessfully. So in the end, only one option was possible: In the early morning hours of 13 August 1961 East German workers guarded by armed soldiers built a barbed-wire fence and closed the border between the Eastern and Western sectors. Soon after, the fence was replaced by a brick and then concrete wall.

The Results

The Western Allies were taken by surprise. They protested, but could do nothing to re-open the border. Any serious actions could have caused a war between the great powers – a risk nobody wanted to take. After the completion of the wall, border guards in more than 300 watchtowers and 50 bunkers made sure nobody could leave the Eastern sector, which was now called "Berlin, the capital of the German Democratic Republic".

The wall achieved its purpose. The flood of refugees stopped. But the wall also provided the West with a propaganda victory over a Communist state that was forced to build barriers to keep its citizens from running away. Nevertheless, Western politicians reacted only reluctantly to the provocation.

From 1961 to 1989 when the wall came down, about 5,000 East Germans managed to cross it and reach West Berlin safely. Another 5,000 were arrested and 191 were killed while attempting to cross.

M 1 Peter Fechter Bleeds to Death at the Berlin Wall, 17 August 1962
Photograph

Building the Berlin Wall – working with visuals

On this page this book offers you three pictures. They were all taken in Berlin when the wall was built.

M 2

M 3

M 4

Tasks

1. **Building the Berlin Wall**
   a) Describe the pictures (M2–M4).
   b) Analyse the pictures: Explain what you can see and from which side they were taken.
   c) Comment on the pictures: Say how you feel, which of the three touches you most.
   d) Decide: Which of these would you put on the cover of a book about the wall?
   e) Research the death of Peter Fechter. Discuss the events (M1).

M 1   The Grand Coalition 1966
From left to right: Foreign Minister and Vice-Chancellor Willy Brandt (SPD), leader of the SPD in the Bundestag Helmut Schmidt, and Chancellor Kurt-Georg Kiesinger.

Info

Fifth Bundestag 1965 – 1969
518 Seats
SPD: 217
CDU: 251
FDP: 50

Info

Emergency Acts (Notstandsgesetze): Until 1968, the Western Allies had the right to control West Germany in an emergency. The Acts were necessary for the FRG to become sovereign.

West Germany in the 60s – a time of change?

In nearly all Western countries, a change of values disturbed society in the 1960s. In some countries this happened peacefully, in some others more serious issues caused violence. Different developments from all over the world were mixed to form a "counterculture".

A New Generation

Young people were no longer content with traditional authoritarian and hierarchical structures, with the central role of the family, with the sexual morality of their parents' generation and with the dominance of consumption and achievement. Simultaneously, new styles of music (rock music) and fashion (the mini skirt) emerged. People born between 1940 and 1950 – the first generation without a memory of the Second World War – left university or school in those years. Many of these young people used these changes to provoke the older generation and to question the system of state and economy. But not only the young demanded change; in literature and the social sciences revolutionary ideas spread. Some foundations of the political system were questioned, like West Germany's ties to the USA or its official doctrine of anti-Communism.

The Global Sixties

"We shall overcome" had been the motto of American students in demonstrations against the Vietnam War. From the mid-1960s on, student unrest also swept across Europe. In West Germany students opposed not only the war in Vietnam. Other goals were rooted in German politics and society. Following the students at the Free University of Berlin, who rejected the old-fashioned organization of the university, the younger generation and many intellectuals formed a movement with very diverse aims. Some fought against the growing influence of the extreme right and demanded that their parents and grandparents face their Nazi past. Others demonstrated against press concentration. Their idols were often revolutionary leaders like Che Guevara (Cuba) or Ho Chi Minh (Vietnam) who had led their countries from colonial rule to freedom. Others related to the civil rights movement in the USA: Its most prominent figure, Martin Luther King, was assassinated in 1968.

The Grand Coalition

When Ludwig Erhard's CDU/CSU/FDP government collapsed in 1966, the CDU/CSU and the SPD, the two largest parties, agreed to form a **Grand Coalition**. They accepted an unusually strong government (90% of the seats in the Bundestag) for a limited period of time because they confronted unusual problems: An economic recession, a budget deficit and sudden growth of a neo-nationalist party ("Nationaldemokratische Partei Deutschlands", NPD). In addition, the coalition intended to use its large parliamentary majority to enact Emergency Acts which required changing the Basic Law. Kurt-Georg Kiesinger (CDU) was elected Chancellor, former Berlin Mayor Willy Brandt (SPD) became his Foreign Minister and Vice-Chancellor. The economy quickly gained strength again, but the peaceful days of the Grand Coalition were short-lived.

M 2 **International Vietnam Congress in Berlin**
In 1968, the "Socialist German Student Association" ("SDS") organized an International Vietnam Congress in Berlin. It was directed against US politics and the war in Vietnam. SDS leader Rudi Dutschke during his speech, 17 February 1968.

Protests by the APO

During the Grand Coalition there was hardly any opposition in parliament, so some students founded an **extra-parliamentary opposition (APO)**. The group organized demonstrations, staged discussions and debated the use of violence, especially after a Berlin demonstrator was killed by the police in 1967. Some even turned to violence against department stores and publishers.

People from all walks of life united to oppose the passage of the Emergency Acts. The protesters feared the loss of their liberties, as the new laws allowed the government to impose emergency measures if civil order broke down. Protesters were reminded of the emergency powers of the Weimar Constitution that had brought Hitler to power. The year 1967–68 was marked by a wave of demonstrations.

The assassination attempt against Rudi Dutschke, an APO leader, by a young anti-communist in 1968 again set off large demonstrations against the **establishment** in general and against the conservative press in particular. But without the charismatic Dutschke, the movement soon disagreed about its aims.

The members of the APO separated into different directions. The most extreme decided that change could not be achieved without the use of violence. They turned to terrorism in the **Red Army Faction**, killing representatives of the political and economic system and causing considerable unrest in the FRG in the 1970s. Other former members of the APO became founders of the Green Party, which emerged in the 1980s. Some began what Dutschke called a "march through the institutions" to gain influence and change the system from within.

The End of the Grand Coalition

The Grand Coalition had seemed to signal unity in the face of growing economic difficulties, but after the necessary reforms of the Basic Law, the leaders of the SPD saw the coalition as too conservative. Willy Brandt pushed for "more democracy". The SPD also supported détente with Eastern Europe, which the CDU/CSU regarded with suspicion. Together with the liberal Free Democrats (FDP), who had moved more to the left under their party leader Walter Scheel, they elected Gustav Heinemann (SPD) President in May 1969. The following general elections provided SPD and FDP with a narrow majority over the CDU/CSU, which had to leave the government after dominating West German politics for twenty years.

Historical Terms

Grand Coalition: Große Koalition

extra-parliamentary opposition: Außerparlamentarische Opposition, APO

the establishment: das Establishment: an elite group holding most of the power and influence in a government or society

Red Army Faction: Rote Armee Fraktion, RAF

West Germany in the 60s – a time of change?

M 3 German Generations

	1890	1910	1914–1918	1933	1939–1945	1945	1968
Grandparents	Born	Youth	War experience	Adult	War experience	German defeat	Senior
Parents		Born		Youth	War experience	German defeat	Adult
Children						Born	Age 23

M 4 Demonstration of the Extra-parliamentary Opposition (APO) against the Vietnam War
Photograph, 1968

M 5 The Question of Violence

a) The magazine "Der Spiegel" wrote this shortly after the assassination attempt against Rudi Dutschke:

"There were street battles: West Germany had not seen such scenes since the Weimar Republic. These left two dead, over 400 injured. Injured as well was the claim of the Federal Republic to be an intact democratic state. [...] Immediately after the assassination attempt on Rudi Dutschke leftist students moved to the West Berlin Springer house in the Kochstraße near the Wall. Stones broke the windows of this *stronghold* of *dumbing down* and hate. Delivery vans were set on fire. 800 kilometers away, 300 students invaded the Munich printing company where 'Bild' was edited and printed for southern Germany. In the offices, *raiders* tore files from the cabinets and threw them out the window."

Der Spiegel 17/1968, pp. 25ff. (transl. by Matthias Bode).

b) The Federal Minister for Justice, Gustav Heinemann (SPD), had this to say about the events:

"These days of shattering events and increased unrest force us all to rethink. Those who point with their index finger of general allegations to the alleged *plotters* or *masterminds* should remember that in the hand with the outstretched forefinger three other fingers point back at you. [...] The fundamental rights include the right to demonstrate to mobilize public opinion. The young generation, too, has a right to be heard and taken seriously with their wishes and suggestions. However, violent acts are deeply wrong and stupid as well. Long experience shows that riots and violence create exactly the opposite public opinion of what their initiators want."

Quoted from: Bulletin des Presse- und Informationsamtes der Bundesregierung. 17. April 1968, p. 393 (transl. by Matthias Bode)

Vocabulary

stronghold: fortress
to dumb down: making sth. simpler
raider: sb. who steals or plunders
plotter: person who makes plans to do sth. bad
mastermind: person who thinks up and/or carries out an idea or project

---

Tasks

1. **German Generations**
   a) Explain this generational model (M3). Use it to look at one of the biographies of Daniel Cohn-Bendit, Petra Kelly, Gudrun Ensslin, Andreas Baader, Hans-Christian Ströbele and Joschka Fischer. Show how historical events shaped his or her political life.
   b) Identify the faces shown on the posters. Explain why these demonstrators seemed so provocative for the older generation (M4).
   c) Role-play: A child born in 1945 asks his parents and grandparents about their lives.

2. **The Global Sixties**
   a) Project: The Global Sixties. Research events and developments in other parts of the world during the late 1960s. Analyse how these developments influenced each other. Design a poster exhibition. Work in groups.

3. **The Question of Violence**
   a) Explain the problem of violence in Der SPIEGEL (M5a) and in Heinemann's speech (M5b).
   b) Discuss the idea that the protesters in Germany identified with armed resistance in the third world because their parents had failed to resist Hitler.

4. **The Grand Coalition**
   a) Explain the role of the opposition.
   b) Explain why the "APO" was founded.

East Germany after 1961: Losing a Second Chance?

After the borders were sealed off, leaving East Germans no escape, the economy of the country was given a second chance. The people of the GDR had to refocus their lives on the situation they found themselves in.

The Power of the State

Living conditions were improved by a series of economic and political reforms: A modernization of the legal code, and more incentives for young people to participate in politics. Election reform gave voters in regional elections the right to reject individual candidates on the single list. But power still remained in the hands of the SED.

While these new ideas looked promising, a new definition of "crimes against the state" meant that simple criticism of the government could lead to prison sentences. When Ulbricht's "economic miracle" did not materialize, the GDR was again in trouble. The 1968 Warsaw Pact invasion of Czechoslovakia (see pages 206–7) also disturbed many East Germans.

The "Stasi"

Opposition in East Germany had to be suppressed ruthlessly because the SED could not be sure that people wanted to live in a Communist state. In 1950, the party leaders founded the **Ministry of State Security (Stasi)**, which became their most important and effective tool for domestic control. After the 1953 East German uprising, the work of the Stasi intensified. Its methods were perfected, resulting in a system of surveillance that detected any form of opposition. However, this also created an atmosphere of widespread mistrust and fear. It seemed as if everybody was watching or being watched – even among friends and relatives people hesitated to say frankly what they thought. Dissidents were *tried* in **show trials**; thousands were spied on and prosecuted because of their political beliefs.

Even watching Western TV programs could be sanctioned. In the 1950s and 60s groups of Free German Youth members looked for *TV aerials* turned in the wrong direction and sometimes destroyed them. If offenders were lucky, they only had to answer embarrassing questions from the "party executive" of their **work collective**.

While the changes in the West were also recognized in the GDR, no such movement like in the West became visible. Some young people tried to imitate Western changes, as they could not lead their lives in a free and self-determined way. They were soon detected by the police and were cut off from the development in the West.

M 1 Coat of Arms of the State Security Service of the GDR

Vocabulary

to try: (here) to bring a case to a court of law; to find guilt or innocence in a court of law

TV aerials: antenna on a rooftop for getting TV signals

Historical Terms

show trials: Schauprozesse
Work collective: Kollektiv (ein DDR-spezifischer Begriff, der eine organisierte Gruppe beschreibt)

M 2 Prison Cell in the Youth Prison in Torgau
Photograph, 1990

M 3 The Role of Western Media: Letters to the BBC (British Broadcasting Corporation)

a) The German language service of the BBC aimed at informing East Germans. One programme was "Briefe ohne Unterschrift" in which letters from the GDR to the BBC were read out and commented on. Most were very critical of the GDR. But also positive ones reached London. The following letter from "Bücherfreund" reached the BBC on 5 October 1963:

"Allow me to say a few words about your programs. You receive letters from the GDR (I do not write SBZ, because our state exists, whether you recognize it or not, and without negotiation with the government of this state there will be no reunification Germany, which you are not interested in). In these letters, it says that people live in distress, hunger, worry and what-not. That is all a lie – like the Bible. Those who work with us live decently. Those who complain and moan about the GDR today would be anarchists even in capitalism or would be convinced communists. I do not agree with everything that is done here. But I do not complain, I criticize, I show ways to improve. Socialism is the fulfillment of the wishes and dreams of humanity, socialism is prosperity, happiness, satisfaction, security. Your tactics are the quiet lie on a grand scale, they want to make people stupid. If you were always telling the truth, I would certainly accept you."

Quoted from: Susanne Schädlich, Briefe ohne Unterschrift, München: Knaus 2017, pp. 94ff. (transl. by Matthias Bode).

b) The following weeks, many letters from the GDR reached the BBC that referred to this letter (see left). Among them, from 20 October 1963, was the following:

"I'm probably one of the listeners who have listened to London Radio the longest. When we were still living on the coast of the Baltic Sea, we were looking forward to [the spokesman for the BBC] every evening, because we recognized him as a friend of the Germans rather than an English enemy. We had to be so careful listening to the BBC, because we were surrounded by spies, as it is today. Unfortunately I can not listen to BBC on a regular basis, […] but I heard by chance the letter from Bücherfreund you read out last Friday. I am appalled that such idiots turn to you. This poor *lunatic* wants to communicate his *atheistic* dogmas he had been told as a way of life to others. You see, that's the sort of people you're dealing with here and now. They adore everything Khrushchev says, they glorify the insane theories of an Ulbricht. This type believes such nonsense. […]"

Quoted from: Susanne Schädlich, Briefe ohne Unterschrift, München: Knaus 2017, pp. 94ff. (transl. by Matthias Bode).

Vocabulary

lunatic: a crazy person
atheistic: not believing in god; unreligious, godless

Tasks

1. **The Power of the State**
   a) Explain why building the wall can be seen as a second chance for the SED government (text).
   b) List the methods the Stasi used (text).
   c) Analyse the way the government of the GDR treated its people (text).

2. **The Role of Western Media**
   a) Summarize the points made in the two letters (M3).
   b) Analyse how different perspectives affect the way history is told (M3).
   c) Assess what western listeners would understand about the situation in the GDR (M3).

Info

Reform laws enacted or started during Brandt's term in office
- Age of majority lowered to 18
- Liberalization of sexual laws
- Equality of husband and wife in marriage
- More rights for children of unmarried parents
- Introduction of student grants (Bafög)
- Reform of upper secondary school

A New Government, a New Ostpolitik

The victory of the SPD and FDP in the 1969 general elections led to a Social Democratic Chancellor for the first time in West German history. It was the first SPD chancellor after more than 40 years, and Willy Brandt (SPD) had promised a new start in West German politics.

Willy Brandt and his Foreign Minister Walter Scheel (FDP) led the Social-Liberal Coalition to reforms in many fields of domestic politics. They expanded the provisions of the welfare system, reformed criminal law, moved toward greater gender equality and made grants available for poorer students to study. The common theme of these reforms was a new fairness, a new openness, as it had been promised during Brandt's election campaign.

A New "Ostpolitik"

However, the most important achievement of the coalition was the new course in foreign policy with Eastern Europe. Egon Bahr, Brandt's closest foreign policy advisor, had called it **"change through rapprochement"**. Brandt declared in his policy statement on taking office that the new government was willing to move beyond earlier offers not to use force. He would accept existing borders in Europe, including the existence of the GDR as a state. This was new: Based on the Hallstein Doctrine, earlier CDU governments had tried to ignore as much as they could that the GDR even existed. There had been no official meeting between East and West German government representatives for 20 years. Brandt and the East German Chairman of the Council of State, Willy Stoph, agreed to meet in person. To avoid meeting in Berlin and Bonn, the negotiations took place in Erfurt and Kassel in 1970. But it was Egon Bahr who finally achieved a breakthrough with the Soviet Union. The Treaty of Moscow was signed in August 1970 and became the centrepiece of a system of treaties with Eastern European states and East Germany. All of them were linked by the same idea: The promise of peaceful negotiations with existing governments to make it easier for people, ideas and business to cross borders between east and west. During Brandt's visit to Warsaw he fell to his knees in front of the memorial for the victims of the Warsaw ghetto. This gesture became famous, but the GDR government did not allow the picture to be printed in East Germany. In the West, it helped to secure West Germany's international reputation for dealing with the past. In 1971 Brandt was awarded the Nobel Peace Prize for his Ostpolitik and in 1973, both the GDR and the FRG finally joined the United Nations.

Selling out German Interests?

From the beginning, the CDU/CSU and conservative pressure groups opposed the negotiations with the Eastern states fiercely and launched a heated debate over what they called Brandt's "sellout of German interests". Their point was that both, the FRG and the GDR, were seen as provisional states and that the Potsdam Agreement in 1945 had said that the final German borders would be set in a future peace treaty. Especially sensitive was the "refugee community", groups of people who had been forced to leave the former eastern provinces. Brandt's policy was seen as giving away their homeland a second time. The government's argument was that in order to reach something at all, the current deadlock had to be overcome. The debate in Germany was fierce.

Some FDP politicians left the party and joined the CDU. Brandt's Bundestag

Historical Terms

change through rapprochement:
Wandel durch Annäherung

M 1 "One Day We Will Have to Tell Them…"

In the back, with the poster: "Accepting the Oder-Neisse-Border is selling out Germany" are Franz-Joseph Strauß (CSU), Rainer Barzel (CDU) and Kurt Georg Kiesinger (CDU).

In the front Walter Scheel (FDP) and Willy Brandt (SPD) talking to each other: "One day we will have to tell them, very calmly: Germany lost the war in 1945."

Cartoon by Horst Haitzinger, West Germany 1970

Info

A new "Ostpolitik"

1970: Treaty with USSR in Moscow

1970: Treaty with Poland in Warsaw

1971: Four-Power-Agreement on the status of Berlin

1971: Transit Agreement with GDR

1972: Basic Treaty with GDR

1973: Treaty with CSSR in Prague

Historical Terms

constructive vote of no confindence: Konstruktives Misstrauensvotum

Vocabulary

referendum: an occasion when everyone in a country can vote on an important issue

majority was thin, and the CDU saw their chance: A **constructive vote of no confidence** in April 1972 aimed at replacing Brandt with CDU leader Rainer Barzel as Chancellor, but failed narrowly. After Brandt won, the Bundestag ratified the treaties on 17 May 1972.

In November, Brandt risked a general election, which actually became a *referendum* on the Ostpolitik. The Social-Liberal Coalition won the election, proving that West Germans supported the changes. The SPD was for the first time the largest party in West German politics, and many people associated it with progress and peace.

Although Brandt succeeded internationally, he faced serious domestic difficulties. Rising inflation, the oil crisis of 1973 and trade union demands for wage increases caused problems. Two opposing wings of his party disagreed on the course of the SPD, and Brandt became isolated. He resigned when his personal assistant was exposed as an East German agent.

A New Government, a New Ostpolitik

M 2 Ostpolitik – the hidden agenda

In a research project, German historian Oliver Bange worked on the beginnings of the "new Ostpolitik". In a presentation, he presented the two sides of the strategy (2003):

"One might compare the 'New Ostpolitik' of Willy Brandt and Egon Bahr with a coin: the currency, or ultimate goal, imprinted on it is called 'unification' (for obvious reasons Brandt refused to speak about 're-unification', preferring 'unification' or 'Zusammenwachsen' – growing closer). The coin itself represents the two long-term strategies to achieve it.

Undermining Communism by exposing the people under its rule to Western values was one side of the coin. However, the eventual break-down of the Communism itself would not suffice to guarantee for German unification.

The other side of the coin was therefore to devise an all-European Security System, taking care of the legitimate security concerns of all nations concerned by a prospective unification of the two German states.

This, and only this it was argued at the time, could possibly ease the way to unification after an eventual collapse of the regimes in Eastern Europe. Of course, with a secret agenda like this, Brandt and Bahr had to play their cards very close to their chests. This is the reason why the best evidence for this double sided-strategy is not so much found in the German archives (for obvious domestic and party political reasons) but in the archives of the Western allies, particularly in Washington and Paris, where this strategy had to be 'sold' and defended, and those in Eastern Europe, where the success of the strategy – once it was recognised – became a reason for great concern."

Dr. Oliver Bange, Mannheim University (Project "Ostpolitik and Detente"), open paper delivered at the London School of Economics, February 26th, 2003. http://www.ostpolitik.net/ostpolitik/publications/download/article3.pdf [August 21, 2018].

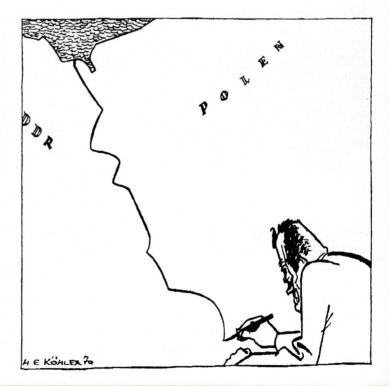

M 3 "Signature of the Year"
Cartoon by Hanns Erich Köhler, West Germany, 1970

Tasks

1. **The Hidden Agenda**
   a) Explain the two sides of the coin as the author sees them (M2).
   b) The author says that this strategy had to kept hidden: Explain why.

Willy Brandt in Warsaw

M 4 "A Good Idea"?

In December 1970, the German news magazine "Der Spiegel" asked: "Should Brandt have knelt down?" The magazine presented the following answers to a representative poll in West Germany.

Have you seen a photo of Brandt kneeling in Warsaw?	84%
Do you think this was appropriate?	41%
Do you think this was overdone?	48%
No answer	11%

Der Spiegel 51/1970 (14.12.1970), Umfrage: Durfte Brandt knien?

M 5 Chancellor Brandt in Warsaw

During his visit in Warsaw Willy Brandt laid a wreath at the memorial for the victims of the Warsaw Ghetto uprising.
Photographs, 7 December 1970.

Tasks

1. **The German Question**
   a) Explain to an English speaker the German position concerning the Potsdam Agreement.
   b) Show the change in West German policy towards the East at the end of the 1960s (text).

2. **A New Policy**
   a) Explain why East Berlin and Bonn were not seen as appropriate meeting places in 1970.
   b) Analyse and compare the two cartoons (M1 and M3). Decide which aspects the artists wanted to stress.

3. **Willy Brandt in Warsaw**
   a) Willy Brandt was followed by cameramen from many TV stations and newspapers. Therefore, there are different photos from different angles. Assess the different perspectives.
   b) Photos of this gesture were not published in the GDR. Explain why.
   c) Comment on the results of the Spiegel poll.

Historical Terms

Conference on Security and Cooperation in Europe (CSCE): Konferenz über Sicherheit und Zusammenarbeit in Europa (KSZE)

developing countries: Entwicklungsländer

Yom Kippur War: Jom-Kippur-Krieg (1973)

M 1 **Chancellor Helmut Schmidt and Chairman Erich Honecker at the CSCE in Helsinki, 1 August 1975**
Photograph

Vocabulary

vulnerability: sth. that can be wounded or hurt

famine: little or no food for a long time

The Limits of Growth

After Willy Brandt was forced to resign, Helmut Schmidt, also from the SPD, replaced him as Chancellor. He led the West German government through difficult times. Not only West Germany, but also other Western states faced multiple challenges.

Co-Existence

In 1973 both German states joined the United Nations, which showed that the whole world acknowledged and confirmed the new political situation in Germany. Two years later they took part in the **Conference on Security and Cooperation in Europe** in Helsinki as delegations on an equal level. The following year the GDR eliminated every reference to reunification from its constitution. East German leaders pursued a policy of separation and emphasized that the GDR was a permanent and an independent state. Most countries established diplomatic relations with the GDR. No longer claiming to be the sole representative of Germany, West Germany also benefited from co-existence by intensifying political and economic links to Eastern Europe. Within the difficult field of inner-German politics, things looked promising. The superpowers also seemed to find more opportunities for agreement.

The Limits of Growth

Other international factors, however, were less favourable. The international monetary system fell into a crisis in 1971: Paying for the Vietnam War had increased the US debt and so the USA had to change the rules of international finance. Global inflation was the consequence. This led to increasing debts in **developing countries**, where development had already slowed after a decade of independence.

In 1972, the "Club of Rome" published the report "The Limits of Growth". It raised public awareness of the limits of industrial development and natural resources as well as the threat of over-population. It cast doubt on the industrialization-based path of development. As if to illustrate the *vulnerability* of industrialized states, in 1973 Arab Middle East countries reduced the amount of oil produced and sold to the West. They wanted to put pressure on the West for supporting Israel in the **Yom Kippur War** of 1973. The dramatic rise in the price of oil made the recession in the West even worse. In addition, a *famine* in the Sahel Zone in 1974 and bad harvests in South Asia marked a worldwide food crisis. It became clear that the fruits of technological progress do not benefit all people in

M 2 **Car-free Sunday**
Cyclists on the Kurfürstendamm in West Berlin.
Photograph, 25 November 1973

a fair way. It seemed impossible to achieve a balanced development of the international community.

There were obvious and short-term consequences in West Germany. On four consecutive Sundays in 1973 it was forbidden to use cars privately because there was not enough fuel. This was the beginning of a serious economic downturn. Chancellor Helmut Schmidt faced growing national debt, a high inflation rate and rising unemployment.

The Green Movement

In the long term, the oil price crisis of 1973 also started an environmentalist green movement that changed the political scene of the FRG. The diverse groups that had formed after 1968 found a common ground in criticizing the environmental consequences of modern industrial society. The appeal of this movement broadened after the Three Mile Island accident in 1979, when a nuclear power plant in Harrisburg (USA) had a serious accident and the dangers of nuclear technology became apparent. Together with the older peace movement, these **grass-roots movements** eventually *merged* between 1976 and 1980 into the West German Green Party.

Terrorism

The biggest challenge for West German society came in autumn 1977 when the RAF, a group of terrorists, attacked various leading representatives of the West German economic and political system. Chancellor Schmidt made it absolutely clear that the state should not give in to terrorist demands. Security became a major issue because some people thought that the anti-terrorist measures went too far in restricting civil rights.

The "German Autumn"

On 5 September 1977, RAF terrorists kidnapped Hanns Martin Schleyer, the president of the **Confederation of the German Employers' Associations**. Three policemen and his driver were killed in the kidnapping in Cologne.

The terrorists demanded that the government release other terrorists from prison. Chancellor Schmidt publicly stated that he would not negotiate with terrorists. When Palestinian terrorists hijacked a German airplane and flew it to Somalia, the German government sent specially trained policemen to rescue the passengers. All the hijackers were shot. Upon hearing this, the terrorists in prison committed suicide and Schleyer was found dead in a car on 19 October 1977.

Historical Terms

grass-roots movements: Bürgerbewegung, politische Bewegung "von unten"

Confederation of the German Employers' Associations: Bundesvereinigung der Deutschen Arbeitgeberverbände (BDA)

M 3 **Election Poster of the Green Party**
Federal Election 1983

Vocabulary

to merge: to combine

M 4 **Scene of the Kidnapping of Hanns Martin Schleyer**
Photograph, 5 September 1977

The Origin of the Green Movement

M 5   The Limits to Growth

In their 1972 book "The Limits to Growth", Dennis Meadows and his colleagues published a forecast of what the world would look like at the beginning of the 21st century. Especially the following illustration became famous:

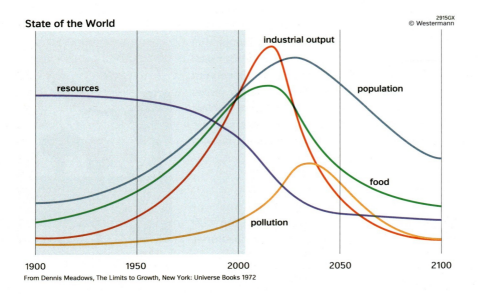

From Dennis Meadows, The Limits to Growth, New York: Universe Books 1972

M 6   "Silent Spring?"

In her book "Silent Spring" (1962), Rachel Carson wrote about the effect humans had on nature, especially about the use of pesticides. It was translated in many languages throughout the 1960s:

"Only within the moment of time represented by the present century has one species – man – acquired significant power to alter the nature of his world. During the past quarter century this power has not only increased to one of disturbing magnitude but it has changed in character. The most alarming of all man's assaults upon the environment is the contamination of air, earth, rivers, and sea with dangerous and even lethal materials. [...] In this now universal contamination of the environment, chemicals are the *sinister* and little-recognized partners of *radiation* in changing the very nature of the world – the very nature of its life. [...] chemicals sprayed on croplands or forests or gardens lie long in soil, entering into living organisms, passing from one to another in a chain of poisoning and death. Or they pass mysteriously by underground streams until they emerge and, through the alchemy of air and sunlight, combine into new forms that kill vegetation, sicken cattle, and work unknown harm on those who drink from once pure wells. As Albert Schweitzer has said, 'Man can hardly even recognize the devils of his own creation'. [...]

In each of these situations, one turns away to *ponder* the question: Who has made the decision that sets in motion these chains of poisonings, this ever-widening wave of death that spreads out, like ripples when a pebble is dropped into a still pond? [...] Who has decided – who has the right to decide – for the countless legions of people who were not consulted that the supreme value is a world without insects, even though it be also a sterile world ungraced by the curving wing of a bird in flight? The decision is that of the *authoritarian* temporarily entrusted with power; he has made it during a moment of inattention by millions to whom beauty and the ordered world of nature still have a meaning that is deep and imperative."

Rachel Carson, Silent Spring, Boston: Boston: Houghton Mifflin 1962, p. 5 and 105.

The Challenge of Terrorism

M 7 Prisoner of the RAF
Kidnapped Hanns Martin Schleyer, the president of the Confederation of the German Employers' Associations. Photograph, 1977

M 8 A Statement

On 20 October 1977, Chancellor Helmut Schmidt tried to explain his decisions:

"We have not *surrendered* the eleven prisoners who were convicted of murder or who are strongly suspected of *assassination* [...]. They are charged with the killing of 13 people and another 43 assassination attempts. Killing 13 people and 43 more murder attempts! Three of the prisoners committed suicide yesterday. We had to fear and do still fear that the 11 captured terrorists would commit further serious crimes after their release, just as those who were freed by the kidnapping of Peter Lorenz[1] after they were released. The latter are now being charged with the killing of nine people and four more attempted murders. In other words, the release of the eleven would, according to this experience, have created a new danger to the lives of many others."

[1] Peter Lorenz (CDU) was a politician in Berlin. Two days before an election in 1975, terrorists kidnapped him. He was released when the government released five terrorists from prison. Some of them continued to commit terrorist acts after the release.

Deutscher Bundestag, Plenarprotokoll 8/50, Stenographischer Bericht 50. Sitzung. Bonn, Donnerstag, den 20. Oktober 1977, pp. 3756f. (transl. by Matthias Bode). http://dipbt.bundestag.de/doc/btp/08/08050.pdf [August 21, 2018].

Vocabulary

sinister: nasty, evil
radiation: radioactivity
to ponder: to think and reflect
authoritarian: a ruler, a dictator

Vocabulary

to surrender: (here) to give sth. up
assassination: murder, especially killing a political person

Tasks

1. **The Origin of the Green Movement**
   a) Analyse the chart (M5).
   b) The chart M5 provoked discussion in 1972. Does it do so today? Why/why not?
   c) Summarize Rachel Carson's line of argument (M6).
   d) Explain why "Silent Spring" (M6) has been called the starting point of the modern environmental movement. Explain this idea.
   e) A big issue for her was "DDT". Research the story of this pesticide.
   f) Show how Carson mixes environmental and political ideas in her book.
   g) Some critics at the time said that the book was exaggerated in the short term, but not exaggerated enough in the long term. Discuss her book from today's perspective.

2. **The Challenge of Terrorism**
   a) Research the events of 1977. Write a detailed timeline (text, Internet).
   b) Describe the photo the terrorists sent to newspapers (M7).
   c) Discuss why they sent this photo.
   d) Outline Helmut Schmidt's reasoning (M8).
   e) Discuss Helmut Schmidt's principle of not negotiating with terrorists.

Vocabulary

sophisticated: refined, cultured

collaborator: person who works with sb. else (sometimes meant negatively)

collectively: together, in a group

A Dictatorship to Live with?

In 1961, it became apparent that the East German state had to build walls and fences to stop people from leaving. In direct competition with West Germany, the GDR looked less dynamic, less open, less friendly, less free and less successful. There were no free elections, no free media and no freedom of travel for its citizens. It looked like a dictatorship. On the other hand, even while they were watching Western television and listening to Western radio, the vast majority of East Germans did not leave and did not protest. One way to explain it is to call the GDR a dictatorship to live with.

The Honecker Era

Since 1971, the new head of state Erich Honecker emphasized the leading role of the Soviet Union in politics and economy. He stopped nearly all reform projects of the Ulbricht era. His policies began well. The Basic Treaty was signed. It led to membership in the UN and many countries opened embassies in East Berlin. Following the Basic Treaty the number of visitors from the West grew constantly. This was welcome on the one hand, because the visitors brought Western money with them, but it also proved a threat to the system: People could see directly what the West was like. Egon Bahr's idea of "change through rapprochement" seemed to work. Even raising the amount of money Western visitors had to exchange for East German currency did not stop them from coming.

M 1 Erich Honecker (1912–1994)
Photograph, 1975

Living and Working in the GDR

"Work, learn and live in the socialist way" was the slogan according to which East Germans were to organize their lives. Everybody had to have a job. Those who did not were regarded as anti-social and could be punished. Ninety per cent of the women were working. The state-organized educational system cared for children throughout the day, so no mother had to stay home to do so. Equality of men and women was considered a socialist achievement. But the "improvements" for women often led to overwork as they had to organize family affairs while working a full-time job.

People's spare time was organized collectively. Neighbours from the same house or district cleaned their environment together voluntarily, went to the theatre or organized parties. Everything was set out in the collective schedule. But what seemed to be community living also provided a network of political surveillance.

Under Honecker the system of surveillance became more and more *sophisticated*. Apart from the official members of the Stasi, thousands of unofficial *collaborators* provided information. Moreover, the quality of the observation equipment was very high.

M 2 Woman Working in Production
A woman working in a factory, producing bathing suits.
Photograph 1966

Economy

One of the many peculiar aspects of the GDR economy was that the country was indeed able to produce goods that were sold in the West. Quite a few West German companies used GDR production facilities, sometimes even in prisons. Textiles, washing machines, furniture, even food: production in the GDR was much cheaper. But these goods were sold solely in the West. The population in East Germany were not able to buy these goods. Only for those privileged enough to have access to West

German currency, the "D-Mark", it was possible to buy Western products in so-called "Intershops". This system created a two-class society of those who somehow had access to Western money and the vast majority of those who did not.

Opposition

Churches were important places for people to speak out freely. In many church congregations "peace libraries" or "environmental libraries" gave **dissidents** a chance *to reveal* their inner lives and thinking. Most of the churches had close relations to churches in the West, which apart from their spiritual support also funded a lot of the work of their Eastern partners. Not surprisingly, many of the churches were observed permanently by the Stasi.

Artists of all kinds were especially discontented with the party-controlled state. Those who agreed were rewarded with advantages, sometimes even travelling occasionally to Western European states. But those who refused to go along or criticized party decisions often left the country, either because they were forced out or because they chose more rewarding work in the West. The actors, writers, painters and musicians who stayed behind had to cope with limitations on their artistic freedom.

Many East Germans were unwilling to support Communist ideas, were unhappy with the constant *harassment* by officials, with the inefficiency of the economy and with the lack of opportunities. They were faced with the question of how to deal with the demands of the state. One option was *to pay lip-service*: to do in public what was demanded, but to think differently in private. This caused a widespread "doublethink": Sometimes schoolchildren were torn between what their teachers told them and what their parents wanted them to think. As a result, many people in the GDR withdrew from public life to cozy, private niches, such as to little cottages in the countryside that they had managed to build.

The existence of two German states was an important factor for any form of opposition: Life in the FRG was always present as an example. Furthermore, the possibility to leave the GDR meant that the opposition of those who stayed was always weakened by those who left.

Vocabulary
to reveal: to show or inform
harassment: mistreatment
to pay lip-service: to say sth. without really meaning it

Historical Terms
dissidents: Dissidenten, Oppositionelle

M 3 "In the Country Cottage"
Photograph, East Germany, 1980s

A Dictatorship to Live with?

M 4 The Stasi

*Timothy Garton Ash (*1955) is a British historian and Professor of European Studies at Oxford University. While writing a book about Berlin and the Nazis, he worked in both West and East Berlin. There he was under surveillance from the Stasi. They suspected him to be a British spy. In his 1997 book "The File" he describes the file the Stasi kept on him:*

"My opening report dates from March 1981. Prepared by one Lieutenant Wendt, it gives my personal details, notes that I have been studying in West Berlin since 1978, and lived from January to June 1980 – actually it was October – in the
5 'capital of the GDR'. I travel frequently from West Berlin to East Berlin and Poland. I have repeatedly 'made contact with operationally interesting persons'. Consequently there are 'grounds for suspecting that G. [for Garton Ash, otherwise 'the object' or 'Romeo'] has *deliberately* exploited
10 his official functions as research student and/or journalist to pursue *intelligence activities*'. [...]
Raw material follows later in the file: observation reports, summaries of intelligence from the files on my friend Werner Krätschell, a Protestant priest, and on the British
15 Embassy; photocopies of articles about Poland that I wrote for the West German news magazine Der Spiegel; copies of my own Polish notes and papers, photographed during a secret search of my luggage at Schönefeld airport, from where I was flying to Warsaw; even copies of the references
20 written by my Oxford tutors for the British Council. In all, there are 325 pages.
Wendt's report pays special attention to information supplied by the Stasi's own informers, known as Inoffizielle Mitarbeiter – literally 'unofficial collaborators' – or IM for
25 short. They were sub-divided into several categories: security, spezial, operative, conspirative, even the informer for running the informers. Since 1989, the initials have entered the German language. SS is the synonym in every European language for the loud, violent, outright bestiality of Nazism. IM has become, in German, the synonym for
30 the routine, bureaucratic forms of *infiltration*, *intimidation* and collaboration which characterized the German communist dictatorship; the quieter corruption of mature totalitarianism. In the early 1990s it was a regular occurence for a prominent East German politician, academic, journalist
35 or priest to be identified through the Stasi files as an IM and to disappear from public life as a result. IM is the black spot."

Timothy Garton Ash, The File, London: Harper Collins 1997, pp. 11f.

Vocabulary

deliberately: intentionally, on purpose
intelligence activities: finding out information about an enemy or potential enemy; spying
infiltration: secretly becoming part of a group to get information or to influence the way the group thinks or acts
intimidation: the act of bullying, frightening

M 5 Timothy Garton Ash
Photograph, 2016

Tasks

1. **The Stasi**
   a) Analyse the way the government treated its people (text, M4).
   b) Discuss what the methods of the Stasi meant for everyday lives of ordinary people.
   c) The author decribes the GDR as "mature totalitarianism". Comment on this choice of words.
   d) In the case of Timothy Garton Ash, the security officers produced 325 pages of material just about a history student in his late 20s writing a book about Berlin's Nazi past. Assess the efficiency of these security officers.

M 6 Pupil in Pioneer Uniform Giving his Teacher the Pioneer Salute
Photograph, 1987

M 7 School life

The educational system became more ideological and influenced young people from a very early age.

"We were eight and fourteen years old. We knew what was allowed and what was forbidden. What children had to do and what they had not to do. But television was a paradox. It was the permitted forbidden, open and clearly defined by the parents. Doing the forbidden thing was fine in this case, as long as we did our part and did not talk about it. We were quiet about the family show 'Einer wird gewinnen'[1] with Hans-Joachim Kulenkampff, who made our Saturday night so enjoyable. We were quiet about 'Raumpatrouille Orion'[2] and of course about football – the Bundesliga and the international matches. And about the news. At seven or at eight o'clock. There was a trick question, which many students of the GDR had to pass. It was: 'Did the clock have points or dashes at the beginning of the news?' Anyone who prematurely called 'dashes' into the classroom had made a serious mistake. The 'Tagesschau' of the ARD had lines, whereas the GDR news of the 'Aktuelle Kamera' started with a clock that represented the minutes in dots. Never once did I let anyone in the school know that we were watching Western TV at home. I was proud of that."

1 "Einer wird gewinnen" with Hans-Joachim Kulenkampff: popular ARD Saturday evening show, 1964–1987
2 "Raumpatrouille Orion": popular West German science fiction series with seven episodes, 1966

Roland Jahn, Wir Angepassten. Überleben in der DDR, München: Piper 2014, pp. 52 (transl. by Matthias Bode).

Tasks

1. School life
   a) Describe the photo (M6).
   b) Compare your school rituals with the one shown in this picture.
   c) Analyse the memories of Roland Jahn (M7). Discuss the "permitted forbidden" and the position of the children and the parents regarding West German TV.
   d) Discuss how people can live with a dictatorship.

The Two Germanies within Europe

A New Cold War – and a new détente

International and inner-German politics of the 1970s had looked promising: An international détente seemed to promise an end to the Cold War. That changed in the early 1980s.

A New Cold War

Towards the end of the 1970s the Soviet Union stepped up its rearmament programme. New weapons were set up. The USA responded with a nuclear missile programme in Europe to stop the Soviets from stationing missiles threatening the Western sphere of influence.

The Soviet invasion of Afghanistan in 1979 revived the Cold War. As a reaction, many Western states boycotted the 1980 Moscow Olympics. In addition, the US government started to finance Afghan resistance against the Soviet occupation army. In the end, the Afghanistan war lasted 10 years. Many thousands of people died and millions had to leave Afghanistan.

At the same time, the two German states were burdened with the stationing of missiles, because they had to act according to the decisions of their blocs. On the other hand, the challenge was to maintain the achievements of the early 1970s.

M 1 "The Chancellor Creates Trust"
Election poster, Federal Election 1983

Rearmament

During these tensions on the international level, the West German government coalition of FDP and SPD fell apart: The FDP joined the CDU and agreed on a new Chancellor: Helmut Kohl (CDU). He immediately faced serious opposition from those who opposed the new American missiles, the Pershing II rockets and new **cruise missiles**. Both could be equipped with nuclear weapons and both were targeted at East Germany, where Soviet nuclear missiles were stationed.

The Western governments had offered not to install all these new weapons on the condition that the Soviet Union would eliminate their **middle range nuclear weapons**. Talks about this topic did not reach any conclusions, so more than 500 missile systems were stationed in Europe.

Protests Against Rearmament

Protests against these new weapons spread through West Germany. In October 1981, about 300,000 people demonstrated in Bonn against rearmament, and in June 1982, the largest demonstration in German history of about 500,000 people assembled again in Bonn. At least 300,000 people formed a human chain in October 1983, from the US Army headquarters in Stuttgart to Neu-Ulm, where Pershing II missiles were stationed. In Mutlangen, demonstrators organized a sit-in in front of the barracks gates. The police carried them away, but the peaceful demonstrators were charged with the use of force and thousands were found guilty. This caused an uproar in Germany. People from all walks of life found themselves together: especially young people, the old and new Left, the SPD, the trade unions, the Protestant church. This movement was the beginning of the success of the Green Party. In the end, however, the large protests failed and the missiles were stationed.

M 2 Peace Demonstrations in Bonn
Photograph, 10 October 1981

Chernobyl

When in 1986 a nuclear power station in Chernobyl, Ukraine, exploded, it sent a large cloud of radioactive dust all over Europe. While soldiers were fighting for

M 3   Nuclear Power Plant Chernobyl
View of the destroyed reactor.
Photograph, September 1986

their lives against the nuclear fire near Kiev, reactions were mixed in Western Europe. The French government declared that the cloud had missed France, the East German government tried to avoid this topic. In West Germany, however, a discussion erupted that showed that fear of any sort of nuclear technology, military or civilian, had *gripped* society. The end of nuclear power became an important part of the party programmes for SPD and the Greens. Ironically, it was the CDU government of Helmut Kohl that, due to this public pressure, introduced a **Ministry of the Environment**.

Contradictory Politics

Ridiculed especially by the young and by the left, Helmut Kohl still had enormous power to shape policy, even with some contradictions. He had come into office to replace the SPD. But he did not change the SPD "Ostpolitik". Instead, the CDU government tried to consolidate the West German state in the Western alliance. So together with France, he went further towards European integration. It was his business-friendly government that took measures to reduce toxic gases from car motors and power plants. It was his conservative government that introduced private TV and cable TV in Germany.

Born 1930, Helmut Kohl was the first leading German politician without any involvement in the Second World War. During his term in office, West Germany tried to leave the past behind and *come to terms* with the status quo. A new parliament building was planned to replace the old one from 1949, and in 1987, for the first time, the leading politician of the GDR, Erich Honecker, visited Bonn. The government had dealt with rearmament and the anti-nuclear protests well. The general feeling was that of a stable state without any surprises.

Nobody expected that changes in the East would put German reunification back on the political agenda.

Historical Terms

cruise missile:
Marschflugkörper: guided missile which flies at low altitude and cannot be tracked by radar

middle range nuclear weapons:
Mittelstreckenwaffen: ballistic missiles with a range between 800 and 5,500 km

Ministry of the Environment:
Umweltministerium

Vocabulary

to grip: to grasp, to hold

to ridicule: to make fun of sth. or sb.; to mock or scorn sb.

to come to terms: to reach an agreement or make an arrangement

A New Cold War – and a new détente

M 4   Helmut Kohl on the Current Situation of the Nation, March 1984

Despite anti-Communist rhetoric and an emphasis on reunification, Helmut Kohl's conservative coalition government held to the policy of German cooperation, to further humanitarian concessions from the GDR through economic incentives:

"We stand behind the agreements we have signed. We hope to further *tighten* the network of relationships. [...] We hope to preserve and increase what we have achieved; we want to *utilize* the opportunities created by the Basic Treaty and other inter-German treaties and agreements. We are prepared to develop further our relations with the GDR on the basis of balance, fulfillment of treaties, and *predictability*, with the goal of *attaining* practical results of immediate value to the people. The FRG and the GDR form a community of responsibility for peace and security in Europe; both must make efforts to reduce international tension. [...]

By agreeing to more than a billion marks in *loans* from West German banks, the Federal Republic sent a clear signal to the GDR leadership last summer. At the same time, this decision was a message to the Germans in the GDR, which they interpreted correctly: We will protect our security and alliance interest but are of course prepared to cooperate in inter-German relations."

Quoted from: Joachim Nawrocki, Die Beziehungen zwischen den beiden Staaten in Deutschland, Berlin: Holzapfel 1986, pp. 64ff. Translation quoted from: Konrad H. Jarausch/Volker Gransow (eds.), Uniting Germany. Documents and Debates 1944–1993, New York/Oxford: Berghahn Books 1994, p. 24.

Vocabulary

incentive: help, motivation
to tighten: to make tighter, stronger
to utilize: to use
predictability: (here) reliability, the state of being reliable
to attain: to reach
loans: money lent for interest, for credit

M 5   Friendship Between France and Germany

On 22 September 1984, German Chancellor Helmut Kohl and French President François Mitterand visited Verdun, the site of a horrible battle in the First World War.

M 6 Sting: Russians (1985)

"In Europe and America, there's a growing feeling of hysteria
Conditioned to respond to all the threats
In the rhetorical speeches of the Soviets
Mr. Krushchev said we will bury you
I don't subscribe to this point of view
It would be such an ignorant thing to do
If the Russians love their children too

How can I save my little boy from Oppenheimer's deadly toy
There is no monopoly in common sense
On either side of the political fence
We share the same biology
Regardless of ideology
Believe me when I say to you
I hope the Russians love their children too

There is no historical precedent
To put the words in the mouth of the President
There's no such thing as a winnable war
It's a lie we don't believe anymore
Mr. Reagan says we will protect you
I don't subscribe to this point of view
Believe me when I say to you
I hope the Russians love their children too

We share the same biology
Regardless of ideology
What might save us, me, and you
Is if the Russians love their children too"

"Russians", from the Album "Sting: The Dream of the Blue Turtles" (1985)
©EMI Music Publishing Germany GmbH & Co. KG, Hamburg.

M 7 "Rattle! Rattle!"
Cartoon, USA, about 1985

Tasks

1. **Helmut Kohl on the Current Situation of the Nation**
   a) Point out elements of the SPD "Ostpolitik" in Kohl's speech (M5). Show how his interest in reunification is made clear. Explain his references to the political situation at the time.
2. **The Visit at Verdun**
   a) Put the visit in its historical context (M5).
   b) Explain the gesture of the two politicians.
   c) Compare to Willy Brandt's gesture in Warsaw (p. 155).
3. **Rearmament**
   a) Analyse the cartoon M7.
   b) Analyse the song "Russians" (1985) by Sting.
   c) Assess what it tells us about the time that this song became a Top Ten hit in various countries in 1985/86.
4. **1983 – a project**
   Looking back, the year 1983 was marked with many seemingly unrelated events. But on closer inspection, they all seemed to fit into a pattern of crisis. Ask parents and grandparents about their memories of that year. A project on the mood of 1983 might include the following topics:
   Movies: The Day After, Wargames
   Pop song: Nena – 99 Luftballons
   Book: Gudrun Pausewang – Die letzten Kinder von Schewenborn
   Incidents: US occupation of Grenada, the Able Archer Crisis, the Stanislav Petrov incident, the incident with Korean Airlines Flight 007

Vocabulary

appliance: equipment
lignite: a soft dark brown type of coal
to ignite: to go up in flames
dismantle: to take apart

M 1 Meeting of Strauß and Honecker
During a private trip of Strauß into the GDR, he discussed the loan of a billion German marks with the SED government. Photograph, 1983

The Crisis of the SED Government

During the 1980s, the GDR ran into trouble, at first gradually, in the end faster and faster. While other countries of the Warsaw Pact had financial and economic problems, too, the existence of two German states created a serious threat to the GDR.

Western Financial Aid

The more the global recession after the oil crisis of 1973 affected the Communist states, the less the GDR was able to continue improving the living conditions for the working population. As many raw materials, especially oil, became more expensive, the GDR had serious difficulties paying foreign debts. As early as 1983, the GDR was bankrupt. Surprisingly, it was the CDU government of Helmut Kohl that supported a credit of about a billion German marks that had been organized by the Bavarian Minister-President Strauß (CSU). While both the CDU and CSU opposed the SED government, there was an element of fear in Western governments that a collapse of the East German economy would create massive problems. In the end, this credit gave the GDR another six years.

Supply Problems

As the economic problems of the GDR became more noticeable, dissatisfaction grew. The longer people waited in queues to buy ordinary goods, the less they supported the government and the whole system. Unlike in the West German TV commercials they watched, people in the GDR constantly had to find ways to organize things that were in short supply. While basic food like potatoes and flour was cheap, imported fruit was hard to find and extremely expensive. Technical *appliances* and building materials were in short supply as well so that many older buildings fell into a state of disrepair. East German city centres looked grey and shabby; in some areas older houses looked like ruins. Cities smelled of burning *lignite*, the only cheap source of energy. The promises of the 50s and 60s, the idea of overtaking the West, were obviously not met.

Ecological Collapse and Opposition

The stubborn attempts of the government to increase industrial production caused pollution of rivers, and air quality became worse through the 80s. So in the mid-eighties, the issues of the green movement were expressed in the GDR as well. This was possible only within the framework of the churches, where environmental libraries gradually became the meeting places for dissidents. Because of the state pressure, this movement remained on a much smaller scale than in the West. But because it was publicized by West German TV correspondents, issues like the lignite mining in Saxony or the effects of uranium mining in the Erzgebirge became known in both states. Growing awareness of the catastrophic ecological situation gave the opposition even more motivation.

The Crisis of 1989

In the 1980s many people in the GDR tried to leave East Germany legally, others fled. Many who remained were encouraged by the reforms Mikhail Gorbachev made in the Soviet system. Only a spark was needed to *ignite* the continuing crisis into a revolution. In May 1989, regional elections were held in the GDR, resulting

M 2 Decaying Inner-city Houses
Photograph, Leipzig 1977

in the usual 98.7% consent to the official ballot. But this time the outcome was criticized openly. Opposition became visible.

Many frustrated people used the summer holiday season of 1989 to seek refuge in West German embassies in Prague, Budapest and Warsaw, hoping to be transferred into the FRG from there. When Hungary *dismantled* its border fences in summer 1989, thousands of East Germans fled from there to Austria. The holes in the Iron Curtain became bigger and the authority of the SED government crumbled.

This open flight of thousands of people created a new reaction within the GDR: Growing crowds demonstrated in the streets every Monday against the SED government, shouting "We are the people" ("Wir sind das Volk") and "We are staying" ("Wir bleiben hier"). The obvious alternative now was to leave the country or to change the country.

In October 1989, the GDR wanted to celebrate its 40th birthday. While the official festivities to celebrate the 40th anniversary of the founding of the GDR were as orderly as planned (6 Oct), the situation in Leipzig and many other cities got out of control. On 9 October, about 70,000 people demonstrated in Leipzig for changes in state and society. One week later, there were 120,000 people. The East German leaders were no longer able to control events in the streets, but to their credit, did not use force. And as news spread, people in other cities followed the example of Leipzig.

The Fall of the Berlin Wall

The Politburo tried to survive by removing Erich Honecker in October 1989 and replacing him with Egon Krenz, but it was too late. During a press conference on 9 November 1989, the press speaker of the Politburo said that it was now possible to leave East Germany at any time. Thousands reacted immediately and went to the Berlin Wall. Border guards had not been informed but decided to open the gates. Again, miraculously, there was no violence. The Berlin Wall had fallen – the crowds climbed onto it, celebrated and picked it apart to take pieces home as souvenirs. The most prominent symbol of the Cold War and of German division had disappeared that night. But what about the two states?

M 3 „Tank Man"
Photograph, Beijing, 1989

"Chinese solution": The Tiananmen Massacre 1989

In summer 1989 protests against the traditional rule of the Chinese Communist party erupted in Beijing. Thousands of people protested on Tienanmen Square in the heart of the city. The Chinese army cleared the city centre by force. There was bloodshed, but it is still unclear how many people died – maybe hundreds, maybe thousands. Since June 1989, this has become the "Chinese solution" to civilian protest.

M 4 The Fall of the Berlin Wall
People celebrating the opening of the border on 10 November 1989. Photograph, taken from the west.

The Crisis of the SED Government

M 5 **The Alexanderplatz Rally**

On 4 November, a large rally took place on Alexanderplatz in East Berlin. The square was packed with people, East German TV broadcast live. Author Christa Wolf spoke:

"My dear fellow citizens: Every revolutionary movement also liberates the language. Suddenly, that which has been so difficult to say up to now rolls freely from our lips. It amazes us to hear what we have apparently been thinking
5 all along, and what we can now shout out loud: Democracy now or never! And we mean people power. We can remember the attempts in our history which *faltered* or were beaten down, and we don't want, yet again, to sleep through the opportunity presented by this crisis which has awakened
10 all our productive strength (applause). […]
I would speak of revolutionary renewal (applause). Revolutions begin at the bottom. Top and bottom are reversed in the value system, turning the socialist society upside down, back onto its feet. Major social movements
15 are growing (applause); people in our country have never before spoken so much as in the last few weeks. Never before really spoken with each other, with such passion, such anger and sadness, but also with such hope."

Translation quoted from: Konrad H. Jarausch/Volker Gransow (eds.), Uniting Germany. Documents and Debates 1944–1993, New York/Oxford: Berghahn Books 1994, p. 70.

M 6 Alexanderplatz, 4 November

The biggest demonstration in the history of the GDR, probably as many as 500.000 people. Photograph, East Berlin, 1989

M 7 **The 40th Anniversary of the Founding of the GDR**

Reviewing stand with Erich Honecker and Mikhail Gorbachev, 7 October 1989

M 8 **Erich Honecker's anniversary speech**

Erich Honecker, the Head of State and of the Party, spoke at the 40th anniversary celebrations (7 October 1989):

"Today, the GDR is an outpost of peace and socialism in Europe. We will never forget this fact; this keeps us, and should also keep our enemies, from misjudgment.
Like the Soviet Union, which liberated us, and the People's Republic of China, which is also celebrating the 40th 5
anniversary of its founding, the People's Republic of Poland, the Czechoslovak Socialist Republic, and other socialist countries, the GDR will also cross the *threshold* into the year 2000 with the certainty that socialism is the future. Socialism is a young society, and yet it *exerts* a great 10

Vocabulary

to falter: to hesitate for too long

threshold: the floor at the entrance to a room or building

to exert: (here) to show, to have

influence on international developments. It has brought about significant social change and will continue to do so. Its existence gives hope, not only to our people, but to all of humankind. [...]

15 Just when the influential powers in the FRG sense the chance *to annul* the outcome of World War II and post-war developments through a *coup*, they have again had to realize that reality cannot be changed, that the GDR, on the western boundary of the socialist countries in Europe,
20 remains firm as a dam against neo-Nazism and chauvinism. The GDR's solid position in the Warsaw Pact cannot be shaken."

Translation quoted from: Konrad H. Jarausch/Volker Gransow (eds.), Uniting Germany. Documents and Debates 1944–1993, New York/Oxford: Berghahn Books 1994, p. 51.

M 9 Leipzig Militia on the Monday Demonstrations, 6 October 1989

The following "Letter to the Editor" appeared in the Leipziger Volkszeitung. It claims to be from workers, but in reality it was published by the "worker's militia"[1]:

"Workers of the District Demand:
Cease Tolerating Activities Hostile to the State
The members of the 'Hans Geiffert' Militia Unit *condemn* the actions which have been organized for some time by
5 unscrupulous elements in the city of Leipzig. We are in favor of Christian citizens gathering in the Nikolai Church to show their reverence in prayer. This is guaranteed by our constitution and the authority of our socialist GDR. However, we are opposed to having the church misused to
10 hold events hostile to the state of the GDR. We feel harassed when we are confronted with such things after a hard day's work. Thus, we expect that everything possible will be done to secure public order and safety, in order to protect the values and achievements of socialism in the GDR which
15 have been attained after forty years of hard work, so that

M 10 "We Demand Free Elections Without Fraud"
Photograph, Leipzig, October 1989

we can continue to work, determined and according to plan, for the well-being of all citizens. We are willing and able to protect effectively that which we have created through the work of our own hands, in order to stop these
20 counterrevolutionary actions once and for all.
If necessary, with weapons in hand!
We deny these elements the right to use the songs and slogans of the working class. In doing this, they are only trying to conceal their true goals."

1 "worker's militia" ("Kampfgruppen der Arbeiterklasse"): A reserve unit consisting of older men with military training and equipment, in the 1980s about 200,000 men.

Translation quoted from: Konrad H. Jarausch/Volker Gransow (eds.), Uniting Germany. Documents and Debates 1944–1993, New York/Oxford: Berghahn Books 1994, p. 56.

Vocabulary

to annul: to cancel, to end
coup: overthrow, regime change
to condemn: to find guilty

Tasks

1. **Two Speeches**
   a) Assess the role of media in the developments in 1989 (text, M5–M10).
   b) Contrast the mood of the two speeches by Wolf (M5) and Honecker (M8). Wolf uses the word "revolution". Do you think that is justified?
   c) Explain why many people were disappointed by Honecker's speech (M8).

2. **Letter to the Editor**
   a) Summarize the main points of this text (M9).
   b) Show the aim of this text.
   c) Assess the dangers this text represents.

German Unity – a question of speed?

After the fall of the Wall the new leaders of the GDR took part in round-table talks with all significant political groups. Practically every day, new ideas were presented, but also new truths emerged about how the state had been run by the ruling group. How could the demand for an answer to the German question be met that kept the peace in Europe?

An Ambitious Time Frame?

During the winter, Helmut Kohl and a close circle of advisors developed an ambitious schedule. They decided to try to achieve the maximum possible result – unification before the West German general election planned for December 1990. Equally important, they wanted continued membership of a unified Germany in the European Community and in NATO. Developments in the GDR, too, made it clear that time was pressing. On 18 May 1990, East Germany held its first free elections. During the election campaign the Eastern parties were supported by West German parties: It was obvious that apart from a small minority only the ex-SED stood up for an independent development in the GDR. With a participation of more than 90%, the CDU-led "Alliance for Germany" got 48% of the votes. The newly-formed East German SPD, which had been reluctant about unification, got only 22%, and the ex-SED, now called the "Party of Democratic Socialism" (PDS) gathered 16% of the votes. East Germans preferred a speedy unification.

M 1 Helmut Kohl in Leipzig, During the Election Campaign
Photograph, March 1990

Economic Troubles

The realities of the East German economy made this even clearer, as the number of people moving west did not decrease. More than 300,000 East Germans left between November 1989 and March 1990, creating bigger and bigger problems in the GDR. Quite early, the slogan "If the German mark does not come to us, we will go to it" appeared. East Germany was tumbling towards a social crash.

After the election, a grand coalition paved the way to unification with the decision to set up a monetary, economic and social union. It came into effect on 1 July 1990, when East Germany introduced the German mark. This was seen as a radical step and was widely critized by economists and the SPD-opposition. As a measure to convince people to stay at home, it was more or less successful. The outdated and ineffective GDR economy was too weak to survive this sudden contact with a Western economy and integration into the European market. It still is a matter of debate whether any other option could have worked: Would the people in the GDR have had the patience to wait even longer for access to the wonders of the market economy they had dreamed about for so long?

M 2 Demonstration for the Introduction of the German Mark in the GDR
Photograph, Leipzig, 1989

Joining? Or a New Start?

While it became clear during the winter and early spring of 1990 that some sort of unification was unavoidable, it was still a matter of debate how this unification should work. During the spring of 1990, two alternatives appeared:

One was a National Assembly, elected in a nationwide election, to establish a new state and a new constitution. The international questions could be dealt with in a big international conference. This idea had some supporters among the East German opposition, but the internal developments in the GDR created enormous time pressure.

So over a few months, this idea lost ground to another option: At the time Article 23 of the Basic Law said that "other parts of Germany" could simply join the existing FRG. This had a number of practical advantages. Not the least among them was that it provided an easy answer to the border question with Poland. The decision of the East German parliament to join the FRG on the basis of Article 23 of the Basic Law (23 August) was only the logical consequence of the monetary union. The Unification Treaty which set out details for the union (31 August) finalized the developments of that summer.

The International Framework

The time pressure generated by the collapse of East German economy and the proposals of Helmut Kohl seriously annoyed the other European countries, especially Britain and France. Unexpected Western criticism disturbed the picture of harmony the West German government was trying to create. Only the US government stood firmly behind Kohl. His argument was that a united Germany within the European Community and within NATO was the most stable option available. Not everybody agreed. Miraculously, the Soviet leader Mikhail Gorbachev supported Helmut Kohl. The existence of 300,000 Soviet soldiers in the GDR, armed with nuclear weapons, forced all politicians to cooperate for a peaceful solution. Mikhail Gorbachev decided in July 1990 that a peaceful and happy Germany was in the best interest of the Soviet Union. So he let the Germans deal with all the inner-German issues. He only insisted that foreign NATO troops should not be stationed on the territory of the ex-GDR.

Gorbachev received the Nobel Prize for Peace in 1990, but many politicians in the Soviet Union saw his policy as a defeat. After the Iraqi dictator Saddam Hussein ordered his army to invade Kuwait in summer 1990, the remaining negotiations were dealt with in enormous haste. All the major powers now had to manage a serious international crisis. Germany had been comparatively calm. In the end, it benefitted from this distraction and the **2+4 Treaty** was signed in Moscow on 12 September 1990, ending the post-war era and giving Germany full sovereignty. The new state agreed that it consisted of only the two German states and that the Polish border was guaranteed. Germany would reduce its army and would not build nuclear weapons. On 3 October 1990, these treaties came into effect and East Germany ceased to exist. Germans now celebrate 3 October, the Day of Unification, as their national holiday.

M 3 **Mikhail Gorbachev**
Photograph, 1991

Historical Terms

2+4 Treaty: Zwei-plus-Vier-Vertrag: Signatories were the FRG and GDR, as well as the former Four Powers – the USSR, the USA, Great Britain, and France.

M 4 **Day of Unification**
Photograph, Berlin, 3 October 1990

German Unity – a question of speed?

M 5 "Policy Failure"

Margaret Thatcher was British Prime Minister from 1979 to 1990. In her memoirs published in 1995, she looks back on 1990 and her attitude towards reunification:

"If there was one instance in which a foreign policy I pursued met with unambiguous failure, it was my policy on German reunification. This policy was to encourage democracy in East Germany while slowing down the country's reunification with West Germany. With the first half of that policy no one disagreed. Nor at the time did everyone disagree with the second, to which indeed lip service was paid. Most observers were unaware of the nationalist passion for German unity that burned in the East.

Indeed, even the dissident leaders of the East German demonstrations that led to freedom were themselves unaware of it, being in favour of a free, reformed, independent East Germany, rather than a larger Federal Republic. And Germany's neighbours all hoped to avoid this latter outcome because they saw it as destabilizing an already unsettled continent.

In the event, the desire for unity among Germans on both sides of the Elbe proved irresistible. So the policy failed.

But was the policy wrong? […] Look first at the consequences of the rapid reunification as they worked themselves out. West Germany's absorption of its next-door relation has been economically disastrous, and that disaster has spread to the rest of the European Community via the Bundesbank's high interest rates and the ERM ('Exchange Rate Mechanism'). We have all paid the price in unemployment and recession. East German political immaturity has affected the whole country in the form of a revived (though containable) neo-Nazi and xenophobic extremism. Internationally it has created a German state so large and dominant that it cannot be easily fitted into the new architecture of Europe."

Margaret Thatcher, The Downing Street Years, London: Harper Collins 1993, pp. 813f.

M 6 "Collapse"

The French newspaper "le Monde" wrote about the immediate consequences of the fall of the Berlin wall (11 November 1989):

"What now? Gone the emotion at the sight of gaping holes in the Berlin Wall and the Fort Knox-style border between the two Germanies, but the question remains. Where does this leave us? What next? The answers are not very clear, which no doubt accounts for the cautious Western reactions, starting with that of President Bush, confronted by high-speed history in the making, destination unknown. For all that the situation is confusing and disorienting there are a number of quite probable outcomes. The first is that the two Germanies will swiftly reunite their economies. The machinery is in place and will start moving very soon: since the GDR has promised its citizens freedom of movement and free elections, Chancellor Kohl will have no short-term alternative but to keep his promise of massive aid to the East German economy.

Unless West Germany wants to see hundreds of thousands, even millions of East Germans bursting onto its own labour market, with all of the political consequences that that would entail, it will have to do something to improve living standards in the East."

"Effondrement", in: Le Monde Nr. 13.931, 11 November 1989, S. 1.; transl. by Centre Virtuel de la Connaissance sur l'Europe (CVCE), at https://www.cvce.eu/content/publication/2002/4/11/e4d9b937-e6d2-446e-bb83-42cc945a0e87/publishable_en.pdf [August 22, 2018].

M 7 George Bush

Even before the fall of the Wall, US President George Bush talked about the chances for Germany in an interview with the New York Times (24 October 1989):

"**Question**: Let me give you two things that are being discussed within your Administration, among the Europeans, among professors. Can you see, presuming that you're here for eight years, any beginning of American troop withdrawal from Europe, or troop reduction?

George Bush: We've already seen that in our proposal […]. So my answer would be definitely yes.

Question: Can you see any changes in the status of Germany?

George Bush: Yes […] I don't share the concern that some European countries have about a reunified Germany, because I think Germany's commitment to and recognition of the importance of the alliance is unshakable. And I don't see Germany, in order to get reunification, going off onto what some are concerned about, and that is a neutralist path that puts them at odds, or potentially at odds, with their NATO partners […].

And yet, I don't think we ought to be out pushing the concept of unification, or setting timetables, or coming from across the Atlantic over here making a lot of new

pronouncements on this subject. It takes time. It takes a prudent evolution. It takes work between them [...] and understanding between the French and the Germans and the Brits and the Germans on all of this.
25 But the subject is so much more front and center because of the [...] rapid changes that are taking place in East Germany: [...]

And who knows how Mr. Krenz is going to turn out to be? Is he going to be just a perpetuation of the Honecker view, or is he going to be something different? I don't think he can 30 resist total change."

Quoted from: Konrad H. Jarausch/Volker Gransow (eds.), Uniting Germany. Documents and Debates 1944–1993, New York/Oxford: Berghahn Books 1994, p. 63.

M 8 **On the Way to Unity**
Cartoon by Walter Hanel, West Germany 1990.
The man skiing downhill is Helmut Kohl.

Tasks

1. **The International Reaction**
   a) Discuss the pros and cons of the GDR joining the FRG (text).
   b) Contrast the views of Margaret Thatcher (M5) and George Bush (M7).
   c) Use the texts and the cartoon on this page to outline the international reactions to German unity.
   d) From your position today, discuss whether the international reactions in 1990 were justified.

Historical Terms

Treuhandanstalt:
Treuhandanstalt

Stasi Records Act:
Stasi-Unterlagengesetz

Social Upheaval in United Germany

The quick unity with Article 23 seemed to promise that things would go smoothly, and life in the West could go on as before. But political unity did not solve all the problems. Rather, it became clear that the new state was facing entirely new challenges.

Changes in the Political System

Helmut Kohl had ruled out that the West Germans would have to pay higher taxes to finance unification. Instead, the campaign for the December election focused on his promise of "flourishing landscapes" in the East. The party spectrum of the new Germany changed. In addition to the old Western parties came the "Party of Democratic Socialism" (PDS), as the old SED had called itself. It was successful mainly in elections in the Eastern German states. The ruling CDU/CSU/FDP coalition won the first all-German election on 2 December 1990 and Helmut Kohl remained Chancellor. The Green party lost, as it had not focused on unification issues. The SPD lost as well for insisting that unification would be much more difficult and expensive than Kohl had promised. This was hard to tell the voters, but in the end it proved to be true.

M 1 Economic Dead End
The Trabant, the East German car, is no longer needed. Photograph, mid-1990s

Economic Problems in the East

The transformation of the GDR economy from a planned economy to a market economy proved particularly difficult. The production sites of the GDR were outdated, quite a few of the factories were in ruins and the infrastructure was in a miserable condition. In addition, there was considerable environmental damage. Thus, the East German economy could not withstand the Western competition, especially as its former markets in Eastern Europe broke away. Many people had believed the SED propaganda about its industrial success.

The state-owned **Treuhandanstalt**, founded in 1990, was supposed to rehabilitate and privatize GDR businesses. The result was the closure of many East German companies, as profitable production was usually not possible. At the same time, speculators took advantage of the situation to get rid of unpleasant competitors. Unemployment reached over 30 percent in some regions. Contrary to Kohl's promises, the restructuring of East Germany had to be financed by taxes. And it took much longer than anticipated.

Dealing With the Past

Coming to terms with the GDR past proved to be difficult. Who was "guilty", who was responsible for the way that the state had treated its people? Leading politicians of the GDR, but also border guards, had to face lawsuits in which they were held responsible for the use of firearms on the Berlin Wall and the inner-German border.

Already during the revolution, the civil rights movement in the GDR had demanded from the State Security Service ("Stasi") the complete opening of the archives. In 1991 the **Stasi Records Act** gave every citizen the Stasi had persecuted the opportunity to view his personal documents.

Bitter stories were told. The 1990s were a time when many thousands of East Germans found out who had spied on them – often friends and even family members. And many careers came to a sudden end when it emerged that people had been unofficial collaborators with the Stasi.

M 2 "Where is my File?"
In front of the former Stasi headquarters in Normannenstraße, Berlin, 19 February 1990

M 3 "German Unity"
Cartoon by Walter Hanel, 1990

Different Mentalities?

Many people in the East were disappointed with their economic and social situation. This led to the bitterness of former GDR citizens, who felt like "second-class citizens" in the new Germany. For many, the story of their lives was worthless now: Everything they had achieved was no longer needed. The success of the PDS in the new federal states can be traced back to several factors. On the one hand, it presented itself as the "East German Party" and on the other hand, it took advantage of the fact that some politicians did not take the new living conditions of the people and the resulting concerns seriously enough.

For some West Germans, the cost of reunification seemed too high and some even called into question the sense of unification. The different ways of life and experiences of the Germans in East and West sometimes made an understanding difficult. This was made worse by the fact that the people in the West had for too long thought that nothing would change.

But not only West Germany changed. In the following decade, the five new East German provinces achieved a higher standard of living. Many of the improvements took much longer than hoped for by the East Germans and much longer than promised by West German politicians. Poland, Hungary, Slovakia and the Czech Republic faced similar problems and they, too, slowly managed to improve the living conditions of the people. Infrastructure was rebuilt, environmental standards were installed, wages rose slowly. Even at the beginning of the 21st century, the economic differences between countries of the former Soviet bloc system and those in Western Europe are still visible.

Tasks

1. **The Stasi Files**
   a) Discuss the opening of the Stasi files. Was it a good idea? A necessary idea? Or should the old files have remained closed (text, M2, see page 161–162)?
2. **Flourishing Landscapes**
   a) Assess the differences between the eastern and the western part of Germany still visible today (text).
   b) Interpret the cartoon (M3).
   c) Discuss how the developments of the 1990s still affect your life.
3. **Oral History Project: Changes**
   Ask people like your grandparents how they remember the changes of the 1990s.

A Monument to German Freedom and Unity?

Politics and the Past

In 1871, Germany was united in one country, dominated by Prussia. Throughout the 19th century, German unity had in one way or another been a topic of debate. Now, after the creation of the German Empire, many people in Germany wanted to celebrate this. Monuments were built all over the country: The Walhalla near Regensburg, the Hermannsdenkmal near Detmold in 1875, many Bismarck monuments, the Kyffhäuser-Monument. One memorial, however, was especially built to commemorate German unification in 1871: the Niederwalddenkmal near Rüdesheim, in 1883. A colossal statue of Germania dominates the monuments on the hillside, overlooking the Rhine valley.

M 1 **Niederwalddenkmal**
Photograph, 2017

In the following decades, the idea of unity remained an important aspect of German political debates. It became important again after 1949, when two opposing German states were founded.

On 3 October 1990 Germany was united again. But how do Germans commemorate this? There is a national holiday, but there is no monument. Is one necessary many years after unification? The model below is for a "Monument to Freedom and Unity" in the centre of Berlin.

M 2 „Scale"
Design for the Monument to Freedom and Unity by Milla & Partner, 2014

Tasks

1. **A Monument to German Freedom and Unity?**
   a) Hold a panel discussion: "Do we need a monument to German unity?"
   b) Write an invitation for artists to present ideas for such a monument. Decide what elements of history should be included, where it should be put, how "commemoration" should be achieved.
   c) Create a draft version of such a monument.
   d) Do some research into the initiative for a "Monument to Freedom and Unity".
   e) Discuss how appropriate a moving scale is for such a monument.

Europe 1945 – 1967: United in Diversity

Already in the 1920s, after the First World War, European politicians and thinkers suggested a federation of European states to prevent a new war. The "Pan-European Movement" was founded in 1923. Politicians such as Gustav Stresemann and Aristide Briand found it attractive, but the movement had no success. It took another war for the idea to become popular.

A Question of War and Peace

In 1946, Winston Churchill proposed a "United States of Europe" in a famous speech in Zurich. Four years later, the French Foreign Minister Robert Schumann, convinced that the historic hatred between France and Germany had to be overcome, suggested merging both nations' coal and steel production and establishing an independent institution to supervise it.

Other leading European politicians, such as the Italian Prime Minister Alcide De Gasperi and the West German Chancellor Konrad Adenauer, all had seen two world wars in their lifetimes. They were all open to radically new ideas. So they saw the chance to integrate West Germany in a pan-European structure. Adenauer had his own motive. He liked the idea that close European cooperation including West Germany could overcome the status left to Germany by the Nazi regime. Another motive was fear. The West was afraid of a Soviet threat. Only the joined forces of Western Europe could defend themselves against the Soviet Union. The ultimate aim was to make war in Europe impossible.

Towards Integration

In 1952, the **European Coal and Steel Community (ECSC)** was founded. In 1957, its members – West Germany, France, Italy, Belgium, the Netherlands and Luxembourg – signed the Treaty of Rome. This treaty further advanced European integration into the **European Economic Community** (EEC). The signatory countries agreed on several basic principles:
- free trade by reducing customs and export/import limitations
- free payment and capital flow by reducing limitations in currency and stock trade
- freedom of labour by granting "market citizen rights", i.e. people could work within Europe and keep social security in all member states.

After the ECSC, the EEC, and the European Atomic Community (EURATOM which was set up to free atomic energy trade) were merged in 1967, the combination of the three was often referred to simply as the **European Community (EC)**.

M 1 Treaty of Rome, Photograph, Rome, 25 March 1957

Historical Terms

European Coal and Steel Community (ECSC):
Europäische Gemeinschaft für Kohle und Stahl (EGKS), kurz: Montanunion

European Economic Community (EEC):
Europäische Wirtschaftsgemeinschaft (EWG)

European Community (EC):
Europäische Gemeinschaft (EG)

M2 Britain and the "United States of Europe"

a) Winston Churchill had left his office of Prime Minister in 1945. So when he was speaking in Zurich to the Academic Youth on 19 September 1946, he was not a member of the government:

"Mr. President, Ladies and Gentlemen,
[…] I wish to speak to you today about the tragedy of Europe. This noble continent, comprising on the whole the fairest and the most cultivated regions of the earth, enjoying a
5 temperate and *equable* climate, is the home of all the great parent races of the western world. It is the fountain of Christian faith and Christian ethics. It is the origin of most of the culture, the arts, philosophy and science both of ancient and modern time. If Europe were once united in the
10 sharing of its common inheritance, there would be no limit to the happiness, to the prosperity and the glory which its three or four hundred million people would enjoy. Yet it is from Europe that have sprung that series of frightful nationalistic quarrels, originated by the Teutonic nations in
15 their rise to power, which we have seen in this twentieth century and even in our own lifetime, wreck the peace and *mar* the prospects of all mankind."

A Speech at Zurich University, in: Winston Churchill, Post War Speeches Vol I. The Collected Works Vol. XXVIII, London: Library of Imperial History in Association with Cassell & Company Ltd. 1975, S. 163.

M3 Winston Churchill (1874–1965)
Photograph, 1950

Vocabulary

equable: (here) neither too hot nor too cold
to mar: to spoil
sterling: currency in the UK

b) Excerpts from a statement by the British Foreign Office on European integration (1951):

"The United Kingdom cannot seriously contemplate joining in European integration. Apart from geographical and strategic considerations, Commonwealth ties and the special position of the United Kingdom as the centre of the
5 *sterling* area, we cannot consider submitting our political and economic system to supranational institutions. Moreover if these institutions did not prove workable, their dissolution would not be serious for the individual countries which would go their separate ways again; it
10 would be another matter for the United Kingdom which would have to break its Commonwealth and sterling area connexions to join them. […] Moreover, although the fact may not be universally recognised, it is not in the true interests of the continent that we should sacrifice our
15 present unattached position which enables us, together with the United States, to give a lead to the free world.
But while it is neither practicable nor desirable for the United Kingdom to join the integration movement, there would seem to be advantage in encouraging the movement
20 without taking part in it. This, in fact, is the policy which the United Kingdom is now following. […]
But while emphasising our support for European integration, we must at the same time take every opportunity to propagate the idea of the Atlantic community
25 and, in particular, to point out that the NATO is not merely a short-term body set up to organise the defence of Western Europe. We should therefore do all we can to further the development of the economic, social and cultural sides of the NATO. […] Thus, by giving encouragement and support
30 to the integration movement on the continent, we shall be in the best position to prevent it becoming exclusively European and to ensure that it develops as part of the Atlantic community."

Source DBPO (1986), series II, Vol. I, no 414. Quoted from: David Gowland/Arthur Turner (eds.), Britain and European Integration 1945–1998: A Documentary History, London & New York: Routledge 2000, p. 29.

Tasks

1. **Europe 1945–1967 – united in diversity**
   a) Explain why the beginnings of European integration were seen as a question of war and peace (text).
   b) Outline Churchill's reasoning (M2a).
   d) Explain the British dilemma (M2b). Draw a diagram to illustrate the position of the British government.

Broadening and Deepening

During the second half of the 20th century, two different political consepts shaped the development of the European institutions. First there was the idea of a broader trade area that should include as many European countries as possible, the second idea was that EC member states should intensify their cooperation.

The First Enlargement
Britain had not taken part in founding the EEC in the 1950s. After practically all colonies had become independent and the old British Empire had disappeared, Britain applied for membership in 1967, together with Ireland, Denmark and Norway. The French president Charles de Gaulle feared that Britain would bring American interests into the EC and vetoed British membership. Only after de Gaulle had left office, was Britain able to join in 1973, together with Denmark and Ireland. After a referendum, Norway decided to withdraw its application. At that time, Britain was in serious economic trouble. Inflation was at 15%, 1.5 million workers were forced into a three-day-workweek because of energy shortages. Unemployment was rising and Britain faced the biggest trade deficit in its history.

The Mediterranean
After decades of political unrest or dictatorships, Greece, Spain, and Portugal became democratic societies in the late 1970s. These countries wished to stabilize their newfound democracy by joining the EC. The founding members faced a dilemma: Economically, these countries were different, sometimes backward. They had to modernize. But could they do that on their own, outside the EC? In the end, the EC decided to export stability by enlargement. Greece joined the EC in 1981, followed by Spain and Portugal in 1986.

What to Do With Butter Mountains?
As early as 1962, the first market regulations for agricultural products came into force. Governments across Europe tried to protect their farmers against competition and, at the same time, tried to guarantee the European food supply. The Common Agricultural Policy (CAP) meant that farm products from outside the EC could not reach the market, and it guaranteed prices for the farmers. This policy was highly controversial, because it had far-reaching consequences. Guaranteed sales made farmers produce more than they could have sold in a free market. The results were a "butter mountain" and a "wine lake" – food nobody needed, but which was paid for by European taxpayers. It was sold cheaply to other parts of the world, thereby ruining prices in third world countries. In the 1960s and 1970s, the largest part of the EC budget was used for the CAP. On the one hand, it kept farmers all over Europe in business. On the other hand, it was enormously expensive. But because "butter mountains" and the destruction of food just to keep prices up seemed bizarre, the CAP became the focus of criticism against the EC. For some people, the CAP seemed to show how impractical and bureaucratic the EC had become. What made matters worse, agriculture was less important in Great Britain than in other large member countries. Understandably, the British government complained that they were paying for the subsidies for French and German farmers. In the end, the CAP achieved its original aims, but still became a symbol for a dysfunctional EC during the 1970s and early 1980s.

M 1 "The Common Agricultural Policy"
Cartoon by Horst Haitzinger, West Germany, 1987

Vocabulary

Language help:
overproduction,
reduction of production,
reduction of subsidies,
price reduction,
subsidies,
EC agricultural policies

M 2 A Common Vision of Europe

On 29 December 1975, the Belgian Prime Minister, Leo Tindemans, published his report on European Union. In it he tried to create a vision for the future of the EC. The following text is from the first page of his report:

"Europe today
Why has the European concept lost a lot of its force and initial impetus? I believe that over the years the European public has lost a guiding light, namely the political *consensus* between our countries on our reasons for undertaking this joint task and the characteristics with which we wish *to endow* it. We must first of all restore this common vision if we wish to have European Union.
In 1975 the European citizen does not view the reasons for the construction of Europe in exactly the same way as in 1950. The European idea is partly a victim of its own successes: the *reconciliation* between formerly hostile countries, the economic prosperity due to the enlarged market, the détente which has taken the place of the cold war, thanks particularly to our cohesion, all this seems to have been achieved and consequently not to require any more effort. Europe today is part of the general run of things; it seems to have lost its air of adventure.
Our peoples are concerned with new problems and values scarcely mentioned by the Treaties. They realize that political union does not automatically follow from economic integration; too many fruitless discussions cast doubt on the credibility and *topicality* of our joint endeavour: to this extent the European idea is also a victim of its failures. [...]
An unfinished structure does not *weather* well: it must be completed, otherwise it collapses. Today Community *attainments* are being challenged. Basically, however, Europeans are still in favour of closer links between our peoples as laid down in the Treaties of Paris and Rome, first between the Six, later between the Nine. [...] A return to selfish national attitudes, to national barriers, and to the antagonisms which they have frequently engendered would be seen as a historic defeat, the collapse of the efforts of a whole generation of Europeans. [...]
Europe must find its place again among the major concerns of public opinion thus ensuring that it will be the focal point of the political discussions of tomorrow. We must listen to our people. What do the Europeans want? What do they expect from a united Europe?"

Quoted from: Bulletin of the European Communities. Dir. of publ. Commision of the European Communities. 1976, Supplement 1. Bruxelles: European Communities. "Report on European Union", pp. 11–35.

Vocabulary

consensus: agreement
to endow: to equip sth. with sth.
reconciliation: a situation of becoming friends again after having been enemies
topicality: relevance
to weather: to survive bad weather
attainment: achievement

M 3 "Butter Mountains"
Cartoon by Karl-Heinz Schoenfeld, about 1980

Tasks

1. **Tindemans' Report**
   a) Point out how Tindemans sees the situation of Europe (M2). Explain why it was regarded as a victim of its success.
   b) Answer his last questions.
   c) Europe in in the 21st century: Is it different to Tindeman's view?

2. **Two Cartoons**
   Work as partners.
   a) Describe one of the cartoons (M1 or M3).
   b) Compare your cartoon with your partner's.
   c) Analyse the cartoonists' views on the Common Agricultural Policy.

After the Cold War: From Cooperation to New Nationalism

For many years, the history of European integration was told as a success story. History textbooks for schools ended with a positive chapter. It showed how a continent in ruins had united in the 1950s, had rebuilt through close cooperation, and achieved a common currency in the end. This book, however, will not only deal with positive aspects.

The old European Community of 12 west European countries saw its first growth in 1990, when the former GDR joined not only West Germany, but also the European Community.

Since 1990, the European Union, as it was called in 1992, has admitted countries in Central and Eastern Europe. The new focus was a better standard of living in the new member states. This included modernization of the outdated economies, democratic reforms, and the free movement of people across the continent.

In 1992, in the Treaty of Maastricht, European leaders decided on the introduction of a single currency, the **euro**, in the European Union. Most of the rest of the 1990s was spent on the preparation for this. Many economists had warned that this might pose problems for the weaker economies, especially in southern Europe, but at the time, the political decision to unite the continent seemed more important. So in 2002, the euro was introduced in most, but not all EU countries.

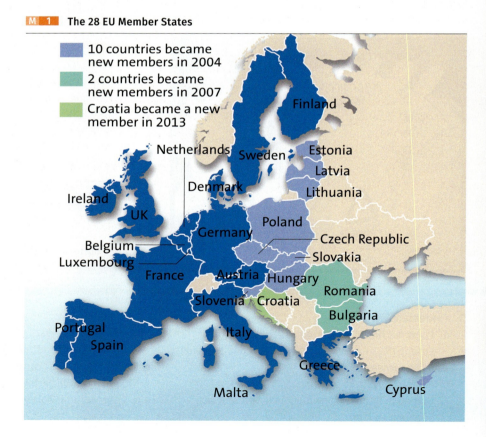

M 1 The 28 EU Member States

M 2   European Debt Crisis
Protests in Athens against the government. Photograph, 2011

Historical Terms

euro: Euro(currency)
International Monetary Fund (IMF): Internationaler Währungsfonds (IWF)

A New Economic Crisis

In the early 2000s, the euro seemed to work. Unemployment went down in many countries, the economy grew and life got better. But in the US, a catastrophe was brewing. After 11 September 2001, the US Federal Reserve (Fed) followed a policy of low interest rates to stimulate the economy. Many people had taken on debt to buy houses and cars. Housing prices grew fast, but some US banks had taken too many risks and had financial problems. In 2007, the US financial sector began to have serious trouble and in 2008 the consequences reached Europe. The economy slowed down, unemployment rose in all of Europe. Faced with this crisis, governments decided to help big banks and insurance companies with public money. They were considered "too big to fail", because their collapse would have caused even more trouble. The debts of private companies were thus taken over by the states – by the taxpayers.

The measures taken by the states to rescue the private banking sector caused a sharp increase in public – i.e. state – debt and resulted in the European debt crisis in 2010.

The Greek Crisis

Greece was particularly affected by this crisis, because Greece had had a very high level of debt during the previous years. To avoid a state bankruptcy, the countries of the Euro-group and the **International Monetary Fund** helped Greece with more than 200 billion euros. But Greece had to undergo serious reforms. Not all European politicians wanted to help Greece indefinitely. For the first time the question was discussed under what conditions a country would have to leave the common currency. Other countries in the Eurozone had also suffered severely under the economic crisis, especially Spain, Ireland, Italy and Portugal. Many people in northern countries questioned the idea of economic integration and solidarity in Europe, whereas many people in southern Europe felt threatened and oppressed by the economic policies forced through by the EU.

The Two Germanies within Europe

A New Nationalism – Hungary and Poland

The end of the Cold War also ended Soviet domination in Central and Eastern Europe. So it came as no surprise when Poland and Hungary applied for EU membership in 1994.

The transformation of these economies was not without problems. Many people have migrated west, looking for work. They have benefited from the freedom of movement guaranteed for all EU citizens. On the other hand, hardly any foreigners have moved into Poland and Hungary.

When this book was written, both countries had fiercely nationalistic and xenophobic governments. While both countries have been net recipients of EU funds since 2004, both governments tried to implement anti-EU policies, because of their fears of foreign domination. How this will affect the future of the EU is unclear.

Brexit

Another serious blow towards the European project came from another source: Britain. For a long time the United Kingdom had been less enthusiastic about the European project than the continental states. Since the 1980s, the UK had enjoyed a "rebate", a reduced membership fee for the EU, and had not introduced the euro. It had, however, opened its job market for Polish workers when Poland joined the EU in 2004. Poles were the largest immigrant group in Britain.

In 2015 Prime Minister David Cameron faced pressure from within his Conservative Party, the Tories. A populist party called UKIP, xenophobic and hostile to the EU, challenged the traditional Tory position. In desperation, Cameron called for a national referendum on the question of whether to leave the EU or to remain. The Brexit (= British Exit) became a possibility. The following campaign became especially nasty. Hardly any prominent politician made a serious case for the Remain side, while the Leave campaign resorted to "fake news", obviously false claims. The "Leave" promises were seen by many as wildly unrealistic. On the one hand, the campaign concentrated on the immigration issue, the question of whether the UK would be able to control immigration into the country. On the other, an unusual British dilemma became apparent. Immigration was seen less as a threat to a national identity, because people from Commonwealth countries had been present in Britain for many decades. It was a more a direct challenge in the job market by Polish workers, who worked for lower wages. In addition to that, the UK had lost its former role as a global power; it was now a partner in a union together with a Germany it had beaten in two world wars. In the end, the vote in the referendum was most likely a protest vote against the situation in the country. The outcome – 48% Remain, 52% Leave – shows how divided the country was then and is now.

It is still unclear what the future of the United Kingdom will look like. The border with Ireland is once again a serious problem, the question whether Scotland will remain part of Great Britain is equally troublesome. The promises of the Leave campaign look hopelessly unrealistic: "Take back control" seems less likely every day. The most likely outcome may be that Great Britain will have to follow the rules of the European Union without being able to influence them anymore. At the same time the United Kingdom may be at risk because the **Irish question** has been opened again.

M 3 "We Want Our Country Back"
Pro-Brexit demonstrators protest outside the Houses of Parliament on 23 November 2016. Photograph, London

---

Info

Irish question
Ireland became independent in 1922, but Northern Ireland still belongs to the United Kingdom. During the 1970s and 1980s, there was a civil war in Northern Ireland between pro-British and pro-Irish groups. Both states joined the EC together, and Brexit will create problems at the border.

Brexit – working with cartoons

M 4 **Brexit in Free Fall**
Cartoon by Martin Erl, Germany, 2016

M 5 **Brexit**
Cartoon by Walter Hanel, Germany, 2017

Tasks

1. **Brexit**
   a) Analyse the cartoons.
   b) Explain the different perspectives.
   c) When you look at this book, some time will have passed since the Brexit discussion. Decide which of the two cartoons comes closer to reality today.

188 SUMMARY — The Two Germanies within Europe

The Two Germanies within Europe – the historical map

Germany Today

Summary

Between 1945/1949 and 1990, the fate of the two German states – the FRG and the GDR – can only be explained and understood as a part of the ongoing Cold War between the superpowers. The two German states soon established themselves as members of opposing military alliances and opposing ideologies. Ideas for a neutral but reunited Germany remained hypothetical in the 1950s.

In both states in Germany, rebuilding the war damage became the most important aim in the 1950s. The "economic miracle" in West Germany was mirrored by much slower progress in the East. There, too, living conditions improved, but as long as the border between the two states was open, many East Germans left the country to escape the demands of the socialist state.

The Berlin Wall in 1961 closed the last loophole in the border. East Germans lived with increasing state control of all aspects of life. It became harder and harder to express opposing views, while the goal of a better life than in the West was not achieved.

Faced with the realities of German and international politics, the new SPD/FDP government with Chancellor Brandt (after 1969) developed new ideas to cooperate with the GDR government, hoping that one day these contacts would help with the ultimate goal of reunification.

Social changes in the 1960s brought new challenges. The environmental movement, terrorism, and economic problems characterized the 1970s in West Germany as well as in other Western states.

The collapse of the GDR economy and the inability of the GDR government to adapt its ideology to new circumstances led to a serious crisis in the late 1980s. A peaceful revolution by the people in the GDR forced the SED government to open the borders. This was only possible because the Soviet Union chose not to interfere. Combining domestic and international aspects, Germany unified in 1990.

Since the 1950s, the idea of European integration had been turned into reality – slowly and not without problems. In the end, however, the European Union became the organization to cope with change on the continent.

A historical era can be defined as a time when basic patterns of political and social life remain stable. With the fall of the Berlin Wall and the end of the Cold War, the basic pattern of international politics became unstable and changed. The end of an era had been reached.

DATES

17 June 1953:
Uprising in the GDR
1955:
West Germany joins NATO
13 August 1961:
Building of the Berlin Wall
9 November 1989:
Fall of the Berlin Wall
3 October 1990:
Day of Unification

HISTORICAL TERMS

planned economy
collectivization
Ministry of State Security
Hallstein Doctrine
social market economy
guest workers
People's Chamber
Free German Youth
Iron Curtain
extra-parliamentary opposition
Red Army Faction
change through rapprochement
Conference on Security and Cooperation in Europe
dissidents
Treuhandanstalt
Stasi Records Act

PERSONS

Konrad Adenauer
Willy Brandt
Helmut Schmidt
Erich Honecker
Helmut Kohl
Mikhail Gorbachev

M 1 "Arms Race: Help, I'm being chased"
Cartoon by Horst Haitzingen, about 1980

M 2 "Perestroika"
Cartoon by Karl-Heinz Schoenfeld, 1987

05

SUPERPOWER RIVALRY
Two Systems Divide The World

The world had changed after World War II. Not only was Nazi Germany defeated and the horrors of the Holocaust ended, there was hope that the Allies would make the world a better and safer place. This hope didn't last long. Instead of a peaceful cooperation between the Allies a confrontation of two very different political views determined the fate of the world: capitalism vs. communism.

Historical Terms

proxy war: Stellvertreterkrieg

Each of the sides found supporters that joined either NATO or the Warsaw Pact. That meant that the two ideologies were supported militarily, which led to many **proxy wars** and crises in the world. Some of these confrontations such as in Korea have had lasting results up to this day. In other situations like the Cuba Crisis the world found itself on the brink of nuclear destruction. Other wars such as the Vietnam War are still present in today's media world.

This shows that many of the challenges we face today originate from events during the Cold War. Some people even claim that the Cold War has never ended.

This chapter deals with many questions such as:
- Was the Korean War the first proxy war?
- Why is Korea still a divided country today?
- What factors led to national uprisings and reform attempts in the Eastern Bloc?
- Why did all of the attempts fail?
- Why did the USSR put down any opposition or national form of socialism?
- How could a small country such as Cuba almost cause a nuclear war?
- Why did the USA become involved in Vietnam?
- How did the confrontation between NATO and the Warsaw Pact develop?
- What factors influenced the collapse of the Soviet Union?

Vocabulary

sphere of influence: area/territory where you have influence and power

to pursue: to continue with an action or plan

offensive: attack

to withdraw (withdrew, withdrawn): to pull out; to move back from a place or situation

stalemate: a situation in which neither side can win or make any progress

on the brink: in a new, dangerous or exciting situation

relentless: refusing to give up; determined not to stop one's attempts to achieve sth.

Historical Terms

containment: Eindämmung
demarcation line: Demarkationslinie
UN Security Council: UN Sicherheitsrat

Superpower Rivalry

In 2018 after decades of separation North and South Korea were brought closer during the Olympic Games in South Korea. They even competed together with one common ice-hockey team. Despite the uniting factor of sports, Korea is still a divided country today. What are the reasons?

The Cold War Continues – the Korean War 1950–53

By the end of the 1940s the former Allies USA and USSR had become rivals trying to secure their *spheres of influence* in the world. The USA *pursued* a policy of **containment**, introduced by President Truman (Truman Doctrine) in 1947 in order to limit further Communist expansion. Chinese Communists, led by Mao Zedong, founded the People's Republic of China, which the USA refused to recognize. On the other hand, the USSR tried to form all Communist countries into a Soviet bloc, if necessary by military means. The Western powers feared a worldwide Communist *offensive*, especially after 1949, when both superpowers had nuclear weapons. One year later the conflict worsened in Korea.

Development

Japan surrendered on 2 September 1945, after atomic bombs were dropped on Hiroshima and Nagasaki. The superpowers agreed to divide Korea temporarily: The North came under Soviet and the South under US occupation. The **demarcation line** was to be the 38th parallel of latitude. Each of the two occupying powers influenced their parts of Korea and threatened the other with war. The country stayed divided even after the USA and the USSR *withdrew* their troops.

The elections that were supposed to take place in all of Korea were held only in South Korea. Syngman Rhee became President of the Republic of Korea with strong backing from the USA. Rhee's authoritarian regime was supported by rich landowners and the military. The North in turn founded the Democratic People's Republic of Korea, led by the Communist Kim Il Sung. The North Korean government, supported by the USSR and China, demanded power over all of Korea, as did the South.

In June 1950 North Korean troops attacked and occupied most of South Korea within a few days. Many in the West saw this as an action initiated by Moscow and considered it proof of Communist aggression. The **UN Security Council** condemned the invasion and sent troops under US command to Korea.

M 1 The Korean War 1950–1953

The Korean War 1950-1953

- South Korea
- North Korea
- line of demarcation to 25 June 1950 / 38th parallel
- line of demarcation from 27 November 1951, border since ceasefire of 27 July 1953

The counteroffensive on land and sea drove the North Korean troops back behind the 38th parallel. The USSR accused the USA of interfering in the internal affairs of foreign countries. When the US army drove the North Korean forces close to the Chinese border, Chinese "volunteers" – China did not want to risk open war – entered the war and the front was forced back to almost its original location. Here the battles ended in a *stalemate*.

The world was *on the brink* of a new global war. President Truman feared the conflict would escalate, because by 1951 Soviet pilots assisted the Chinese air force. In public, US General MacArthur demanded a nuclear attack on China, but Truman replaced the outspoken general.

Several chances for peace were passed. The war lasted until 1953, when an armistice was finally signed. The border was reset at the 38th parallel with a few minor changes, and a four-kilometre-wide demilitarized zone was agreed upon. Negotiations for a peace treaty failed in 1954.

Results

To this day Korea is a divided country. About two million people died in the conflict. The war had other far-reaching effects: The USA gave up its policy of demilitarization in both Japan and West Germany in order to avoid a Communist take-over. The superpowers became even more suspicious of each other.

The USA built up military bases around the Soviet sphere of influence and by 1955 had signed military treaties with forty-three countries. The USSR continued to maintain its power in its dominated territory *relentlessly* putting down demonstrations in East Germany on 17 June 1953 and a revolt in Hungary in October 1956.

M 2 Kim Il Sung (1912–1994)
was an active fighter against Japan and was supposedly trained by the Soviet Red Army. Not much is known about his early years. In 1946 he became the leader of the Korean Communist Party and in 1947 the official head of government. He secured his power by eliminating political opposition as well as opponents in his administration. After his death he was declared "eternal president of the republic".

M 3 Syngman Rhee (1875–1965)
was born to an impoverished aristocratic family. In his youth he fought against the monarchy and spent six years in prison for treason. In 1910 he got his doctorate from Princton University in the USA. Still he was always involved in Korean politics from abroad/exile. As president after 1948 he ruled oppressively and undemocratically. It is said that he manipulated the elections in 1956 and 1960 to be reelected.

The Korean War

M 4 "Massacre in Korea"
Painting by Pablo Picasso, 1951

M 5 The Korean War in Contemporary Accounts

a) Harry S. Truman, President of the United States:

"In my generation, this was not the first time that the strong had attacked the weak. I recalled some earlier instances: Manchuria, Ethiopia, Austria. I remembered how each time the democracies failed to act, it had encouraged the aggressors to keep going ahead. Communism was acting in Korea just as Hitler, Mussolini, and the Japanese had acted […] If this were allowed to go unchallenged it would mean a third World War, just as similar incidents had brought on a Second World War."

Harry S. Truman, Years of Trial and Hope 1946–1953, New York: Doubleday 1956, p. 351.

b) Mao decides to send Chinese troops to Korea, October 1950:

"We have decided to send a portion of our troops, under the name of Volunteers [sic], to Korea […] If Korea were completely occupied by the Americans and the Korean revolutionary forces were substantially destroyed the American invaders would be more *rampant*, and such a situation would be unfavourable to the whole East […] Meanwhile our troops will be awaiting the arrival of Soviet weapons and becoming equipped with those weapons. Only then will our troops launch a counteroffensive […] The enemy will control the air while our air force, which has just started its training, will not be able to enter the war with some 300 planes until February 1951."

Quoted from: Shu Guang Zhang and Jian Chen (eds.), Chinese Communist Foreign Policy and the Cold War in Asia: New Documentary Evidence 1944–1950, Waterloo: Imprint Publications 1996, pp. 162f.

M 6 N. S. Khrushchev on the Korean War

N. S. Khrushchev remembers in 1971:

"The North Koreans wanted to give a helping hand to their brethren who were under the heel of Syngman Rhee. Stalin persuaded Kim Il Sung to think it over […] Kim returned to Moscow when he had worked everything out […] Stalin had his doubts. He was worried that the Americans would jump in, but we were inclined to think that if the war were fought swiftly – and Kim Il Sung was sure it could be won swiftly – then intervention by the USA could be avoided. Nevertheless Stalin decided to ask Mao Zedong's opinion about Kim Il Sung's suggestion. I must stress it wasn't Stalin's idea, but Kim Il Sung's. Kim was the initiator. Stalin, of course, didn't try to dissuade him […] Mao Zedong also answered him affirmatively. He approved Kim Il Sung's suggestion and put forward the opinion that the USA would not intervene since the war would be an internal matter which the Korean people would decide for themselves."

Nikita Sergejevich Khrushchev, Khrushchev Remembers. With an Introduction, Commentary and Notes by Edward Crankshaw, transl. by Strobe Talbott, Boston/Toronto: Little, Brown & Company 1971.

M 7 "America at its Best"

US President Bill Clinton gave a speech on the 50th anniversary of the beginning of the Korean War at the Korean War Memorial in Washington, D.C., in 2000:

"[...] the leaders of the communist nations did not believe America would stand up for South Korea. After all, America didn't want another war; the blood still hadn't dried from World War II. Nobody wanted more rationing, nobody wanted more Western Union boys riding up with telegrams from the War Department. Americans wanted to start families. They wanted to see gold stars on report cards, not gold stars in windows.

But from the moment Harry Truman heard the news at home, on his first trip to Missouri since Christmas that year before, he knew this was a moment of truth. If an invasion was permitted to triumph in Korea without opposition from the free world, no small nation again would have the courage to resist aggression. He knew American boys didn't fight and die to stop Nazi aggression only to see it replaced by communist aggression.

So Korea wasn't just a line on a map. It was where America drew the line in the sand on the Cold War; and where, for the first time, the nations of the whole world, together at the then newly-created United Nations, voted to use armed force to stop armed aggression. [...] There is no question: Korea was war at its worst. But it was also America at its best."

William J. Clinton, "Remarks on the Observance of the 50th Anniversary of the Korean War", June 25, 2000; quoted from: Gerhard Peters and John T. Woolley (eds.), The American Presidency Project: http://www.presidency.ucsb.edu/ws/?pid=58158 [July 19, 2018].

Vocabulary

(in M5b) rampant: spreading in an uncontrolled way

M 8 Korean War Memorial in Washington, D.C.
Photograph, 1995

Tasks

1. **Conflict in Korea**
   a) Show how the war developed (M1).
   b) Explain the word "volunteers" (Text, M5b).
2. **Perception of the Korean War**
   a) Analyse the painting by Picasso. What is his accusation (M4)?
   b) Explain why Truman refers to Manchuria, Ethiopia and Austria (M5a).
   c) Compare Khrushchev's perception of the war with Clinton's (M6, M7).
   d) Comment on Clinton's perception of the Korean War (M7).
3. **Is Korea Comparable to Germany After 1945?**
   a) Find out about the situation in Korea today.
   b) Compare the situation of Korea with the situation in Germany in regard to the division of the countries.
   c) Project: Compare South Korea's and North Korea's political structures today. You may present your results in any form you like (presentation, poster, essay).

The Cuban Crisis 1962 – 13 days on the edge

In October 1963 the world was on the brink of a nuclear war, because the two superpowers came close to a hot rather than cold war over the matter of stationing nuclear weapons on each other's borders. So both countries felt threatened directly. What prevented this direct confrontation of the superpowers from escalating into a nuclear war?

Origins of the Crisis – why Cuba?

During the 1950s the USSR and USA confronted each other with an **arms race**. By the 1960s both sides had enough bombs to destroy the world. At the time long-range missiles could fly thousands of miles, but it took about thirty minutes to reach a *target* on the other side of the globe. This gave the enemy too much time to react, so both powers tried to station their weapons closer to the enemy.

Turkey allowed the Americans to set up missiles on the Turkish-Soviet border. A missile launched from there could reach Moscow within five to ten minutes. As a result the USSR looked for a missile site closer to the United States. Cuba seemed ideal.

Cuba was considered part of the American sphere of influence and had been economically dependent and politically linked to the US. In 1959 Fidel Castro led a revolt and made Cuba a Communist country. In April 1961 the USA invaded Cuba at the Bay of Pigs with the help of exile Cubans in the USA. The attempt failed and embarrassed the USA, which broke off diplomatic and trade relations. This drove Cuba into the arms of the USSR, which began to supply planes and petrol to the country. Additionally, Khrushchev made it clear that the USSR would support the Cuban people if the USA did not withdraw from the island.

The October Crisis – the world on the brink of nuclear destruction

On 16 October 1962 President Kennedy was shown aerial photographs of nuclear missiles under construction. More weapons were on their way to Cuba on Soviet

---

Historical Terms

arms race: Wettrüsten

M 1 Soviet Missiles to Cuba?
A US-plane flies over the warship USS Barry and the Soviet cargo vessel Anosow, which is suspected of transporting Soviet missiles to Cuba. Photograph, October 1962.

ships. In September Khrushchev had reassured the Americans that he had no intention of stationing any Soviet weapons on Cuba. In the eyes of the US government the Soviets had lied.

This situation brought the two superpowers to the brink of nuclear war and the world to the edge of destruction. It was in the hands of the two leaders to either save or destroy the world.

M 2 Range of Soviet Missiles in Cuba, 1962

Info

- 22 October: Kennedy decides to blockade Cuba. He warns Khrushchev that all Soviet ships will be searched and sent back if any missiles are found. Searching Soviet ships as well as the embargo are regarded as acts of war.
- 23 October: Khrushchev replies to Kennedy, saying that the Soviets will ignore the blockade and sail to Cuba.
- 24 October: The first Soviet ships near the blockade, stop and turn around.
- 25 October: The question of the missiles already installed in Cuba remains open. Some of Kennedy's advisers urge him to invade Cuba and destroy the sites.
- 26 October: Khrushchev offers to remove the missiles from Cuba if Kennedy lifts the blockade and promises not to invade Cuba. Later he also demands that the USA remove missiles in Turkey.
- 27 October: Kennedy's advisers insist on invading Cuba and *urge* him to ignore Khrushchev. Instead, Kennedy decides to accept Khrushchev's first offer. He also sends his brother Robert to the Soviet embassy to agree secretly to remove the missiles from Turkey after the crisis has ended.
- 28 October: The two leaders come to an agreement, ending the crisis that brought the world to the brink of destruction. Both sides manage to save face.

Viewpoints on the Cuban crisis vary. Some think Kennedy saved the world by putting pressure on the Soviets through the blockade and his strong threats. At the same time, he gave the Soviet Union enough time to react. Others think that Khrushchev saved the world by backing down from a nuclear war when he realized that Kennedy would not be pushed around.

Results: The Hotline

Following this major crisis, both sides realized how dangerously close they had come to destroying the world. The two leaders set up a "hotline" between Washington and Moscow.

The hotline enabled the leaders of the superpowers to contact each other within seconds before deciding to *launch* a nuclear *strike*. Kennedy and Khrushchev also agreed to ban all nuclear tests above ground.

However, relations between the superpowers remained cool for the following decades.

Fidel Castro had no say in the settling of the crisis, so the Soviet-Cuban relations suffered. Cuba had been put under economic pressure even before the crisis in order to prevent the "communist virus" from spreading across South America. After the crisis an embargo was enforced by the USA even more vigorously. Only in 2016 did President Obama of the USA resume diplomatic relations with Cuba.

Vocabulary

target: an object, a person or a place that people aim at when attacking

to urge sb.: to push for sb. to do sth.

to launch: to send a missile or a spacecraft into the air or space

strike: a military attack, esp. by aircraft dropping bombs

The Cuban Crisis 1962

M 3 John Fitzgerald Kennedy Jr (1917–1963)
was US president from 20 November 1961 until 22 November 1963 when he was shot in Dallas, Texas.

M 4 Nikita Sergeyevich Khrushchev (1894–1971)
was the First Secretary of the Communist Party of the USSR from 1953 unit 1964. He made some liberal reforms in domestic policy and was removed from office in 1964.

M 5 Fidel Alejandro Castro Ruz (1926–2016)
was a communist revolutionary. From 1959 until 1976 he ruled Cuba as Prime Minister and from 1976 until 2008 as President, until 2011 he was also the First Secretary of the Cuban Communist Party.

M 6 **Kennedy**

Transcript of Kennedy's motives on Friday, 19 October 1962:

"If we attack Cuban missiles, or Cuba, in any way, it gives them a clear line to go ahead and take Berlin, as they were able to do in Hungary under the Anglo war in Egypt [...] We would be regarded as the trigger happy Americans who lost
5 Berlin. We would have no support among our allies. We would affect West Germans' attitudes towards us [...] If we go in and take them out [...] We increase the chance greatly [... of] their just going in and taking Berlin by force. Which leaves me only one alternative, which is to fire nuclear
10 weapons – which is a hell of an alternative – and begin a nuclear exchange."

Quoted from: Mike Sewell, The Cold War, Cambridge: Cambridge University Press 2002, p. 90.

M 7 **Khrushchev**

Khrushchev's letter to Kennedy, 26 October 1962:

"I propose: we will declare that our ships bound for Cuba are not carrying any armaments. You will declare that the United States will not invade Cuba with its troops and will not support any other forces which might intend to invade Cuba. Then the necessity for the presence of our military
5 specialists in Cuba will be *obviated* [...] You and I should not now pull on the ends of the rope in which you have tied the knot of war [...] thereby dooming the world to the catastrophe of thermonuclear war."

Quoted from: Laurence Chang and Peter Kornbluh (eds.), The Cuban Missiles Crisis 1962. A National Security Archive Documents Reader, New York: New Press 1992, p. 188 (Document 44).

M 8 **Fidel Castro**

Fidel Castro recounts a conversation with Khrushchev in 1963:

"[He read a message from Kennedy]: He said 'we have fulfilled our commitments and we have withdrawn, or we are withdrawing, or we're going to withdraw the missiles from Turkey and Italy.' [...] When I heard that, I imagine that
5 Nikita realized that that was the last sentence I wanted to hear. He knew how I thought and how we were totally against being used as a bargaining chip. That ran counter to the theory that the missiles had been sent to defend Cuba. You do not defend Cuba by withdrawing missiles from
10 Turkey [...]. Defending Cuba would have been accomplished

by insisting that the United States withdraw from its base at Guantanamo, stop the pirate attacks, and end the blockade [of Cuba]. But withdrawing missiles from Turkey completely contradicted the theory that the main objective of the deployment had been defending Cuba."

Quoted from: James G. Blight, Bruce J. Allyn and David A. Welch (eds.), Cuba on the Brink. Castro, the Missile Crisis and the Soviet Collapse, New York: Pantheon Books 1993. pp. 224f.

Vocabulary

to obviate: to get rid of sth. such as a problem

M 9 "Okay, Mr. President, we want to negotiate."
British caricature, 1962

Vocabulary

Useful words
arm wrestling
hydrogen bomb

Tasks

1. **Parties Involved**
   a) Explain why Cuba came under Soviet influence (text).
   b) Find out more about the personalities involved: J. F. Kennedy, N. Khrushchev, F. Castro (Internet, text, M3 – M5).
   c) Speculate in what way their personalities contributed to the conflict or to its outcome (research, text).
   d) Assess why it was so important for the USA and the USSR to save face.

2. **Confrontation and Crisis**
   a) Analyse the map (M2). Why was the range of the weapons so important (text, M2)?
   b) Explain Kennedy's argumentation (M6).
   c) Give your opinion on Khrushchev's offer (M7).
   d) What do Castro's comment (M8) say about the standing of Cuba?

3. **Cuba – the eye of the storm**
   a) Interpret the cartoon (M9).
   b) Find out what role Cuba played during the later years of the Cold War (Internet).
   c) Give a presentation about the situation in Cuba today.

Vocabulary

omnipresent: to be seen, heard, felt, noticed everywhere

to intend to do sth.: to have a plan to do sth.

to shore up: to support sth. that is weak or going to fail

foe: enemy

napalm: a liquid chemical that burns the persons that it hits

escalation: increase, making sth. larger or more serious

Agent Orange: a chemical that destroys herbs, plants and makes trees lose their leaves

repression: the use of force or violence to control people

The Vietnam War 1964–1973

- Democratic Republic of North Vietnam, controlled by Communists since autumn 1970
- Vietcong
- Pathet Lao
- Red Khmer

⊕ US air base
⊕ US naval base
⫶ US airstrikes (after Feb.1965)

M 1

American Involvement in Vietnam 1962 – 75

In many US films and TV series (i. e. "Good Morning Vietnam" or "Magnum P.I.", to name a few) the Vietnam war plays a major role. This war is often referred to as "the American nightmare", because the US military was not able to win this war. Why is this war still *omnipresent* in US everyday life?

The French in Vietnam

Vietnam was part of the French Empire in Indochina before World War II. Japan occupied the country during the war. The Vietminh, Vietnamese Communists led by Ho Chi Minh, tried to drive the Japanese out and found an independent Vietnam. Because Japan was also at war with the USA, the latter supported the Vietminh.

After the surrender of Japan in 1945, the French returned to Vietnam to reclaim Indochina. A bitter guerilla war ended with the defeat of French forces in 1954.

In Geneva, Switzerland, a peace conference divided Vietnam at the 17th parallel north latitude and ordered free elections by 1956. Cambodia and Laos became independent, neutral states and all foreign troops were to be withdrawn.

Ho Chi Minh set up a Communist government in the North, *intending to* unite Vietnam in the forthcoming elections. He encouraged a Communist guerilla force, the Vietcong, to fight in the South. There, the government led by President Ngo Dinh Diem increasingly relied on corruption and the military *to shore up* its power. The South Vietnamese government became so unpopular that the Vietcong won support among the peasants.

Fearing a "domino effect" in south-east Asia, the USA tried to prevent a Communist victory in the elections. After supplying money and weapons proved ineffective, President Kennedy sent military advisors to assist the South Vietnamese troops against the Vietcong. Regular troops followed in 1962.

Full Scale War

In 1964 Kennedy's successor, Lyndon B. Johnson, increased the number of American soldiers to a full scale war on land and in the air. By 1967 over half a million US troops fought in Vietnam. By 1973 US planes had dropped more bombs on Vietnam than they had dropped during World War II.

President Johnson had hoped that the war could be won quickly. But several errors in judgement prevented victory: 1) American soldiers destroyed not only the land but also killed many innocent people, because they could not distinguish between friend and *foe* among the Vietnamese; 2) the US government believed the war could be won, although France had been defeated in a guerilla war; 3) US leaders were convinced that victory was worth any sacrifice.

By the end of the 1960s the American public strongly opposed the war, because many soldiers lost their lives and the American people were not told the truth about the course of the war. The US army won some battles, but could not win the war. Additionally, many horrible pictures of the war were published or broadcast on TV. The world witnessed executions and the horrible effect of *napalm* bombs.

Not only Americans opposed the war. The USSR and China had supported the Communist fighters. They competed for more influence in Vietnam. By the end of the 1960s all the parties involved feared an *escalation* of the conflict. This finally opened the way to peace negotiations with North Vietnam. After a decade of fighting and many dead (about 58,000 US soldiers, more than 2,000,000 Vietnamese) the USA withdrew in 1973, turning over responsibility for the war to the South Vietnamese.

Consequences of the War

On 30 April 1975 North Vietnamese troops invaded Saigon. The South surrendered unconditionally. But the end of the war did not mean the end of misery.

Napalm bombs and *Agent Orange* had killed and injured thousands of Vietnamese, had turned fertile farm land into poisonous deserts. Fearing Communist *repression*, hunger and worsening living-conditions, many people fled from Vietnam. More than 1.6 million refugees, called boat people, tried to get away in old boats. This exodus lasted well into the 1980s – an estimated 25% of these boat people died during storms at sea or when attacked by pirates.

The war had also long-term effects on the USA. The Vietnam war was regarded as the first war the USA had ever lost. American loss of confidence in foreign affairs took different forms in the following years. At first, US leaders showed more humility in foreign affairs (for example, Jimmy Carter); later others returned to conventional power politics (Ronald Reagan, George W. Bush).

M 2 US Soldiers in Vietnam
Photograph

M 3 "Boat People"
Refugees later received in the FRG on the freighter Hai Hong.
Photograph, 1978

American Involvement in Vietnam 1962–75

M 4 **The Origin of Eisenhower's "Domino Theory"**

Communist domination, by whatever means, of all South-east Asia would seriously endanger in the short term, and critically endanger in the longer term, United States security interests (1953):

a) "The loss of any of the countries of South-east Asia to communist aggression would have critical psychological, political and economic consequences. In the absence of effective and timely counteraction, the loss of any single country would probably lead to relatively swift submission to or an alignment with communism by the remaining countries of this group. Furthermore, an alignment with communism of the rest of South-east Asia and India, and in the longer term, of the Middle East (with the probable exceptions of at least Pakistan and Turkey) would in all probability progressively follow. Such widespread alignment would endanger the stability and security of Europe."

b) "Communist control of all of South-east Asia would render the US position in the Pacific offshore islands precarious and would seriously *jeopardize* fundamental US security interests in the Far East."

c) "South-east Asia, especially *Malaya* and Indonesia, is the principal world source of natural rubber and tin, and a producer of petroleum and other strategically important commodities. The rice exports of Burma and Thailand are critically important to *Malaya*, Ceylon and Hong Kong and are of considerable significance to Japan and India, all important areas of free Asia."

d) "The loss of South-east Asia, especially of *Malaya* and Indonesia, could result in such economic and political pressures as to make it extremely difficult to prevent Japan's eventual accommodation to communism."

NSC 12/2, June 1953, quoted from: https://history.state.gov/historicaldocuments/frus1952-54v12p1/d36 [July 19, 2018].

Vocabulary

to jeopardize: to risk damaging or destroying sth. important
Malaya: Malaysia (after 1963)
to defoliate: to remove leaves from plants and trees

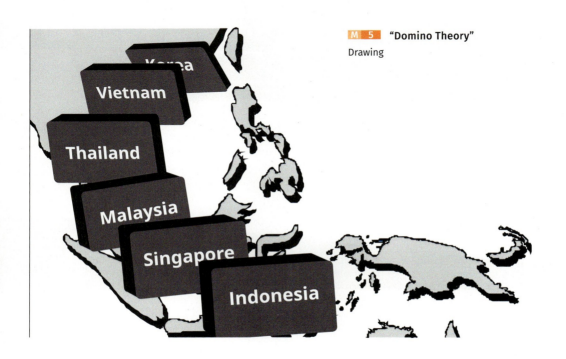

M 5 **"Domino Theory"**
Drawing

M6 Eyewitness Reports from Vietnam

a) The reality of guerilla warfare as reported by two American soldiers:

"[…] this enemy is invisible […] it is not just the people but the land itself – unfamiliar […] frightening […] it can be that field ahead littered with land mines […] The enemy can be the kind who comes out smiling and then lobs a grenade
5 […] or that bent old lady carrying a watermelon. […]
You walk down a road between rice paddies. Vietnamese are in every paddy. Then, a mortar shell lands right in the middle of the patrol. A couple of guys are dead, others are screaming in agony with a leg or arm blown off, or their guts
10 hanging out. Did one of them (the peasants) lob the mortar? If so which one? Should you kill all of them or none of them?"

Quoted from: Peter Fisher, The Great Power Conflict after 1945, New York: Simon & Schuster 1985, p. 47.

b) Richard Hammer, an American journalist, visited Vietnam in 1970:

"To move about Vietnam today is to view the far side of the moon. This is now a land of bomb craters and shell holes, of deserted and ruined hamlets, of abandoned rice paddies. It is a country of refugees […] once the rice bowl of Asia –
5 now unable to feed itself."

Quoted from: Peter Fisher, The Great Power Conflict after 1945, New York: Simon & Schuster 1985, p. 47.

M7 Winning Battles – a losing strategy

Richard Hammer, author and journalist, from: One Morning in the War:

"One does not use napalm on villages and hamlets sheltering civilians […] if one is attempting to persuade these people of the rightness of one's cause. One does not blast hamlets to dust with high explosives from jet planes
5 miles (sic!) in the sky without warning – if one is attempting to woo the people living there to the goodness of one's cause […] One does not *defoliate* a country and deform its people with chemicals if one is attempting to persuade them of the foe's evil nature."

Richard Hammer, One Morning in the War: The Tragedy at Son My, 1970, quoted from: Howard Langer, The Vietnam War: An Encyclopedia of Quotations, Westport/Connecticut: Greenwood Publishing Group, 2005, p. 231.

M8 American Planes Dropping Defoliants in Vietnam
Photograph

Tasks

1. **From Colonial Problem to International Conflict**
   a) Explain why the USA became involved in the Vietnam conflict (text).
   b) List the events of the Vietnam war in chronological order (text, M1).
   c) Explain the "Domino Theory" (M4).
   d) Analyse the drawing (M5).
   e) Make a table in which you list the opposing parties (text).

2. **Warfare – the war itself**
   a) Describe what the eyewitnesses report about the Vietnam war (M6).
   b) Explain the chemical warfare in Vietnam and its consequences (text, research).

3. **The Perception of the Vietnam War**
   a) Show why the American public became more and more weary of the war (text, M3, M8, research).
   b) Find out about references to the Vietnam War in TV shows and films (research) and report your findings to the class.

4. **The Consequences**
   a) Find out about the Vietnamese perspective on the war (Internet).
   b) Divide into groups and discuss the problems of boat people today (text, M3, research).

HISTORICAL WORKSHOP — Superpower Rivalry

M 1 **9-year-old Kim Phuc Running from a Napalm Attack on her Village**

Photograph, taken by Nick Ut in 1972.

M 2 **Eyewitness Report 1**

Kim Phuc remembers this day in an interview with the BBC in the year 2000:

"In 1972 a napalm bomb was dropped on my village in south Vietnam. A photographer, Nick Ut, took a picture of me running away from the fire and that photo is very famous. I remember I was nine years old, just a child. That night we heard the Viet Cong were coming and that they wanted to use the village. And then in the daytime, the soldiers came in and there was fighting.

We were so scared. I remember my family decided to seek refuge in the temple, the pagoda, because we thought it was a holy place. We could seek refuge there and we could be safe. I did not hear the explosion but I saw the fire around me.

And suddenly my clothes were burnt off by fire. I saw the fire over my body and especially my arm. I remember at that moment I thought I would be ugly, and not normal like other children.

I was so scared because I did not see anyone around me. Just fire and smoke. I was crying and I was running out of the fire and the miracle was my feet were not burned. I kept running and running and running.

My parents could not get past the fire, so they turned back to the temple and they sheltered there. My aunt and two cousins died. One was three years old and one just nine months – two babies.

After that I passed out."

http://news.bbc.co.uk/2/hi/asia-pacific/718106.stm [July 16, 2018].

M 3 **Eyewitness Report 2**

H. Fass and Marianne Fulton report on the events in the picture on the basis of interviews with Nick Ut:

"We passed hundreds of refugees fleeing the village. They cooked and slept outside the village, hoping to return when the fighting stopped. […]

When we moved closer to the village we saw the first people running. I thought 'Oh my God' when I suddenly saw a woman with her left leg badly burned by napalm. Then came a woman carrying a baby, who died, then another woman carrying a small child with it's [sic] skin coming off. When I took a picture of them I heard a child screaming and saw that young girl who had pulled off all her burning clothes. She yelled to her brother […]

Nick Ut recalls that Kim Phuc screamed 'Nong qua, nong qua' ('too hot, too hot') as he photographed her running past him. When the girl had stopped Nick Ut and […] Christopher Wain poured water from their canteens over her burns.

[…] Nick Ut heard her saying to her also injured older brother […], 'I think I am going to die.' […]

Urged on by Kim Phuc's uncle, Nick commandered his car and being one of the few reporters able to communicate with the injured villagers he took over and carried Kim Phuc into the car. Then other members of her family […] rushed into the car. Ut climbed aboard the now overcrowded minibus last and ask [sic] the driver to speed towards the provincial Vietnamese hospital in Cu Chi, halfway to Saigon. 'I am thirsty, I am thirsty, I need water' Kim Phuc continued to cry. When the van moved Kim Phuc screamed out loud, obviously in great pain and then lost consciousness. Nick, beside her, tried to console her saying 'don't worry, we will reach hospital very soon.'

They reached the hospital within the hour. […]

Only when Kim Phuc was on the operating table did Nick Ut leave the hospital and head towards Saigon, to bring his film to the AP."

Horst Fass, Marianne Fulton, The Bigger Picture – Nick Ut recalls the Events of June 8, 1972; on: www.digitaljournalist.org/issue0008/ng2.htm [July 16, 2018].

Oral History

Historical events happen all the time. There are always people involved who witnessed special events or even took part in them. By questioning people new sources are created, which often reflect daily events, routines or atmospheres at a certain time. Usually there are only very few official written sources. Newspaper reports, books, TV news or even laws do not give historians any idea about how the people felt about a certain event.

Still there are quite a few dangers, which have to be kept in mind when dealing with eyewitnesses. Some witnesses might lie for different reasons. Often they want to present themselves in a better light, to keep personal failure secret or even to avoid prosecution.

Memories reported by eyewitnesses now and then are hard to prove, because there are no statistics or they are not defined facts in themselves. In addition to that they are subjective. Different people will always experience events from different prespectives and therefore their memories will differ.

The photograph of Kim Phuc (the "girl in the picture") taken during the Vietnam war shows us one instance of the war, that became known all around the world as a symbol of the horrors of war. It was taken 8 June 1972 by the young Associated Press photographer Nick Ut. He is still working for the AP today.

In the 1980s a Dutch film crew set out to find "the girl in the picture". When the Vietnamese government found her, she was used for propaganda purposes in the Soviet world to demonstrate how evil the USA and respectively capitalism were. On the flight back to Cuba, where Kim Phuc attended university, she and her husband stayed behind in Newfoundland. They were granted asylum in Canada, where she has lived since then.

M 4 Eyewitness Kim Phuc
Kim Phuc has founded the Kim Phuc Foundation to help children that are/were traumatized by war. She even became a "goodwill ambassador" for UNESCO. Photograph, about 2000

Historical Workshop

Analysing Eyewitness Reports

1. Describing the Reports
a. Name the person and the event that the person talks about (M2, M3).
b. Define the circumstances in which the report is given (M2, M3).
c. Say how much time lies between the report and the event (M2, M3).
d. Sum up the main points in your own words (M2, M3).

2. Analysing the Reports
a. Analyse the eyewitness' perspective: Was the eyewitness personally involved, did he/she watch an event, etc. (M2, M3)?
b. Examine which facts the eyewitness could not have known at the time of the event. List them (M2, M3).
c. Point out whether there are any facts that do not correspond with accepted historical facts (M2, M3).
d. Find out more about the background of the eyewitness (M2, M3).
e. Look at the content and the language of the eyewitness. Show what both say about him/her (M2, M3).
f. Find out in which context the eyewitness talks about an event (interview, memoirs, etc.).

3. Evaluating the Reports
a. Discuss whether the report is important for the understanding of a context (M2, M3).
b. Find arguments for or against the credibility of the eyewitness (M2, M3).
c. Compare several sources to get more than one perspective (M2, M3).

Vocabulary

to legitimize: to justify sth.

to exploit: to use sth. selfishly for one's own purposes

to decline: to become worse / go down

to lynch: to kill sb. without a trial

thaw: melting of ice

The Soviet Union and Eastern Europe 1955–69

Stalin had created a system which made many countries not only allies but dependants of the USSR. After Stalin's death and after West Germany became a member of NATO things developed differently in the Eastern Bloc. Many countries tried to find their own way.

The Warsaw Pact

The Warsaw Pact, officially known as the **Treaty of Friendship, Co-operation and Mutual Assistance**, was signed by the Soviet Union and its **satellite states** in May 1955, when West Germany joined NATO (North Atlantic Treaty Organisation). The pact not only countered the Western military alliance, it also gave the USSR a means of maintaining influence over the satellite states after the occupation of Eastern Europe ended. For example, it *legitimized* Soviet troops in Hungary and Romania, which otherwise would have had to be withdrawn.

In spite of the fact that Romania opposed and refused to participate in the invasion of Czechoslovakia in 1968, it still remained a member of the Warsaw Pact. East German membership ended with German unification in October 1990. Eight months later, on 30 June 1991, the remaining pact members dissolved the alliance themselves.

Poland and Hungary 1956 – two satellite states

After 1945 Stalin *exploited* the Soviet satellite states. East Germany had to pay reparations in food and goods to the USSR. The standard of living in all the satellite states such as Poland and Hungary steadily *declined*, while farm and factory employees worked harder for less income. The secret police controlled whole societies and were generally feared. In Hungary and in other satellite states many people were executed without trial after 1945.

Following Khrushchev's criticism of Stalinism in his secret speech to the 20th Congress of the **CPSU** (Communist Party of the Soviet Union) in February 1956, people in the satellite states hoped for higher standards of living, fewer economic restrictions and more political independence from the USSR.

In July 1956 a revolt against harsh living and working conditions began in Poland. It was settled when the Soviets granted relative independence to the Poles in domestic and economic policy.

The news spread to Hungary, where an angry crowd pulled down a statue of Stalin and dragged it through Budapest. When the protest grew, Soviet tanks rolled

M 1 Hungarian Revolt
Photograph, Budapest, November 1956

into the city. The Hungarian army backed the rebels, but the security police stayed loyal to the Soviets. Hundreds of policemen were *lynched* by crowds. Both sides battled for five days. When the Soviets realized they were not strong enough to crush the revolt, they retreated.

On 1 November 1956 Hungarians demanded far-reaching reforms, including the end of the one-party system and holding free elections. In addition, they demanded that Hungary leave the Warsaw Pact and become a neutral, independent country. The USSR could not tolerate these demands. Free elections could mean the end of Communism and the Iron Curtain, especially if other satellite states followed. Also, the buffer zone to the capitalistic West would disappear.

On 4 November 1956, Soviet tanks returned and crushed the Hungarian revolt in bitter street fighting. No country came to the rebels' aid, although the USA, for example, had supported the Hungarian revolt earlier. Several thousand people were killed. Nearly 200,000 fled to the West via Austria. The Hungarian Prime Minister Nagy was arrested and later shot. A new government loyal to the USSR was installed.

"Prague Spring" 1968 – an attempt at reforms

In the spring of 1968 the Czechoslovak Prime Minister Alexander Dubcek promised to improve living conditions and establish a better form of socialism, which he called "socialism with a human face". Therefore, he introduced freedom of the press to newspapers, radio and television. Freedom of religion and trade with the West were also part of the new policy. Although still a Communist, Dubcek proposed that the state exercise less control over people's lives. The Czechoslovak people gave Dubcek's government their full support. This reform of Czechoslovak socialism became known as the "Prague Spring".

The USSR distrusted the development, although the Czechoslovaks acted diplomatically and remained a loyal ally in the Warsaw Pact. Especially foreign policy was not changed, because people still remembered how Hungary had been crushed in 1956.

Brezhnev and other Socialist leaders warned Czechoslovakia not to make a "hole in the Iron Curtain". In the end Dubcek's "socialism with a human face" went too far for the other members of the Warsaw Pact. Especially freedom of the press was considered too dangerous. On 20 August 1968 Warsaw Pact forces from Poland, the USSR, and Hungary invaded Czechoslovakia.

The Czechoslovaks decided to resist only passively in order to prevent bloodshed. The passive resistance was organized via radio broadcasts. When the invaders took control, they arrested leading Czechoslovak politicians. The radio stations were found and shut down, breaking the resistance.

Dubcek and other leading politicians were taken to Moscow for discussions and then returned home. They announced measures to normalize the situation. Censorship was reintroduced and Soviet troops remained in Czechoslovakia to keep the country under control.

Reactions to the Prague Spring were manifold: the student Jan Palach protested by setting himself on fire in the centre of Prague; Dubcek resigned in the spring of 1969; China quickly condemned the Soviet invasion, revealing the poor relations between these two countries; the West watched in horror, but did nothing.

The Prague Spring occurred during a phase of improvement in relations between the USA and the USSR. The former knew that an intervention could ruin the *thaw* between the two superpowers and between the East and West in general.

Historical Terms

Treaty of Friendship, Cooperation and Mutual Assistance: Vertrag über Freundschaft, Zusammenarbeit und gegenseitigen Beistand

satellite states: Satellitenstaaten

CPSU: KPdSU, Kommunistische Partei der Sowjetunion

M 2 "Prague Spring"
Demonstrators opposing Soviet tanks. Photograph, Prague, 21 August 1968

The Soviet Union and Eastern Europe 1955–69

M 3 The Soviet Advance in Europe

M 4 US Evaluation of Eastern Europe

An excerpt from a US intelligence report, 1956:

"The elimination of Soviet domination of the satellites is […] in the fundamental interest of the United States […] One alternative is to take direct action for the liberation of the satellite peoples from the USSR by military force, either through direct military intervention or through armed support of revolutionary movements. Such use of military force would in all probability start a global war. This alternative is not in accordance with current US policy and must therefore be rejected […]
In its efforts to encourage anti-Soviet elements in the satellites and keep up their hopes, the United States should not encourage premature action on their part which will bring upon them reprisals involving further terror and suppression […]."

Annex to NSC 5608, 6 July 1956, quoted from: https://history.state.gov/historicaldocuments/frus1952-54v08/d51 [July 16, 2018].

M 5 "If you Hear a New … Voice …, Do not Believe it"

Radio announcements during the "Prague Spring":

"Citizens – go to work normally […] keep calm […] do not give the occupation forces any excuse for armed action […] show the invaders your scorn in silence. […] We do not know how long we will be able to broadcast. If you hear a new unknown voice on this station, do not believe it."

Quoted from: Peter Fisher, The Great Power Conflict after 1945, New York: Simon & Schuster 1985, p. 41.

M 6 Soviet Propaganda

Soviet propaganda to prepare the invading soldiers for their task:

"TASS [Soviet newsagency] is authorized to state that the leaders of the Czechoslovak Socialist Republic have asked the Sovjet Union and allied states to render the Czechoslovak people urgent assistance. This request was brought about by the threat which has arisen to the Socialist system, existing in Czechoslovakia."

TASS, August 21, 1968, quoted from: Peter Fisher, The Great Power Conflict after 1945, New York: Simon & Schuster 1985, p. 41.

M 7 The Brezhnev Doctrine, 1968

In a speech at the Fifth Congress of the United Polish Workers' Party on 13 November 1968, Soviet leader Leonid Brezhnev announced a new foreign policy for the Soviet Union. In the West, this policy was known as the Brezhnev Doctrine:

Socialist states stand for strict respect for the sovereignty of all countries. We resolutely oppose interference in the affairs of any states and the violation of their sovereignty. [...]
5 It is common knowledge that the Soviet Union has really done a good deal to strengthen the sovereignty and autonomy of the socialist countries. The CPSU [Communist Party of the Soviet Union] has always advocated that each socialist country determine the concrete forms of its
10 development along the path of socialism by taking into account the specific nature of their national conditions. But it is well known, comrades, that there are common natural laws of socialist construction, deviation from which could lead to deviation from socialism as such. And when external
15 and internal forces hostile to socialism try to turn the development of a given socialist country in the direction of restoration of the capitalist system, when a threat arises to the cause of socialism in that country – a threat to the security of the socialist commonwealth as a whole – this is
20 no longer merely a problem for that country's people, but a common problem, the concern of all socialist countries. It is quite clear that an action such as military assistance to a fraternal country to end a threat to the socialist system is an extraordinary measure, dictated by necessity; it can be called forth only by the overt actions of enemies of 25 socialism within the country and beyond its boundaries, actions that create a threat to the common interests of the socialist camp. [...]

The Current Digest of the Soviet Press (Columbus, Ohio, 1968); http://modernhistorian.blogspot.com/2008/11/on-this-day-in-history-brezhnev.html [30 Jan 2019].

M 8 "Say that you called me!"
West German caricature by Peter Leger on the Prague Spring, 1968

Tasks

1. **Superpowers as the Leading Forces**
   a) Describe the development in Eastern Europe (M3).
   b) Explain why the USA did not intervene in Hungary in 1956 (M4, text).
   c) Explain what it meant if an "unknown voice" was heard on the radio (M5)?
   d) Examine the reasons why the USSR intervened in such a harsh way (text, M6).
   e) Find out which countries were members of
      – the Warsaw Pact
      – NATO.
   e) Assess the TASS statement (M6).
2. **Satellite States – resistance and change**
   a) Find out about the resistance in other Eastern European countries (M3, research).
   c) Give your opinion: Is passive resistance a sensible measure against military action (M5)?
   d) Show when passive resistance has been successful in the past (research).
3. **The Brezhnev Doctrine**
   a) Summarize Brezhnev's speech (M7).
   b) Analyse the Brezhnev Doctrine and its effect on the Soviet satellite states.
4. **"Say that you called me!"**
   a) Describe the cartoon (M8).
   b) Comment on the cartoonist's view of the end of the Prague Spring.

Vocabulary

to launch: to start a major activity

détente: a situation in which formerly hostile countries become more friendly

setback: a problem that stops progress or makes a situation worse

Historical Terms

SALT (Strategic Arms Limitation Talks): Gespräche zur Begrenzung strategischer Waffen

Helsinki Accords: Schlussakte von Helsinki

glasnost: Offenheit, Transparenz

perestroika: Umbau

M 1 Mikhail Gorbachev (*2 March 1931) was the last leader of the USSR from 1985 until 1991. With his policies glasnost and perestroika he started major reforms in the Soviet Union that helped to end the Cold War and led to the end of the USSR. He was awarded the Nobel Peace Prize in 1990.

From Co-operation to the Collapse of Communist Europe

The Cold War is often described as a fever curve with ups and downs. From the early 1970s until the end of the Cold War there were many of these ups and downs that finally caused the fall of the USSR and the Iron Curtain. What factors played a part?

The 1970s – *détente* and *setbacks*

As a result of the development in the 1960s, the superpowers signed **SALT** I in 1972. In addition, the USA agreed to export grain to the Soviet Union and to improve cultural exchanges. In 1975 American and Soviet astronauts even worked together in space.

In 1975 the **Helsinki Accords**, an agreement to respect human rights and fundamental freedoms, was signed by 35 countries, including the USA and the USSR. While SALT talks continued, US President Jimmy Carter criticized the Soviet government for its treatment of dissidents and linked the talks on arms control to human rights. Shortly before the USA ratified SALT II in 1979, the Soviets invaded Afghanistan, claiming to support the new communist government there. President Carter replied with a boycott of the Olympic Games held in Moscow in 1980.

The 1980s – decade of change

After Ronald Reagan was elected President relations became frostier, because he openly admitted his intolerance of communism, even calling the USSR "the Empire of Evil". Reagan *launched* a new arms race in 1983, which became extremely expensive for both superpowers and was opposed in Europe and the USA. In 1986 the US president claimed that the USSR had violated the SALT II treaty and that the treaty therefore ended. The confrontation between the two superpowers became more pronounced again.

Change in the USSR

The new Soviet secretary-general, Mikhail Gorbachev, had to react to the economic problems of the USSR. In general, low living standards, poor wages, chronic shortages of goods and industrial inefficiency had become unbearable burdens. In particular, mismanagement, self-interest and privileges for the communist leaders were criticized within the Soviet bloc. Most Eastern European leaders put down opposition harshly. However, Gorbachev insisted that **glasnost** (making things public/transparent) and **perestroika** (rebuilding) would slowly start a process of reform within the Soviet sphere.

When iron-clad Communist structures began to crumble, other Eastern Europeans saw the opportunities for reform. In May 1989, Hungary, which had always remained closer to the West, started to remove security measures along the Austrian-Hungarian border. On 27 June 1989 a symbolic act opened the Iron Curtain: the foreign ministers of Austria and Hungary, Alois Mock and Gyula Horn, cut open the barbed wire in front of rolling cameras. In Leipzig East Germans began to demonstrate regularly on Mondays to demand reforms. This came after many East Germans who had spent the summer holiday in Hungary the same year used the opening of the security fence to flee across the border to Austria. In Poland, too, reformers came to power in August 1989 and won the first free elections in 1990.

Poland – an example of change

After the "Prague Spring" workers in Poland kept striking, because the economic situation was unbearable. They were organized in illegal trade unions. In 1980 the independent trade union Solidarność (solidarity) was founded, which criticized the Communist trade union. By 1981 it had about ten million members, which meant about a fourth of the Polish population. One of its leaders, Lech Wałęsa, was awarded the Nobel Peace Prize in 1983.

General Wojciech Jaruzelski imposed **martial law** in order to avoid an invasion of Soviet troops as had happened in all of the workers uprisings during the previous decades. Wałęsa and others were arrested and held prisoners, others were killed. Media were censored, schools and universities supervised, people's actions were observed secretly and industry was placed under military administration. Poland became isolated.

In 1983 martial law was lifted, but the atmosphere of distrust and repression lasted. Solidarność continued underground while the economic situation remained difficult. The development in Poland, on the other hand, showed that the USSR had lost power over the Eastern Bloc.

The Iron Curtain Falls

On 9 November 1989 the Berlin Wall came down between East and West Germany, finally lifting the Iron Curtain in Europe. At the same time in Czechoslovakia, Hungary and elsewhere democratic changes took place. Romania, one of the most repressive regimes, was overthrown and the former leader Ceausescu executed.

The Soviet Union, a multi-national empire, was powerless against national movements within its own borders. Provinces that had been forced into the Union strove for autonomy. By 1991 the basis of the USSR was threatened. The **Communist Secret Service**, the Soviet Army and conservatives wanted to keep the Union together by military force. Because Gorbachev accepted the various national claims to autonomy, Communist forces tried to overthrow him, but failed. During the attempted coup d'état Gorbachev was supported by Boris Yeltsin, who was the elected President of the new Russian Federation. On December 26, 1991 Gorbachev officially declared the end of the USSR and therefore his office was dissolved. By this act, Boris Yeltsin became the new leader of the **Commonwealth of Independent States** (CIS).

In the course of the disappearance of the Soviet Union, the Warsaw Pact dissolved as well. The new national governments pursued their own foreign policies.

M 2 Lech Wałęsa (*29 September 1943)
was born into a Catholic household. After primary school he went to a vocational school and became an electrician. In 1967 he began to work at the Lenin Shipyard in Gdansk. He got married in 1969 and has eight children. Very early on in his career he became involved in illegal strike committees and later he became the leading figure in the Solidarność movement for which he was awarded the Nobel Peace Prize. In 1990 he won the presidential elections and became the President of Poland for five years.

Historical Terms

martial law: Kriegsrecht
Communist Secret Service: Kommunistischer Geheimdienst, KGB
Commonwealth of Independent States (CIS): Gemeinschaft Unabhängiger Staaten (GUS)

M 3 First Meeting of Gorbachev and Reagan
Geneva, 19–21 November 1985, Photograph

Change in the USSR

M 4   End of the Warsaw Pact, 1991

News Report in "Keesings Contemporary Archives", February 1991:

"At a meeting of the political and consultative committee of the Warsaw Treaty Organization in Budapest on 25 February, foreign and defence ministers from Bulgaria, Czechoslovakia, Hungary, Poland, Romania and the Soviet Union unanimously approved and signed a protocol cancelling the validity of all military agreements, organs and structures of the Warsaw Treaty with effect from 31 March.

Moves to dissolve the military alliance, which were first apparent at a Warsaw Pact summit meeting in June 1990, were intensified after January 1991. They were followed by reports on 11 February that the Soviet President Mikhail Gorbachev had written to the leaders of member states recommending 'the liquidation of Warsaw Pact military structures by 1 April'.

A communiqué issued after the 25 February meeting said that the decision to dismantle the Treaty's military organization had been taken by 'member states […] acting as sovereign states with equal rights'. It noted that the 'elimination of Europe's dividedness [sic] offers a historical possiblity to attain a new quality in security relations' based on each state's 'freedom of choice'.

At a press conference attended by participants from all member states except the Soviet Union, Hungarian Foreign Minister Geza Jeszensky revealed that members had held 'different views' concerning the Treaty's political structures, which ministers had agreed to transform temporarily into a purely voluntary consultative organization. It was understood that while ministers from eastern European member states had been keen to dissolve the entire organization, preferably by the end of 1991, the Soviet delegation had expressed a preference for the continuation of a bloc as a counterpart to NATO, at least until the conclusion of the talks related to the Helsinki process."

News Report, Keesings Contemporary Archives, February 1991. http://keesings.com/index_new.php [July 17, 2018].

M 5   Coup d'état in Moscow

Boris Yeltsin (centre, with paper), President of the Russian Federation, in front of the Russian parliament building, standing on a tank. He is addressing the public, speaking against the rebel soldiers who had tried to take over power in Moscow. Photograph, Moscow, 19 August 1991.

M 6 Crowds Lay Siege to Party Offices

Report in "The Guardian", London, 24 August 1991:

"They streamed in from all directions. By mid-afternoon, thousands of exhilarated Russians had converged on Moscow's Staraya Ploshchad (Old Square), the headquarters of the Central Committee of the Communist Party. Brandishing the newly instituted Russian tricolour and chanting "Down with the Communist Party", they linked arms to form a human chain around the giant complex housing the Russian and Soviet Communist Party headquarters. The previous night, the complex had been sealed off by the transport police, when crowds of demonstrators, having succeeded in pressuring Mossoviet (Moscow local council) to remove the statue of Felix Dzherzhinsky, founder of the KGB, had then threatened to break in and take the secret party documents by force – inspired by the storming of Stasi headquarters in East Berlin.

But in the end yesterday's human chain was a peaceful attempt to stop Central Committee members and functionaries from entering to remove or destroy documents containing potentially incriminating evidence. In the old days the Central Committee archives were probably the most closely guarded in the country [...].

One man told me: "For four years they (the communists) have been blocking all attempts at reform. They have raised prices, they've provoked civil war in the republics and now they try to organise a fascist coup. We must make sure that all the documents are not destroyed, so that they can be prosecuted." [...]

Halfway through the afternoon van-loads of militia arrived to evacuate the remaining staff from the complex to applause from the demonstrators who knew once again the authorities had bowed to their demand. [...].

Another police car drew up and an officer announced that Mr Yeltsin had signed a decree, with Mr Gorbachev's blessing, confiscating the Central Committee building from the party and handing it over to the state. The crowd broke again into applause."

"The Guardian", London, 24 August 1991.

Tasks

1. **NATO vs. Warsaw Pact**
    a) Explain why the relationship between the USA and the USSR worsened in the 1980s (text).
    b) List reasons for the dissolving of the Warsaw Pact (M4).
    c) Describe the development of NATO until today (research).

2. **People Involved in World Politics**
    a) Find out about one of the following people and write a text for an "info box" on these people or report back to your class (research):
        – Ronald Reagan
        – Boris Yeltsin
        – Jimmy Carter.
    b) Lech Wałęsa had been politically active all his adult life. Some of his views are controversial, some not. Make a list of topics you agree with and with things you find difficult. Give reasons for your choice (research).
    c) After Michael Gorbachev handed over power to Boris Yeltsin he became "persona non grata" in Russian (research).
        – Make a timeline of his life after 1990
        – Explain why Gorbachev is highly respected in the West and despised in Russia.

3. **The World After 1990**
    a) Show how the author sees the demonstrators (M6).
    b) Point out the importance of the documents mentioned here (M6).
    c) Explain why a new Russian flag – the tricolor – was waved (M5, M6).
    d) Discuss whether Boris Yeltsin's actions mark the end of an era (M5, M6).
    e) Find out about the relations between Russia and the USA from 1990 until today (research).
    f) Pick one of the following former satellite states and present its development until today:
        – Poland
        – Hungary
        – Czechoslovakia
        – Romania.

214 SUMMARY Superpower Rivalry

| 1945 | 1950 | 1955 | 1960 | 1965 |

1945: End of World War II

1950: Korean War

1956: Uprising in Poland and Hungary

1962: Cuban Crisis

1968: "Prague Spring"

The East-West Conflict after 1949
- USA and allies
- Soviet Union and allies
- Communist states in Asia
- strategic US Navy fleets
- ★ Cold War conflicts

Superpower Rivalry – the historical map

1975   1980   1985   1990   1995

1975: Vietnam War   1985: Mikhail Gorbachev becomes leader of the USSR   1989: GDR opens wall

Summary

After the Potsdam Conference in 1945 it became clear that the ideologies of the Western Allies and the Soviet Union were so different that they could not be overcome. This clash of the systems led to proxy wars, the first in Korea in 1950.

North Korea, which attacked South Korea, was supported by the USSR, whereas the USA supported the South. In Korea the superpowers fought indirectly on the two Korean sides. Over the stationing of nuclear weapons on Cuba the superpowers threatened each other with nuclear attacks. The world was on the brink of destruction for thirteen days. When this crisis was over, both powers tried to live peacefully side by side.

In an attempt to contain communism from spreading, the USA later became involved in Vietnam, which turned into a disaster for the US military. Although there were many confrontations between the military alliances of NATO and the Warsaw Pact, there were also times when the superpowers agreed on disarmament and peace talks.

Within the Eastern Bloc there were also many attempts to find a national form of socialism. One was the "Prague Spring" in Czechoslovakia which was violently put down by Soviet military in 1968. In the USSR Gorbachev tried to reform socialism, which in addition to other national uprisings such as in Poland led to the collapse of the Soviet Union in 1991 and with it the Warsaw Pact.

DATES

1950–1953: Korean War
1956: Uprising in Poland and Hungary
1962: Cuban Crisis
1964–1975: Vietnam War
1968: "Prague Spring"
1989: GDR opens wall
1991: Collapse of USSR; end of Warsaw Pact

HISTORICAL TERMS

proxy war
containment
demarcation line
UN Security Council
arms race
Treaty of Friendship, Cooperation and Mutual Assistance
satellite states
CPSU
SALT
Helsinki Accords
glasnost
perestroika
martial law
Communist Secret Service
Commonwealth of Independent States (CIS)

PERSONS

Harry S. Truman
Bill Clinton
J. F. Kennedy
Nikita S. Khrushchev
Fidel A. Castro Ruz
Jimmy Carter
Ronald Reagan
Mikhail Gorbachev
Boris Yeltsin
Lech Wałęsa

HISTORY WORKSHOP

Oral History

06 21ST CENTURY CHALLENGES

People who remember the night of 9 November 1989, will remember it as a moment of change. With the opening of the Berlin Wall, the end of the Cold War had its date and its symbol. However, the years before and after saw more dramatic changes around the globe. New challenges have appeared.

In the decades since 1990, the USA and Russia have remained important: While the US saw itself as the sole remaining superpower, Russia's role and importance has been questioned. The consequences of this still shape today's politics.

Directly related is the question of radical "Islamism". This "clash of civilizations" has become obvious since the 9/11 attacks on New York and Washington in 2001.

Since 2010, political upheaval in Arab countries has led to civil war in some of them. With the breakdown of some of these states, refugees from there and from African countries migrating through northern Africa have created a "refugee crisis", as it has been called since 2015.

These and other 21st century challenges are presented in historical context in the following chapter. The topics can be dealt with separately, in no special order. They can be used as starting points for plenary discussions as well as for group presentations and research projects.

M 1 "Hope for a New Life"
Syrian refugee crossing the border from Serbia into Hungary. Photo by Warren Richardsen, 2015, World Press Photo 2016.

The USA and Russia – from cooperation to a new Cold War

The second half of the 20th century had been characterized by the rivalry of two great powers: the United States and the Soviet Union. At the end of the Cold War, both countries faced the task of reevaluating their roles in the world.

The End of the Soviet Union
The independence of the three Baltic states, Lithuania, Latvia and Estonia, was the beginning of the end of the Soviet Union. Many other regions followed and declared their independence between 1989 and 1991. In the summer of 1991, the Warsaw Pact was dissolved. The USSR collapsed and was officially disbanded at the end of 1991. The military system that had controlled Eastern Europe had ended. However, the Russian Federation has continued to be the dominant power in the region.

A New Policy of Strength
Mikhail Gorbachev, whose reform policies had made this change possible, lost all influence on Russian politics. Many saw in him a man of defeat. His successor, Boris Yeltsin, became an even more radical reformer at the beginning of the 1990s. Vast portions of the old Soviet economy were privatized and fell into the hands of so-called "oligarchs" – extremely wealthy businessmen who control large companies. Big oil companies, for example, changed ownership, often for a small amount. This transition process was not easy, and especially working-class people suffered hardships in the 1990s.

Economic Situation
The Russian economy is still to a large degree based on exports of raw materials, especially of oil and gas to Europe. Despite the enormous sums earned by these exports, there are huge social problems in the country between the super-rich and millions of Russians who live below the poverty line.

War in Chechnya
Under pressure from these economic problems, President Yeltsin increasingly turned towards nationalist positions. In order to prevent a break-up of the country, Yeltsin sent the army to the Caucasus republic of Chechnya in 1991 to prevent this Islamic region from becoming independent from Russia. In the first Chechen war between 1994 and 1996, probably about 100,000 people lost their lives. In 1999, the conflict broke out again and led to the complete destruction of Chechnya, with a loss of life comparable to the first Chechen war. Since 2009, the conflict has not been resolved and fighting has remained on a "low level". Djihadist fighters from Arab countries who joined the fight have complicated the Chechen conflict – and turned a nationalist struggle into a religious one. From Chechnya, terror has reached other parts of the world.

M 2　**Boris Yeltsin**
First President of the Russian Federation (1991–1999). Photograph, about 1995

The Relationship with the West
In the United States, in the meantime, there was a feeling of victory as the Cold War had been won. Western governments hoped to increase stability and security. Various treaties were signed to promote disarmament and cooperation.

However, things changed when some Eastern European countries wanted to join NATO. Russia was very opposed to it, but unable to prevent an expansion of the Western alliance. In 1999, Poland, the Czech Republic and Hungary joined. Five years later, the Baltic states and other Eastern European states followed.

Since the beginning of the 21st century, Russian foreign policy has aimed at limiting a growing US influence close to Russian borders. In 2003, for example, the USA prepared to attack Iraq without a UN mandate. Together with France and Germany, Russia was one of the main opponents of a war against Saddam Hussein. After NATO promised Georgia the chance to become a member in 2008, a short, but brutal war between Russia and Georgia made it clear that Russia would not allow NATO membership so close to Russia's borders.

Russia and the Ukraine Crisis

Since 2014, a crisis in the Ukraine has further complicated world politics. Located between Poland in the west and Russia in the east, two languages are spoken, Ukrainian and Russian. The western half of the country has close economic ties to the European Union, the eastern half with Russia. The corrupt government of the 90s was *ousted* in the so-called "Orange Revolution" in 2004, but new hopes were soon dashed. Here, too, the question of NATO membership, first discussed in 2008, triggered the crisis. It began with mass protests on the Maidan Square in Kiev in November 2013. People in the streets protested President Viktor Yanukovych's decision to stop membership talks with the EU and to resume close ties to Russia. When in February 2014 more than 70 people were killed by unidentified *snipers* in Kiev, President Yanukovych fled to Russia. The presidential election in May resulted in a majority for Petro Poroshenko, a pro-Western candidate.

After the Crimea had been occupied by Russian troops in February 2014, a different form of conflict arose in the eastern regions of the Ukraine. Bloody fighting between government troops and local, pro-Russian forces broke out in the Donetsk and Luhansk regions. While it is clear that these local rebels could not operate without some sort of Russian support, the exact nature of Russian (military) involvement in the eastern Ukraine remains a matter of dispute.

Vocabulary

to oust: to force sb. out of a position of power

sniper: sharpshooter, a fighter skilled in precision shooting

M 3 War in Ukraine
Soldiers of the Ukrainian army in the east of the country. Photograph, February 2015

The USA and Russia – from cooperation to a new Cold War

M 4 Putin's Address to the Nation (excerpts)

In a televised speech in 2005, Russian President Vladimir Putin set out his views on Russian politics:

"The collapse of the Soviet Union was the greatest geopolitical catastrophe of the century. And for the Russian people, it became a real drama. Tens of millions of our citizens and compatriots found themselves outside the
5 Russian Federation. [...]
Russia is a country that, at the will of its own people, chose democracy for itself. It set out on this course itself and, observing all generally accepted political norms, will decide for itself how it will ensure that the principles of
10 freedom and democracy are implemented, taking into account its historical, geopolitical and other characteristics. [...] Russia, connected as it is with the former republics of the USSR, connected as it is today with these independent states, by a single historical destiny, the Russian language
15 and a great culture, cannot stand aside from the general aspiration for freedom [...]:
We want the development of the economy and the strengthening of the international authority of the states that are our closest neighbours. We want to synchronise
20 the pace and parameters of reform processes in Russia and the **CIS states** [...].
International support in guaranteeing the rights of Russian compatriots abroad remains highly important to us. This is not a subject for political or diplomatic bargaining [...].
25 We count on the new Nato and EU members in the post-Soviet area to show real respect for human rights, including the rights of ethnic minorities. People do not have the right to demand observance of human rights by others if they themselves do not respect and observe human rights."

Translation quoted from: http://news.bbc.co.uk/2/hi/europe/4481455.stm [August 22, 2018].

M 5 "Careful, Hard to Digest!"
Cartoon by Jürgen Janson, Germany, 7 April 2014

Historical Terms

CIS – „Commonwealth of Independent States": an association of countries that were formerly part of the Soviet Union: Gemeinschaft Unabhängiger Staaten, GUS

Tasks

1. **Revision**
    a) Explain the relationship between Russia and the Soviet Union on the one hand and the West on the other throughout the 20th century.
    b) Explain the change in the role of the USA after the end of the Cold War.
    c) Comment on the statement: "The end of the Cold War made the international situation uncertain."
2. **Aggressive or defensive?**
    a) Analyse Vladimir Putin's speech (M4). Decide whether it is more aggressive or more defensive.
    b) Discuss whether political developments since 2005 can be explained by this speech (M4).
    c) In March 2014, US President Obama said in a press conference: "Russia is a regional power that is threatening some of its immediate neighbours, not out of strength but out of weakness." Explain this statement.
    d) Discuss whether this statement is justified.
    e) Write a press commentary for a Russian newspaper.
    f) Discuss: What makes a power a world power?
    g) Describe the cartoon (M5). Show how the Russian President Vladimir Putin is characterized.
    h) Explain the title of the cartoon (M5).

Islamism and the "War on Terror"

The creation of Israel in 1948 caused conflicts in the Near and Middle East. But most of the time, these conflicts were national conflicts about who controlled which territory. Social conflicts complicated matters: Since the 1950s, some countries in the region suddenly have become very rich through oil production. Additionally, local governments had to decide during the Cold War which side they were on: Saudi Arabia, for example, was pro-Western, Syria was pro-Soviet. Religion did not matter much, at least not publicly.

This changed dramatically in 1979, when the "Islamic Revolution" in Iran ousted the Shah, the pro-Western king. The new ruler was Ruhollah Khomeini, a Muslim cleric who had come back from exile in France. He established an "Islamic Republic" which was as clearly against the West as it was against Soviet Communism. Political opposition in Muslim countries now had a new role model.

The Soviet Union invaded Afghanistan in 1979. As a reaction, the US government paid and equipped local resistance fighters, the Mujahideen. Muslim countries like Saudi Arabia funded these fighters, too. A Saudi businessman, called Osama bin Laden, organized transports of weapons and money into Afghanistan. Young men taught the local people the form of Islam practiced in Saudi Arabia.

Throughout the 1990s, after the Afghan war had ended, these fighting groups expanded into a global movement. Some reappeared in the early 1990s in Bosnia and in Chechnya, while others participated in the civil war in Somalia. Increasingly, the US became the target of these groups. One of them was al-Qaeda, Osama bin Laden's group. Many of these radicals saw the large US military involvement in the Gulf region after the first Gulf War in 1991 as a step towards Western domination of Islam.

M 1 9/11
Dust cloud above Manhattan after the collapse of the World Trade Center. Photograph, 11 September 2001

11 September 2001

The day of 11 September 2001 has left a mark in the memory of contemporaries. According to the official results of the investigation, 19 terrorists, most of them from Saudi Arabia, hijacked four passenger aircraft to fly as bombs into symbolic buildings in the USA. In the attacks on the World Trade Center, the so-called Twin Towers and a third building collapsed, a further attack occurred on the Pentagon. More than 3000 people died. In the USA, this enormous attack was seen as an "act of war" against the country. Osama bin Laden's terrorist organization al-Qaeda was identified as responsible for the attacks.

War on Terror

A few days after September 11, American President George W. Bush spoke of a "war on terror" throughout the world. Within weeks, British and American air forces bombed al-Qaeda camps in Afghanistan. By December 2001, Western troops occupied Afghanistan. The radical Islamist regime of the Taliban ended.

Immediately after 11 September there was broad international solidarity with the US. The United Nations Security Council established the ISAF mission, a peace-building force deployed in Afghanistan. The German government decided to help the USA and participated in the Afghanistan mission. The mission continues even today: When this book was written, there were still German soldiers in Afghanistan.

The Iraq War

The broad international cooperation against Islamist terrorism was shortlived, however. The situation in Afghanistan was far from clear in 2002, when the US government started a second large-scale war, this time against Iraq. The USA claimed that the Iraqi dictator Saddam Hussein was in possession of weapons of mass destruction, for example poison gas, and that he had supported al-Qaeda terrorists. Both claims were wrong. In contrast to the war against the Taliban in Afghanistan, the international reaction was divided. Great Britain and many Eastern European countries supported the USA; but France, Germany, Russia and China were very critical. In March 2003, the invasion of Iraq started, and in May, President Bush announced victory. It soon became clear, however, that this triumph was too early; the country was by no means pacified. The Iraqi people did not see the Americans as liberators, but as occupiers. The US was unable to rebuild the country. Conflict among the different religious groups (Shiites, Sunnis and Kurds) intensified and in the following years thousands of people died from terrorist attacks.

Damaged Reputation for the US

As weapons of mass destruction never were found in Iraq, American foreign policy lost credibility. The „war on terror" should have been about universal values – such as freedom, human rights and democracy – but these values have been abused by the USA itself all too often. During the wars in Iraq and Afghanistan US agencies tortured and killed terror suspects. The moral authority of the US – an important basis of its leadership in 20th century world politics – thus suffered massive damage in the years after 9/11.

M 2 US Soldier in Iraq
US Marine Corps soldier on patrol in Fallujah. Photograph, October 2014

M 3 US Internment Camp in the Guantanamo Naval Base on Cuba
Photograph 2004

Islamism and the "War on Terror"

M 4 War on Terror

US President George W. Bush spoke on 20 September 2001 about the "war on terror" following the 9/11 attacks:

Tonight we are a country awakened to danger and called to defend freedom. Our grief has turned to anger, and anger to resolution. Whether we bring our enemies to justice, or bring justice to our enemies, justice will be done. [...] On
5 September the 11th, enemies of freedom committed an act of war against our country. Americans have known wars – but for the past 136 years, they have been wars on foreign soil, except for one Sunday in 1941. Americans have known the casualties of war – but not at the center of a great city
10 on a peaceful morning. Americans have known surprise attacks – but never before on thousands of civilians. All of this was brought upon us in a single day – and night fell on a different world, a world where freedom itself is under attack. Americans have many questions tonight. Americans
15 are asking: Who attacked our country? The evidence we have gathered all points to a collection of loosely affiliated terrorist organizations known as al Qaeda. [...] Al Qaeda is to terror what the mafia is to crime. But its goal is not making money; its goal is remaking the world – and
20 imposing its radical beliefs on people everywhere. The terrorists practice a *fringe* form of Islamic extremism that has been rejected by Muslim scholars and the vast majority of Muslim clerics – a fringe movement that perverts the peaceful teachings of Islam. The terrorists' directive
25 commands them to kill Christians and Jews, to kill all Americans, and make no distinction among military and civilians, including women and children. This group and its leader – a person named Osama bin Laden – are linked to many other organizations in different countries, including
30 the Egyptian Islamic Jihad and the Islamic Movement of Uzbekistan. There are thousands of these terrorists in more than 60 countries. They are recruited from their own nations and neighborhoods and brought to camps in places like Afghanistan, where they are trained in the tactics of
35 terror. They are sent back to their homes or sent to hide in countries around the world to plot evil and destruction.... Our war on terror begins with al Qaeda, but it does not end there. It will not end until every terrorist group of global reach has been found, stopped and defeated.

George W. Bush, Address to Joint Session of Congress Following 9/11 Attacks, delivered 20 September 2001; quoted from: http://www.americanrhetoric.com/speeches/gwbush911jointsessionspeech.htm [August 22, 2018].

M 5 "Mission Accomplished"
US President George W. Bush on the aircraft carrier USS Abraham Lincoln. At the time, he claimed that the war in Iraq was over. Photograph, 2 May 2003

Vocabulary

fringe: minor, less important

Tasks

1. **A Case for War?**
   a) Ask adults – parents, teachers, others – what they remember about 11 September 2001. Present your results.
   b) Analyse Bush's speech (M4). Show how the US President argues for a worldwide "war on terror".
   c) Discuss Bush's aim in the "war on terror".

2. **A Damaged Reputation?**
   a) In May 2003, US President George W. Bush proclaimed victory in Iraq with the words "mission accomplished" (M5). Comment on this statement.
   b) Analyse the two pictures (M2, M3).
   c) Assess the effect of these pictures on the image of the USA.

Refugees

People have always been on the move. Migration, also mass migration, has been a fact of life throughout history. For centuries, people have left their homes to search for a better life and to leave persecution, war and violence behind. It is instability that people want to escape from.

Migration in the Cold War Era

The Cold War period in Europe was a period of stability which especially in Germany lasted for a longer time. But even the Cold War era saw mass migrations. First, millions of Germans fled from the former German territories that had been given to Poland by the Allied victors of the war. Second, hundreds of thousands of people left the GDR. Then large numbers of "guest workers" from southern Europe came to Germany and other northern countries. The end of the British and French colonial empires brought many Europeans back to Europe, followed by migrants from Africa and Asia who came to work in Europe.

Civil War in Yugoslavia in the 1990s

Conflicts in Yugoslavia caused the first mass movement of a new type. Thousands of people – Croats, Serbs, and especially Bosnians – were forced to leave their homes. Many came to western and northern Europe looking for protection.

The "Arab Spring"

Northern Africa had a special dilemma. Until 2010, the Arab world was dominated by authoritarian, un-democratic and often corrupt regimes that ruled without participation of the population. On the other hand, these regimes blocked any illegal trans-Sahara traffic.

In December 2010, a Tunisian greengrocer set himself on fire because he no longer saw any perspective in his life. This event triggered protests in many Arab countries. Especially young people demanded political participation and future opportunities. Within a short time, the governments in Tunisia, Egypt, Libya and Yemen collapsed. Only Tunisia has survived these revolutions without further bloodshed. In Egypt, the revolution was very violent, and the protests in Yemen and Syria have turned into bloody wars.

The revolutionaries had diverse ideas for the political future of their countries, especially with regard to the role of religion. What looked like a democratic uprising in 2011 became a religiously motivated power struggle in the region. Iran, Turkey and Saudi Arabia are fighting for dominance in the Muslim world, whereas the roles of Russia and the USA as the old powers have been greatly diminished.

"Islamic State"

The "Islamic State" (IS) is a terrorist group that appeared in the Middle East in the early 2000s. The aim of this group was to abolish the "*Sykes-Picot*" borders to proclaim a caliphate ("an Islamic religious state"), including Syria, Iraq, Lebanon, Israel, Palestine and Jordan. The "Islamic State" has its origin in the Iraq War, where it carried out terrorist attacks in Iraq in 2004. The group then changed its focus to Syria. It took part in the Syrian civil war and publicized its extreme cruelty with the release of execution videos on the Internet.

M 1 Civil War in Syria
Photograph, Damascus, 2014

Info

Sykes-Picot
An agreement (officially called the Asia Minor Agreement) made in 1916 between the United Kingdom and France setting out spheres of interest in Southwestern Asia in case the Triple Entente defeated the Ottoman Empire in World War I. The Russian Empire also approved the terms of the agreement. The regions affected included Palestine, Jordan, parts of Turkey, Iraq, Syria, Lebanon, and Armenia.

21st Century Challenges

M 2 Border Fence
Building a border fence between Hungary and Serbia.
Photograph, Hungary, 2017

Refugee Crisis in 2015

Because of the civil wars in many Muslim states, the terror of the "Islamic state" and the lack of perspectives in other societies, the number of refugees has increased. There have never been so many people on the move in the world as in the 21st century.

In the summer of 2015, over 50 million people left their homes, about half of whom were young people. Of these, more than 16 million had to leave their countries as well. Most of these found refuge in the directly neighbouring country. According to the UN Refugee Agency, 86% of all refugees stayed in developing countries. Only a very small number of the refugees travelled to Europe to apply for asylum. The way to Europe is difficult, often dangerous and in part controlled by criminals. Thousands of refugees have died crossing the Mediterranean, when their overcrowded ships sank.

The growing number of refugees created a serious challenge for Europe. Some states like Poland and Hungary want only a few or no refugees and have closed their borders. Other states like Germany have taken in relatively large numbers of refugees. In 2015, Germans spoke of a new "welcoming culture". Many Germans wanted to help the refugees from Iraq, Afghanistan, Syria, Libya and other countries in Africa. Since then, however, the question of how to deal with this refugee crisis has divided not only German, but also many other European societies. Conservative politicians demand a strict limitation of the refugee flow; others continue to support and help people in need. Xenophobic movements have gained support in many countries.

When this book was written, the topic of migration remained a hot topic of debate.

M 3 "Welcome to Germany?"
Cartoon by Klaus Stuttmann, Germany, 7 September 2015

Tasks

1. **Refugees**
   a) Do some research on the migration of people in the 19th and 20th century. Refer back to this book.
   b) Describe the picture (M2). State your own opinion about these border fortifications.
   c) Interpret the cartoon (M3).

Energy and Climate Change

From coal and horse power to oil, electricity, and beyond – the 20th century has changed the way humans produce and use power like never before in history.

Long into the 20th century, the majority of humans on this planet lived with the energy nature provided – water power, firewood, and the muscle power of humans and animals. Only in small areas of industrialized production, coal was used to produce industrial goods. But even in Western Europe, people used wood to cook and to heat houses well after the Second World War.

Technological Revolutions

The most important aspect of 20th century energy innovations was that households were connected to a *grid*. As early as 1920, Soviet leader Lenin foresaw that electrification of the whole country was a necessary step into the future. This happened all over the world – first in the cities, and after the Second World War, also in the countryside. It occurred in the USA much earlier than in Europe, in other parts of the world even later. Electricity, phone and gas lines all connected individual homes, delivering energy and information to every house.

The mass use of the car changed the world even more. Before 1914, cars were toys for the rich. After 1918 it became clear that the car was the future. The technological advances of another war era made motorized individual traffic the new norm starting in the 1950s. Those who could afford a car owned one, and those who could not dreamt of owning one.

Petrol was cheap. In the 1950s, the USA was the largest producer of oil in the world, but as early as the 1960s, Arab countries produced more.

Oil became the basis for postwar industrial chemistry. Modern plastic culture is based on oil. We think we cannot live without it any more, but we have to do so, because all our natural resources have nearly come to an end.

M 1   Traffic in Lagos (Nigeria)
Photograph, 2003

Vocabulary

grid: network of electricity supply wires

M 2   Traffic in Beijing (China)
Photograph, 2012

21st Century Challenges

Two-faced Progress

For a long time, technological progress promised to make us independent from natural resources. Fossil fuels have nearly achieved this. Never before in history have so many people been warm, well fed, healthy and equipped with technology as today. But the downsides have become apparent as well. Nearly 200 years of unlimited growth have resulted in climate change. While the exact details of this process are still uncertain, the basic fact is clear. The glaciers are melting, sea levels rising. By burning fossil fuels humanity has started a gigantic change of the global climate. And those who are young at the beginning of the 21st century will see the results in their lifetimes.

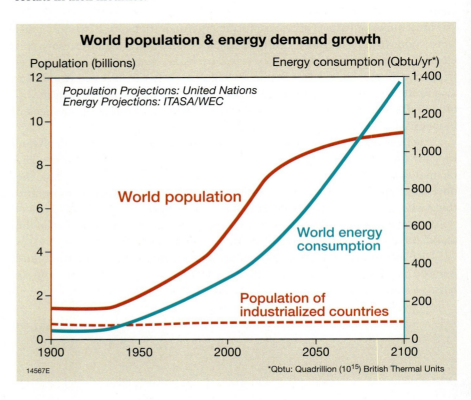

Tasks

1. **Energy and Climate Change**
   a) Illustrate the development of the use of electricity. Refer to illustrations in this book.
   b) Show how cars can be seen as symbols for industrial development. Refer to illustrations in this book.
   c) Analyse the chart. Put the developments into their historical context.
   d) Comment on the use of fossil fuels.
   e) Discuss how globalization and the use of fossil fuels are connected.
   f) Discuss the balance between global prosperity and the threat to the global environment.

Globalization

We all live on one planet – but only in the 20th century have people had the chance to experience this in their everyday lives.

War Brings Change

Before the First World War, Europe managed to influence events in other parts of the world, but the war changed the situation. It was the first time fighting took place all over the world, the first time soldiers from all continents fought on all continents. The USA showed its enormous economic and political power already in the 1920s. When this power failed, a Great Depression was the global result. After the Second World War, the Soviet Union, too, became a global player. Europe was no longer the centre of the world. The 1950s and 1960s brought a transport and communication revolution with jet aircraft, more international telephone communication, and satellite television. People all over the world came into closer contact. The 1964 Olympic Games in Tokyo were the first to be broadcast via TV satellite. The end of European colonial rule meant that countries in Africa and Asia wanted to be taken seriously. The majority of UN member states now were Asian and African. Suddenly, the whole world mattered – in a way it never had before.

M 1 Globalized Events
Live TV broadcast of the Football World Championship. Photograph, Yemen, 2014

The End of the Cold War Opens up Borders

Prior to 1990 Cold War alliances shaped world politics and the world economy. While Japanese industries had taken a lead in, e.g., consumer electronics, and played an enormous role in car manufacturing, the new situation after the end of the Cold War opened up chances for other countries. Since then countries like South Korea and especially China have become economic powers, selling their products, packed in containers, around the world.

The newly liberated economies of many countries also meant that companies could shake off government control and become powerful players in their own right. Investment in other countries and a globally interconnected economy became the norm, moving money and goods around the globe. But people were also on the move. Opened borders brought opportunities for many and mass migrations have become normal.

Into the 21st Century

The latest phase of globalization has brought new challenges for poor and rich countries alike. Since 1990, plain hunger has been reduced in large parts of Africa. On the other hand, an ever-widening gap between the "haves" in the global north and the "have-nots" in the global south has become ever more apparent – not in the least by a spread of information technology such as Internet communication. People all over the world can easily see where life is better. In some parts of the world, a rich nation directly borders a poor one, for example, where the US state of California borders Mexico. The consequence is the return of the border fortification, a military style fence.

M 2 Globalization
Cartoon by Fritz Alfred Behrendt, Germany

Tasks

1. **Globalisation**
   a) Illustrate how the US became a global power in the 20th century. Refer to relevant pages in this book.
   b) Illustrate how Europe lost its world power in the 20th century. Refer to relevant pages in this book.

21st Century Challenges

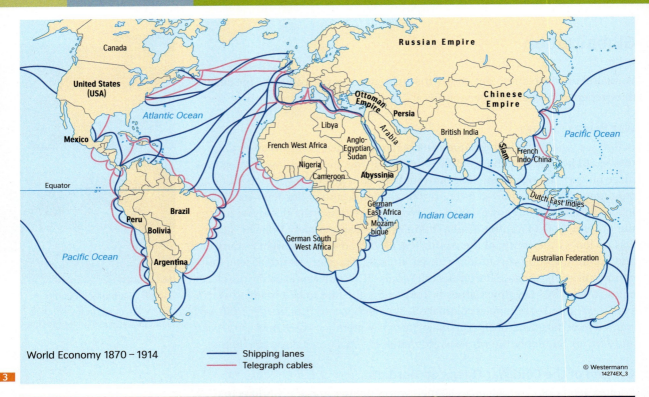

M 3 — World Economy 1870–1914. Shipping lanes. Telegraph cables.

M 4 — Air Traffic Between International Airports (2013). The colour red shows the heaviest traffic, followed by yellow etc.

Tasks

1. **Globalization**
   a) The 21st century: Check where the things in your life – clothing, electronic equipment, food – come from.
   b) Compare the two maps (M3, M4). Explain the "hot spots" and the "dark spots".
   c) Assess the consequences of the globalized economy.

What's Left?

The end of your book at the end of the school year is a good time to look back. History lessons have reached the present, the time when your parents were young.

A Short History of the 21st Century

A lot has happened since 2000, and even more since 1990.

Create a mind map to illustrate the most important developments of the 21st century. Use pages 216–228 in this book.

Do some research on how the topics presented in the last chapter have developed since the book was written.

Tua Res Agitur – it is your history

History is who we are and why we are the way we are.

"The past isn't dead. It isn't even past." (William Faulkner)

"History is written by the victors." (Winston Churchill)

"Not to know what happened before you were born is to remain forever a child." (Cicero)

"The more you know about the past, the better prepared you are for the future." (Theodore Roosevelt)

Choose one chapter in this book. Comment on the quotes – if you want, find better ones – in relation to your chapter.

Convince the others in your group that your topic is the most important in relation to your present.

Discuss the quotes in relation to the last 30 years.

The Second Decade of the 21st Century

Flying cars are still "the future"; there are still no cities on the ocean floor and no astronauts have flown to Mars. But, on the other hand, Europe hasn't seen a serious war since 1945 (apart from the Bosnian Civil War). More than seventy years of peace have brought stability and prosperity to large parts of the continent – and, to a lesser degree – on other continents as well. One hundred years ago, however, the First World War ended in 1918.

Plenary discussion: Discuss whether the 21st century had a better start than the 20th. Refer to the relevant pages of this book.

Inaction

Haile Selassie, then Emperor of Ethiopia, said about doing your share (1963):

"Throughout history, it has been the inaction of those who could have acted; the indifference of those who should have known better; the silence of the voice of justice when it mattered most; that has made it possible for evil to triumph." (Haile Selassie)

Discuss whether he was right. Refer to the history of the 20th century and to relevant passages in this book.

Allied Control Council: Founded in August 1945 as the supreme governmental instrument of the occupying powers in Germany. The Control Council consisted of the four commanders-in-chief of the occupying armies and represented the interests of the USA, the USSR, Great Britain and France. In addition to controlling functions, the council guaranteed uniform treatment of all issues affecting Germany as a whole. Due to increasing disagreement among the Allies (Cold War), the Control Council was unable to act and did not meet from March 1948 until September 1990, when it approved of German unification.

antisemitism: Prejudice, hostility, even hatred towards Jews. Term for racist ideas based on social, religious and ethnic prejudices. Antisemitism played a dominant role in the ideology of the National Socialists and became politically effective with their assumption of power in 1933. It led to the isolation of the Jewish population from political, economic and social life (Nuremberg Laws, 1935), intensified with the pogrom of 9–10 November ("Night of Broken Glass") and finally to systematic mass murder. The 1942 Wannsee Conference in Berlin decided the "Final Solution of the Jewish Question", resulting in the murder of six million Jews in concentration and death camps.

appeasement policy: Term referring to foreign policy concessions granted to Nazi Germany by Britain, especially by Chamberlain. The British Prime Minister gave in to German revisionist claims, because he hoped to avoid a war led by Hitler to achieve his goals (Sudeten Crisis, Munich Agreement, 1938). The policy was harshly criticized in some British circles and abandoned after the German invasion of Czechoslovakia in 1939.

Atlantic Charter: Declaration by Roosevelt and Churchill on board the HMS Prince of Wales in the Atlantic near Newfoundland (1941) on the principles of the future postwar order, including the right of national self-determination, renunciation of force, equality in world trade and the foundation of an international security system. The Atlantic Charter became the central document at the founding of the United Nations (UN).

Basic Law ("Grundgesetz"): The constitution of the Federal Republic of Germany (FRG) written by the Parliamentary Council ("Parlamentarischer Rat") and put into effect in 1949 was called the Basic Law. The term made it clear that the arrangement was only provisional, but necessary because of the division of Germany. The Basic Law stated that the duty of all Germans was to overcome the national division.

Basic Treaty: Treaty on the basis of the relations between the Federal Republic and the GDR in 1972. The Treaty accepted the sovereignty of the GDR for the first time and normalized the relations between both German states according to the goals of the new "Ostpolitik" of the Social-Liberal Coalition.

Berlin Blockade: Imposed on West Berlin by the Soviet occupying power (in response to Western currency reform), closing off all access roads on 24 June 1948. This Soviet attempt to get control over the whole of Berlin failed because of the resistance of the Western powers. They provided West Berlin with all necessary supplies via the Berlin Airlift ('Luftbrücke'); the Soviet blockade stopped on 12 May 1949.

Bolshevism, Bolsheviks (Russian = the majority): Name for the radical Social Democratic followers of Lenin who agreed with his revolutionary tactics at a party conference in 1903. Those who lost by this vote accepted the name of Mensheviks (= minority). According to Lenin's theory the revolution of the proletariat – the working class – must be carried out by a strictly organized hierarchical party, which will be the determining force to socialism and whose party functionaries must control all subordinate social groups. In the Soviet Union (SU) Stalin forced state and society to be reorganized according to Bolshevik principles which were adopted by all countries within the Soviet sphere of influence after 1945.

Brezhnev Doctrine: In 1968 troops of the Warsaw Pact led by the SU occupied Czechoslovakia to end the "Prague Spring" reform movement by force. To justify this invasion later, the Soviet General Secretary Brezhnev supported the theory that all countries within the socialist sphere of influence had only a restricted right of self-determination and that the Soviet Union had the right to intervene whenever socialism in a country was in danger.

claim to sole representation (Hallstein Doctrine): From 1955 onwards the FRG ("Bundesrepublik Deutschland", BRD") claimed it was the sole representative of Germany, as only the FRG had a legitimate government, elected in free elections. This principle of West German foreign policy was formulated by the state secretary Walter Hallstein. It included breaking off diplomatic relations with all states recognizing the GDR ("Deutsche Demokratische Republik", "DDR"). The new "Ostpolitik" of the Social-Liberal Coalition abandoned the Hallstein Doctrine in 1969.

coexistence: Khrushchev proclaimed the "peaceful coexistence" of states with differing social systems as a direction of Soviet foreign policy at the 20th Party Congress of the Communist Party of the Soviet Union. The conflict between socialism and capitalism would be decided along economic and social lines in future, but the ideological struggle was to continue. This policy led to a relaxation of tension in Soviet-American affairs.

Cold War: Term dealing with the political and ideological conflict between the USA and the Soviet Union after World War II. It was set in the global East-West conflict, in which the military blocs of NATO and the Warsaw Pact confronted each other. Due to the destructive power of nuclear weapons the super powers avoided direct military confrontation of each other. Instead each tried to weaken the position of the other through military alliances, infiltration, espionage and economic pressure. The conflicts of the Berlin Blockade (1948–49), the Korean War (1950–53) and the Cuban Crisis all led to the brink of a "hot" war. The Cold War calmed down through the efforts of détente after 1963, but was ended only when the Eastern bloc dissolved in 1989–90.

collective farm ("Landwirtschaftliche Produktionsgenossenschaft", "LPG"): The GDR collectivized agriculture on the model of the Soviet Union. Farms were usually consolidated into larger farms ("LPG") by force, fields were planted and harvested collectively.

collectivization: Turning means of production – especially agrarian private property – into cooperatively cultivated public property. The collectivization of Soviet agriculture occurred largely after 1927 under

Stalin und was mostly a violent form of forced collectivization. The type of farm established was called a kolkhoz. After 1945 the socialist Eastern bloc states also collectivized their agriculture, for example, in the GDR in the form of agricultural production cooperatives ("Landwirschaftliche Produktionsgenossenschaften", "LPG").

communism: Theory formulated by Marx and Engels in which a classless society in takes over private ownership of the means of production (factories, machinery) and converts it into public property. Communism begins with a proletarian revolution. The working class establishes a "dictatorship of the proletariat" and after a transitional phase of socialism, the communist society is gradually formed. In the 20th century the social form established following the 1917 October Revolution in the Soviet Union with its dictatorship of the Communist Party was called communism. The terms communism and socialism are often used as synonyms.

concentration camp: After assuming power in 1933 the National Socialists built concentration camps, at first to imprison political opponents, later to persecute victims of "racial" or religious groups in large numbers (in 1945 there were 715,000 camp prisoners). Camp prisoners were intimidated, eliminated and annihilated under the supervision of the SS. Forced labour, starvation, disease and sadistic torture killed many. As part of the so-called "Final Solution of the Jewish Question" the SS erected death camps in the conquered eastern areas from 1942 on. About six million Jews from all the occupied parts of Europe were murdered in the camps' gas chambers.

containment policy: After World War II the Soviet Union incorporated Eastern Europe into its sphere of influence and tried to affect neighbouring states. To hinder further expansion and the spread of Communism, the US adopted a policy of containment. It was expressed in the 1947 Truman Doctrine, which marks the beginning of the East-West conflict and the outbreak of the Cold War.

Council for Mutual Economic Assistance ("Rat für gegenseitige Wirtschaftshilfe", "RGW"): Also called COMECON. Organisation founded in 1949 by the USSR and 5 countries of the Eastern bloc in reaction to the Marshall Plan, which was rejected by the USSR. The GDR joined in 1950. Goal of the COMECON was the economic integration of the countries of the Eastern bloc within an international socialist division of labour, based on the co-ordination of the separate state economic plans. The sluggishness of the planned economies and the isolation of COMECON from the competition-oriented global economy prevented success. The collapse of the Eastern bloc and the acceptance of a market economy by the Eastern European countries led COMECON to dissolve in 1991.

decolonization: The breakup of colonial empires established since the 16th century in America, Africa and Asia. The process of decolonization was accelerated by World War II, as nearly all colonies reached the political freedom they desired in the years following it.

"degenerate art" ("entartete Kunst"): A Nazi expression to defame modern art, i.e. expressionism, surrealism, as non-German, subversive or Bolshevik. After 1933 there were exhibitions on "degenerate art" in many large cities – among these Munich in1937 – in order to denounce the works shown. Many artists emigrated or withdrew into private life to avoid being forbidden to work or exhibit. The measures against "degenerate art" were accepted because of a defensive attitude toward art based on ignorance and lack of understanding among many middle-class Germans.

de-Stalinization: After Stalin's death the 20th Party Conference of the Communist Party of the Soviet Union ("Kommunistische Partei der Sowjetunion", "KPdSU") rejected his methods of terror in 1956. In addition his personality cult was condemned and political victims of Stalin's dictatorship were rehabilitated. This de-Stalinization was initiated by Khrushchev, spread to other Eastern bloc countries and usually led to the removal of Stalinists. But the system of dictatorship and the dominant role of the Communist Party remained unchanged.

developing countries: Term for the countries of the Third World which – compared to industrial countries – have a low economic stage of development. Due to very low standards of living the population of these countries, which makes up three quarters of the world population, is threatened by hunger, poverty and disease. The problems have various causes: lack of industrialization, backward agriculture, rapid growth of population combined with malnutrition, debts to foreign countries, dependence on the industrial countries and their imports, low rates of literacy and low levels of education, lack of experts for the economy and administration. In addition, feudal upper classes prevent reforms in order to keep their political power. These countries usually export only a few agricultural products from monocultures and cheap raw materials.

disarmament: In the 20th century various attempts were made to reduce tension and secure peace by reducing military arms and placing them under international control. However, neither The Hague Peace Conferences (1899, 1907) nor the efforts of the League of Nations in the 1920s and 30s were successful. The nuclear stalemate ("mutual assured destruction") and fear of nuclear war between the USA and the Soviet Union brought about a change. The decisive breakthrough came with the Nuclear Non-proliferation Treaty (1968) and the Strategic Arms Limitation Talks agreement (1972). Real disarmament agreements came with the foreign policy changes in the USSR under Gorbachev. In 1987 the USA and the USSR agreed to destroy all medium and short-range missiles in the Intermediate-Range Nuclear Forces Treaty (INF).

dismantling: Taking industrial plants apart in a defeated country. The reparations demanded by the Allies from Germany after World War II led to the dismantling of German industry. One plan provided for the dismantling of 1,800 factories and a reduction in production to 50% of the pre-war level. With tension growing between East and West, the Western Allies partly reduced the dismantling in their zones in 1946 and abolished it in1951. However, in the Soviet zone dismantling was thorough and hindered post-war reconstruction considerably. Therefore, the starting position of the GDR was much more difficult than that of the FRG.

Eastern treaties ("Ostpolitik"): Term for various treaties concluded by the West German government under Chancellor Willy Brandt (SPD). These include the Moscow Treaty with the Soviet Union of 12 August 1970, the Warsaw Treaty with Poland of 7 December 1970, the Basic Treaty with East Germany of 21 December 1972, the Prague Treaty with Czechoslovakia of 11 December 1973. In these treaties the Federal Republic accepted the inviolability of the Polish western border and the sovereignty of the GDR, revoking the West German claim to act as the sole representative of all Germany. The Eastern treaties were hotly disputed between the Social-Liberal Coalition and the CDU/CSU, but led to a phase of détente.

emergency decree: According to Article 48 of the Weimar Constitution, if public security and order was endangered, the president was empowered to order the suspension of civil rights completely or partially. The measures decreed had to be rescinded on demand of the Reichstag, but the president could dissolve the parliament at any time, so that Article 48 practically assured him of dictatorial powers. During the final phase of the Weimar Republic (1930–33) emergency decrees became the main method of governing and made the totalitarian state of the National Socialists possible.

Enabling Act ("Ermächtigungsgesetz"): A law authorizing the government to enact laws or decrees without parliament. This abolishes the separation of powers (legislature, executive and judiciary) and endangers the democratic order. The Enabling Act of 24 March 1933 ("Law to Remedy the Distress of the People and the Nation") had catastrophic consequences. It transferred the complete authority of the state to the National Socialist government and thus established the basis of Nazi dictatorship.

European Union (EU): In 1957 the Federal Republic of Germany, France, Italy and the Benelux countries joined together to form the European Economic Community ("Europäische Wirtschaftsgemeinschaft", "EWG"). After its fusion with the European Coal and Steel Community ("Montanunion") and the European Atomic Community ("EURATOM") the European Community ("Europäische Gemeinschaft", "EG") came into existence in 1967; further European countries entered later. In 1992 the Treaty of Maastricht brought fundamental changes; numerous Eastern European countries joined later. The European Union (EU), as the union of the 28 countries is called now, set new goals: In addition to a duty-free European domestic market, a closer economic union and a European constitution, as well as common foreign, security and legal policy. Long-term goal is the complete fusion of the economies.

fascism (Lat. fasces = a bundle of rods carried as a symbol of authority for ancient Roman magistrates): Originally the term means the nationalistic, authoritarian, and leader dominated movement of Mussolini, who came to power in Italy in 1922. The term was soon applied to ring-wing movements in other states which had the same features: an anti-Marxist, anti-liberal and anti-democratic ideology with extreme nationalistic characteristics and imperial tendencies. The goal of fascism is a centralized state with the fascist party holding a monopoly of power over all public life. The state demands complete submission of its citizens, glorifies the people's community ("Volksgemeinschaft") and raises the leader to a mythical figure. Power is maintained by a brutal police and surveillance system, combined with the restriction of human rights and intense propaganda. The result of such a dictatorship is the "total state": loss of democratic freedom, terrorizing of dissidents, and isolation of ethnic and religious minorities. National Socialism is also a form of fascism.

"Final Solution of the Jewish Question" ("Endlösung"): In July 1941 Hitler ordered and Göring directed leading representatives of the German government and the SS to meet at the Wannsee Conference in Berlin on 20 January 1942. The measures approved there aimed at the annihilation of the European Jews through mass murder: "Cleansing" deported Jews from west to east into the occupied Eastern territories for "work detail" and above all for "appropriate treatment", that is, for death in specially built extermination camps. The Wannsee Conference set off the largest genocide in history, during which about 6 million Jews were murdered.

free market: An economic system which is not regulated by the state, but left to the free forces of the market. The type and amount of produced goods are determined by the demand for them, prices are set according to competition with other products. The principles of a free market are private property, freedom to exercise a trade and make contracts, free choice of profession and place of work, as well as free enterprise. The counter model of the free market is the planned economy. In a social market economy the state takes measures to correct negative effects of free enterprise on the population – regulating social policy, supervising competition and other appropriate measures, such as determining business cycle policy for economically underdeveloped regions or implementing economic steps to counter cyclical fluctuations. The goal of these measures is to achieve equitable income distribution, to protect underprivileged social groups and prevent unfair competitive from monopolies or cartels (Federal Cartel Agency, "Bundeskartellamt").

FRG: Federal Republic of Germany, West Germany ("Bundesrepublik Deutschland", "BRD"). On 7 October 1990, both German states were unified within the FRG.

GDR: German Democratic Republic, East Germany ("Deutsche Demokratische Republik", "DDR").

German-Soviet Non-aggression Pact: A treaty, also called the Hitler-Stalin Pact, signed in Moscow on 23 August 1939. Both countries promised each other neutrality in case of war. More important was a secret protocol, which defined both powers' spheres of interest in Eastern Europe and which should be realized "in case of territorial reorganization".

"Gleichschaltung" (literally: synchronizing of gears): The National Socialists aimed at organising all state organs and interest groups to conform with Nazi governmental policies and goals. The synchronisation laws of 1933 set the seats in the provincial parliaments at the same proportion as in the Reichstag, made the Nazi party the only political party, centralised state legislative and administrative functions, and placed the press and culture (theatre, film, literature) under the supervision of the Propaganda Ministry. Interest groups, for example, trade unions, were either dissolved or replaced by Nazi organizations.

Great Depression: At the end of the

1920s the economic data in the USA deteriorated. The causes were high surplus production, declining sales and a credit bubble. The situation was made worse by the destabilizing effects of reparation payments and the debts which the allies still owed the USA from World War I. On 24 October 1929 ("Black Thursday") the New York Stock Exchange crashed, causing a global economic crisis, the Great Depression. The social consequences of the depression contributed considerably to political radicalization and led to the rise of National Socialism in Germany. Mass unemployment and pauperization of wide circles of the population discredited not only the capitalist economic system, but also liberal democracy.

Hitler Youth ("Hitlerjugend", "HJ"): Term for the Nazi youth organization with its various subgroups. Founded in 1926 by the Nazi party, the Hitler Youth was converted into a far-reaching state youth organization after 1933. In 1936 the "Law on the Hitler Youth" determined that the organization was to educate youth beyond the home and school in the spirit of National Socialism. In 1939 service in the Hitler Youth was required and declared to be a "service of honour to the German people". The Hitler Youth included the League of German Maidens ("Bund Deutscher Mädel", "BDM"), the German Young People ("Deutsches Jungvolk", "DJ") for ten to fourteen-year-old boys and the Young Maidens ("Jungmädelbund", "JM") for girls of the same age.

Kapp-Putsch: Attempt of right-wing politician Wolfgang Kapp and dissatisfied military circles around General Lüttwitz to overthrow the Weimar government. On 13 March 1920 a naval brigade occupied the Berlin governmental district and proclaimed Kapp Chancellor. The coup d'état failed after a few days when the army and civil service refused their support.

Locarno Treaty: A treaty signed on 16 October 1925 by France, Great Britain, Italy and Germany explicitly recognizing the Treaty of Versailles and confirming the inviolability of the western German border. The treaty ended German diplomatic isolation, led to German admission to the League of Nations and a phase of détente in Europe. German Foreign Minister Gustav Stresemann and his French colleague Aristide Briand were responsible for the success of the Conference of Locarno.

Marshall Plan: A "European Recovery Plan" suggested by American Secretary of State George Marshall in 1947 to direct economic aid to war-torn Europe. The funds which were sent to Western Europe included raw materials, machinery, food supplies as well as credit and formed the basis of a new beginning. Under pressure from the Soviet Union the Eastern European states refused to join the Marshall Plan and established the COMECON ("Rat für gegenseitige Wirtschaftshilfe", "RGW") under Soviet leadership in 1949.

Munich Agreement: Agreement reached among the leaders of Great Britain (Chamberlain), France (Daladier), Italy (Mussolini) and Germany (Hitler) at the Munich Conference on 29 September 1938. The Munich Agreement ceded the ethnically German Sudetenland to the German Empire from Czechoslovakia, which was not even consulted on the issue.

National Socialism (Nazism): After World War I a German extreme right-wing movement which pursued nationalistic, expansive and anti-democratic goals. National Socialism is a German type of fascism which exceeds fascist ideology by its particularly radical ideas, such as prevalent racism, extreme antisemitism and mythical exaggeration of the Aryan-Nordic master race. After assuming power in 1933 the National Socialists established a dictatorship under their "leader" Adolf Hitler. The system was based on terror and surveillance, imprisoned opponents and minorities in concentration camps and led Germany to destruction in World War II.

NATO (North Atlantic Treaty Organization, North Atlantic Pact): Faced with the expansion of Communism under the Soviet Union, twelve European and North American states formed a military alliance in NATO in 1949. Today the US-led alliance consists of twenty-six states. The Federal Republic of Germany joined in 1955; France seceded from military integration in 1966, considering it incompatible with French sovereignty. NATO proved decisive in stabilizing Western Europe during the East-West conflict. After the dissolution of the Eastern bloc in 1989-90 the alliance tried to redefine its goals. Since then several former Eastern European states have joined NATO.

"Night of Broken Glass" ("Reichskristall-nacht"/"Reichspogromnacht"): A pogrom initiated by the National Socialists against the Jewish population in the German Reich. It introduced a new phase in the persecution of Jews. During the night of 9 to 10 November 1938 National Socialist gangs destroyed about 7,000 Jewish shops, set synagogues on fire and demolished flats, schools and businesses. In the course of the night many Jews were abused or killed, more than 30,000 were put under "protective arrest" without any legal grounds in order to force them to emigrate ("Nuremberg Laws", "Final Solution of the Jewish Question").

November revolution: Uprisings in Germany in November 1918 which ended the monarchy and led to the introduction of a parliamentary republic. The causes were the military defeat in World War I, long-term refusal to institute domestic reforms and economic collapse. Mutinying sailors and revolting workers in Kiel and Wilhelmshaven set off the revolution, which quickly spread to the larger cities. The bearers of the revolt were the spontaneously formed workers' and soldiers' councils which formed a Council of People's Representatives ("Rat der Volksbeauftragten") to act as a national government on 10 November 1918. The conflict of whether the revolution should point towards a soviet system or towards a parliamentary national assembly was decided in favour of the parliamentary solution at the All-German Assembly of Councils in December 1918. While the Social Democratic Party (SPD) approved of this decision, sections of the Independent Social Democrats (USPD) and the Spartacus group preferred a soviet system. Elections to the National Assembly on 19 January 1919 opened the path to the founding of the Weimar Republic.

Nuremberg Laws: After assuming power the National Socialists began to exclude the Jewish population through discriminatory laws. The "Law to Restore the Professional Civil Service" in 1933 excluded all German Jews from civil service jobs. Increasingly Jews were removed from economic and public life. In 1935 the Nazi racial laws reached a climax in the Nuremberg Laws: Essential civil rights were abolished for Jews, reducing them to inferior status as citizens; marriages and sexual relations between Germans and Jews were forbidden as "racial defilement" ("Rassenschande") and punished by imprisonment. Legal discrimination was followed by social isolation, both of which led to genocide for the Jews ("Final Solution", antisemitism).

Occupation Statute: Together with the founding of the FRG in 1949, the three Western powers issued the Occupation Statute. The FRG was given essential sovereign rights, but the Western powers reserved representation in foreign affairs and controlling rights for themselves. The interests of the Western Allies were attended to by a High Commission with three high commissioners. The Paris Treaties finally abolished the Statute in 1955, but the Allies kept certain rights in Berlin as well as emergency powers.

occupation zones: According to an agreement of 5 June 1945, Germany was divided into four zones of occupation administered by each of the four Allied powers. Berlin was divided into four sectors.

October Revolution: Bolshevik revolution in Russia on 25 October 1917 (according to the Western calendar on 7 November 1917), which led to violent social and political change. The economic and military collapse of the Russian Empire during World War I determined the conditions for the revolution. Bolshevik troops and workers' militias occupied the most important buildings in St. Petersburg and stormed the seat of government. Under Lenin's leadership the "Council of People's Commissars" took over the government, which was supported by farmers and soldiers. Immediate decrees expropriated property from large landowners and distributed it to farmers, nationalized banks and industry, eliminated freedom of the press and prepared the peace treaty with the Axis powers.

Oder-Neisse Line: The line of demarcation between Germany and Poland, set at the Potsdam Conference of the victorious Allies of World War II (USA, Soviet Union, Great Britain) in 1945. All German territories east of this line, which followed the Oder and Lausitz Neisse Rivers, fell under Polish administration. The Oder-Neisse Line was a temporary arrangement to be finalized in a peace treaty. It became the internationally binding border in the Treaty on German Sovereignty of 12 September 1990.

Parliamentary Council: A council assembled on 1 Sept 1948 in Bonn on command of the Western Allies to write a constitution for the provinces ("Länder") of the Western German occupied zones. The council consisted of 65 members, who were delegates of the 11 provinces. Konrad Adenauer (CDU) was elected its first president. On 8 May 1949 the council approved the "Basic Law for the Federal Republic of Germany", which was officially announced in a ceremony on 23 May 1949.

people's community: In Nazi-ideology the "fatefully bound people's community" ("Volksgemeinschaft") was constantly called upon to get people to stand above class distinctions and to subordinate themselves to the "Führer". Because Nazis decided who was a member of this people's community, it became a means to isolate minorities and to stigmatize political opponents.

people's democracy: Term for communist ruling system, established mainly in the Eastern European countries within the Soviet sphere of influence after 1945. While the organs of a parliamentary democracy seemed to remain, the Communist Party actually ruled, determining the entire social and economic life. Characteristics of a people's democracy are collectivization of capital goods (planned economy) and the monopoly of power in the hands of the Communist Party, to which several bloc parties are subordinate (single list of candidates). According to Marxist-Leninist theory, the people's democracy ensures the transition from capitalism to socialism.

planned/command economy: Name of an economic system in which the state commands and controls the entire economy. Production, distribution of goods and regulation of prices follow a common plan, the fulfilment of which is supervised by a central agency. Competition and free forces of the market to regulate supply and demand are not part of this system. The command economy – also centralized planned economy – is found foremost in socialist states. The counter model is a market economy.

Potsdam Conference: Meeting of the heads of states of the victorious Allies from 17 July to 2 August 1945 in Potsdam to consider the "German Question" after World War II. Truman (USA), Stalin (USSR) and Churchill (Great Britain) made important decisions, which were expressed in the Potsdam Agreement of 2 August 1945: Establishment of an Allied Control Council, demilitarization, denazification, prosecution of war criminals, payment of reparations, transfer of the administration in the territories to the east of the Oder-Neisse Line to Poland and northern East Prussia to the USSR, expulsion of ethnic Germans from the eastern territories, transforming the economy, establishing German local administration according to democratic principles. The agreements of the Potsdam Conference determined the policy on Germany after 1945, but their importance in many fields faded with the subsequent outbreak of the Cold War and the founding of the two German states.

rollback policy: The American Secretary of State J. F. Dulles designed a concept in 1950 which rejected containment in favour of active power politics. On the basis of its nuclear superiority the USA was supposed to roll back the USSR and liberate the countries that had come under Communist rule. The risk of a new war was accepted. In contrast to his proposed policy, Dulles carefully maintained the status quo during the revolt in the GDR (1953) as well as during the Hungarian and Suez Crises (1956).

socialism: A political movement from the 19th century that intends to overthrow the existing social order to create a socially fair and equal society. The change will occur through the conversion of the means of production into public property, the introduction of a planned economy and the abolition of class distinctions. Since the end of the 19th century more moderate and radical socialist movements formed, whose goals varied from reforming the capitalist economic system to overthrowing this social order entirely. After 1945 a distinction is made between real socialism, as found in the countries of the Eastern bloc, and democratic socialism, as practised in Social Democratic and Socialist Parties in the Western world. In Marxist theory socialism is the transition from capitalism to communism.

soviet republic: Form of government which ensures the direct political participation of underprivileged parts of society (i.e. workers, farmers, soldiers). Elected delegates form a soviet (Russ. = council), which makes all decisions and combines executive, legislative and judicative powers. Therefore there is no longer any separation of powers. The soviets are directly responsible to their voters and can be dismissed at any time. The soviet system is therefore a counter model to a parliamentary democracy. In Russia soviets formed spontaneously in 1905 and during the October Revolution in 1917. They became the instruments of power for the Communist Party. In 1917 the Russian Socialist Federation of Soviet Republics was founded. In 1922 the Union of Socialist Soviet Republics (USSR) was constituted. Since then the soviet system (soviet republic) was the basis for the state organisation, headed by the Supreme Soviet. This parliament was elected every four years; however, the people could only agree to the candidates of the Communist Party and the delegates of the organizations ruled by the Communist Party.

"Stab in the back" myth: After the First World War German nationalists maintained that neither the German army nor the Imperial leadership was responsible for the German defeat, but socialists and democratic politicians. This propaganda helped nationalistic and anti-democratic forces to defame the Weimar Republic.

Stalinism: System of government imposed by Stalin using violence and terror from 1927 to 1953. Stalin proposed the theory of "socialism in one country" to advance industrialization and eliminate the remains of capitalism by a harsh class struggle. The result was a cruel regime of terror, which achieved its goals by propaganda trials, liquidations, deportations and purges, whereas Stalin enjoyed a distinct cult of personality. The 20th Party Conference of the Communist Party of the Soviet Union condemned the terrorist elements of Stalinism in 1956 (de-Stalinization).

Third World: Term for economically and socially underdeveloped countries in Africa, Asia and Latin America. The classification originated in 1945, when the highly developed capitalist industrial countries in the West were called the "First World" and the countries of the once communist Soviet bloc were termed the "Second World". For the underdeveloped countries of the Third World, the expression "developing countries" is more common.

Treaty of Maastricht: The "Treaty on the European Union" signed in Maastricht and effective on 26 June 1993 fundamentally amended the previous European Community (EC). Besides the finalization of a duty-free European single market it envisions intensive European integration to be achieved by the following means: Establishment of an economic and monetary union (already in force), common foreign and security policies, cooperation in domestic and legal policies as well as in environmental and social policies. The long-term goal is economic and political integration, but the final form is still controversial.

Truman Doctrine: Foreign policy principle of the USA during the Cold War, formulated in a speech given to Congress by the American President Harry S. Truman (1945–1952) on 12 March 1947. Regarding the Soviet policy of expansion, the USA promised "to support free peoples who are resisting attempted subjugation by armed minorities or by outside pressures". This US policy of containment was to be accompanied with massive military and economic aid to prevent a Communist infiltration of the Western world.

United Nations (UN): Fifty-one nations founded the UN based on the Atlantic Charter in San Francisco on 26 June 1945. The organization is to secure world peace and insure the respect of human rights. The UN has five main organs: The General Assembly as the central advising authority, which consists of representatives of the member states. It elects the non-permanent members of the Security Council, the members of the Economic and Social Council as well as the Secretary-General. Its decisions are recommendations. The Security Council decides on measures to secure peace. It includes five permanent members with a right of veto (USA, Russia, China, Great Britain, France) as well as ten non-permanent members. Other organs are the Economic and Social Council, the International Court of Justice in The Hague, and the Secretary-General as executive authority. Several special organizations deal with additional tasks for the UN, especially in the fields of foreign aid, education, culture and health.

Warsaw Pact: Military alliance founded in Warsaw in 1955. It consisted of seven Eastern bloc countries led by the USSR. Albania left the alliance in 1968. The pact was founded as a reaction to West German admittance to NATO (North Atlantic Treaty Organisation). Both military blocs influenced the global East-West conflict for a long time. The Warsaw Pact soon proved to be a Soviet instrument of power, when the 1956 rebellion in Hungary was put down. In 1968 troops of the Warsaw Pact invaded Czechoslovakia and ended the reforms of the "Prague Spring". German unification in 1990 caused the GDR to leave the pact, which subsequently dissolved with the collapse of the Eastern bloc in 1991.

Weimar Republic: An era in German history from 1919 to 1933, named after the first city where the constituent National Assembly met in 1919. The November Revolution of 1918, which led to the collapse of the German Empire, marked the beginning of the Weimar Republic. The Weimar constitution, which was passed by the National Assembly in 1919, replaced the monarchy by a parliamentary republic. It lasted until 1933, when it fell victim to the Nazi dictatorship. Despite economic hardship and political opposition, the Weimar Republic gave rise to important cultural achievements, which prospered free from the governmental paternalism of the Imperial era.

INDEX

1968 movement 147 ff., 157
9/11 attacks 216, 220 ff.

Adenauer, Konrad 119, 122, 129, 132 ff., 136 f., 140, 180, 189
Afghanistan 164, 210, 220 ff., 224
Agent Orange 200 f.
air raids 73 f., 77 ff., 80, 82, 86 f., 192, 197, 200 f., 203 f., 220
All-German Assembly of Councils (Allgemeiner Kongress der Arbeiter- und Soldatenräte) 9
Allied Control Council 112, 118, 128, 134
Allies 7 f., 14 f., 45, 74, 76, 90, 94, 101, 103 f., 112, 114, 118 f., 121, 129, 132, 134, 144, 146, 191 f.
al-Qaeda 220 ff.
americanization 136 f.
annexation 69 f., 73, 108
"Anschluss" of Austria 69
anti-Communism 49, 75, 81, 146 f., 166
anti-Fascism 61, 73
anti-Hitler coalition 76
anti-Semitism 48 f., 88
APO, Außerparlamentarische Opposition see extra-parliamentary opposition
appeasement 69 – 72
Arab Spring 223
armistice 8 f., 45, 48, 193
arms race 196, 210
Art Deco 31
"aryanization" 89
Assembly of Councils 9
atomic bomb 77 ff., 104, 164, 173, 191 ff., 196 ff., 215
atomic energy 157 f., 164 f., 180 f.
Attlee, Clement 112
Auschwitz 46, 90 ff., 100
austerity measures 34 f., 38
autarky 65
Autobahn 65
Axis Powers 68, 70, 74 ff.

Baden, Max von 8 ff., 45
Bahr, Egon 152, 154, 160
Balkans 75, 93
Basic Law 121 ff., 125, 136, 146 f., 173
Basic Treaty 153, 160, 166
Battle
■ of Britain 74
■ of the Somme 87
■ of Stalingrad 76, 96
■ of Verdun 166
Bauhaus 31
BDM, "Bund Deutscher Mädel" ("League of German Maidens") 60 ff.
Beer Hall Putsch 24, 26, 49
Berlin Blockade 103, 118 – 121, 129
Berlin Wall 98, 123, 127, 130, 144 f., 149, 160, 169, 172, 174, 176, 189, 211, 216
bin Laden, Osama 220, 222
Bismarck, Otto von 11, 70, 178
Bizone 115, 119
Black Friday 34

"Blitzkrieg" ("lightning war") 74 f.
Bloody Sunday 39
Bolsheviks, Bolshevism 8 f., 73, 75, 84, 88
bombardments see air raids
Bonhoeffer, Dietrich 94
Bosnia 220, 223, 229
boycott 9, 20, 88, 164, 210
Brandenburg Gate 8, 127
Brandt, Willy 130, 146 f., 152 – 156, 189
Brecht, Bertolt 33
Brest-Litovsk see Treaty of Brest-Litovsk
Brexit 186 f.
Brezhnev, Leonid Ilyich 207
Briand, Aristide 28 f., 45, 180
Brüning, Heinrich 34 f., 38 f., 41, 45
Bundestag 98, 110, 122, 125, 146, 152 f.
Bundeswehr 132
bureaucracy 162, 182, 208
Bush, George H. W. 174, 201
Bush, George W. 220 ff.

Cameron, David 186
capitulation see surrender
Carter, Jimmy 201, 210
Casablanca see Conference of Casablanca
Castro Ruz, Fidel 196 ff.
Catholic Church, Catholicism 88, 94, 211
CDU, Christlich Demokratische Union Deutschlands (Christian Democratic Union of Germany) 110, 122, 132, 137, 146 f., 152 f., 164 f., 168, 172, 176
Centre Party see Zentrum
Chamberlain, Arthur Neville 69 f., 72 f.
Chechnya 218, 220
Chernobyl 164 f.
child labour 34
China 169 f., 192 ff., 200, 207, 221, 225, 227
Chomeini, Ruhollah 220
Churchill, Winston 72 f., 74, 87, 102, 104, 112, 115, 180 f., 229
cinema 30, 47, 56, 126 f., 137
CIS, Commonwealth of Independent States see Russia
civil rights 20, 22, 101, 121, 146, 157, 176
civil war 39, 45, 126, 186, 216, 220, 223 f., 229
Clemenceau, Georges 14, 16
climate change 225 f.
Clinton, Bill 195
Club of Rome 156
co-existence 156
Cold War 47, 103 ff., 113, 123, 127 f., 132, 144, 164, 166, 169, 183 f., 186, 189, 191 f., 195 f., 210, 214, 216 – 220, 223, 227
collapse 7, 34, 38, 42 f., 106, 123, 154, 168, 173, 174, 183, 185, 189, 191, 215, 217, 219, 223
collectivization 122, 133, 140, 150, 160
colonialism 15, 45, 50, 146, 182, 186, 223, 227
Comintern 123
Commonwealth 181, 211
Communism, Communists 9, 12, 24,

38 ff., 52 f., 75, 94, 104, 115, 122, 140, 154, 168 f., 191 f., 200, 202, 206 f., 210
Communist Party of Germany see KPD
concentration camps 53, 56, 59, 81, 88, 90, 92, 101, 103
Conference
■ of Casablanca 112
■ of Geneva 200
■ of Helsinki (C. on Security and Cooperation in Europe) 156, 210, 212
■ of Locarno 28, 45, 73
■ of London (Six-Power C.) 112, 118, 121
■ of Munich 68, 70, 72 f.
■ of Potsdam 78, 102 f., 107, 112 f., 215 f., 118, 129, 152, 215
■ of Tehran 112
■ of Versailles see Treaty of Versailles
■ at the Wannsee 89, 101
■ of Yalta 107, 112
Constituent Assembly 8 f., 11, 121
constitution 7, 20 ff., 35, 38, 45, 52 ff., 94, 101, 121 – 125, 147, 156, 171 f.
containment 114 f., 192
Control Council see Allied Control Council
Council of People's Representatives 9
Council of Workers and Soldiers (Arbeiter- und Soldatenrat) 8 ff.
counter revolution 171, 208
coup d'état 23 f., 26, 48, 211
Coventry 46, 74, 80
crisis 23 f., 26, 35, 38, 40, 43, 69 f., 88, 107, 117, 120, 153, 156, 168, 170, 185, 189, 191, 196 ff., 216, 218, 224
CSCE, Conference on Security and Co-operation in Europe see Conference of Helsinki
Cuba, Cuban Missile Crisis 146, 191, 196 – 199, 205, 215
Cuno, Wilhelm 24
currency reform 24, 115, 118, 121, 184 f.
Czechoslovakia 69 f., 72, 150, 170, 206 – 209, 211 f., 215

DAF, "Deutsche Arbeitsfront" ("German Labour Front") 53, 57, 101
Dawes, Charles (Dawes Plan) 28
"Day of Potsdam" 52, 55
DDP, Deutsche Demokratische Partei (German Democratic Party) 24, 38, 41
"Decree for the Protection of People and State" 52, 54
demilitarization 15, 19, 45, 69, 113, 193
democracy 7 – 10, 22 f., 38 f., 42 f., 53, 56, 79, 93, 101, 113, 122, 124, 147, 170, 182, 184, 208, 211 f., 221, 223
demonstrations 9, 12, 14, 43, 140 f., 143, 146 – 149, 164, 169 – 172, 186, 193, 207
denazification 113
deportation 81, 90
depression see Great Depression
détente 147, 164, 166, 183, 210
dictatorship 43, 47 f., 52 ff., 56 f., 69 f., 95, 160, 162, 182, 221
discrimination 88, 101

displaced persons 107 ff., 129
DNVP, Deutschnationale Volkspartei (German National People's Party) 28, 41, 52
Domino Theory 200, 202
Dresden 82, 86
Dubček, Alexander 207 f.
Dutschke, Rudi 147, 149
DVP, Deutsche Volkspartei (German People's Party) 24, 38, 41

East Prussia 15, 19, 70, 76, 95 f., 106 f.
eastern integration 132 ff.
Ebert, Friedrich 9 f., 20 f., 23, 45
Ebert-Groener Pact 9
EC, European Community 172 ff., 180, 182 ff., 186
ECSC, European Coal and Steel Community 180
EEC, European Economic Community 136, 180
Egypt 198, 222 f.
Einstein, Albert 31
elections 8 f., 20 ff., 38 ff., 122 ff., 132 f., 136, 147, 150, 152 f., 172, 176, 200, 210 f.
electricity 34, 81, 119, 158, 225
emergency acts 146 f.
emergency decrees 38 f., 43, 52
emigration 11, 65, 89, 109, 122
Enabling Act 52 ff.
"Entartete Kunst" ("Degenerate Art") 56
environmental movement 147, 157 f., 161, 164, 168, 176 f., 189
Erhard, Ludwig 137 f., 146
"Ermächtigungsgesetz" ("Enabling Act") 52 ff.
Erzberger, Matthias 9, 23
EU, European Union 183 – 186, 189, 218 f.
EURATOM (European Atomic Community) 132, 180
Euro 184 f.
European debt crisis 185
"Euthanasia" 88
EWG, Europäische Wirtschaftsgemeinschaft see EEC
exile 8, 66, 123, 196, 220
expansion 68, 70, 74, 77, 101, 218
Expressionism 30 f.
expulsion 80 f., 106 ff., 110 f., 129
extermination 74 f., 81, 88 ff., 100
extermination camps 90, 100
extra-parliamentary opposition 147 f.
extremism 23 f., 28, 38, 45, 174, 222

Fascism 93
FDGB, Freier Deutscher Gewerkschaftsbund (Free German Trade Union Federation) 133, 141
FDJ, Freie Deutsche Jugend (Free German Youth) 133, 140 f.
FDP, Freie Demokratische Partei (Free Democratic Party) 122, 132, 146 f., 152 f., 164, 176
Federal Constitutional Court 125

Federal Council 122, 125
federalism 11, 20, 21, 53, 121 f., 125, 177
feminism 60
FGY, Free German Youth (Freie Deutsche Jugend) 133, 140 f.
"Final Solution" 88 f., 91 ff.
flight 106–111, 169, 223
Four Powers, Four Power Agreement 103, 114 ff., 118 f., 122, 129
Fourteen Points (Wilson) 14
France 9, 11, 15, 17, 24, 28, 30, 45, 68 ff., 72, 74, 80 f., 112, 115, 129, 165 f., 173, 180, 200, 218, 220 f.
Franco-Prussian War 17
Frankfurt Documents 121
Free Corps (Freikorps) 9, 12, 23, 45
"Führer" 46, 49, 53, 56, 58, 62 f., 96, 101
"fulfilment policy" 23, 28

Galen, Clemens August von 88, 94
general strike 23, 39
genocide 47, 88 ff., 93, 99
German Revolution see November Revolution
German-French Friendship Treaty see Treaty
German-Polish Non-Aggression Pact 68
German-Soviet Non-Aggression Pact 68, 70, 73, 75
Gestapo, "Geheime Staatspolizei" ("Secret State Police") 56, 81, 89 f., 94 f., 111
ghetto 81, 89, 152, 155
glasnost 210
"Gleichschaltung" 53, 101
globalization 226 ff.
Goebbels, Joseph 56, 60, 65
Goerdeler, Carl Friedrich 95
Göring, Hermann 65 f.
Golden Twenties 7, 30 – 33, 45
Gorbachev, Mikhail Sergeyevich 168, 170, 173, 210 ff., 215, 217
grand coalition 24, 38, 146 f., 172
grass-roots movement 157
Great Depression 7, 28 f., 31, 34 – 38, 42 f., 45, 227
Greece 75, 139, 182, 185
Green Party 147, 157, 164, 176
Groener, Wilhelm 9, 39
growth 30, 137, 156 ff., 226
Grundgesetz see Basic Law
Grundlagenvertrag see Basic Treaty
Guantanamo 199, 221
guerilla warfare 200, 203
guest workers 137, 139, 223
Guevara, Ernesto Che 146

Hallstein Doctrine 136 f., 152
Harden, Maximilian 23
Harrisburgh nuclear accident 157
Heinemann, Gustav 147, 149
Heisenberg, Werner 31
Helsinki Accords see Conference of Helsinki

Heuss, Theodor 122, 132
Heydrich, Reinhard 89
Himmler, Heinrich 56, 90
Hindenburg, Paul von 21, 23, 38 ff., 45, 52 f., 55
Hiroshima 77 ff., 192
Hitler, Adolf 7, 28 f., 35, 38 – 42, 47 – 58, 61 – 71, 73 – 77, 82, 88 ff., 94 – 98, 101
Hitler-Putsch see Beer Hall Putsch
Hitler-Stalin Pact see German-Soviet Non-Aggression Pact
HJ, "Hitlerjugend" ("Hitler Youth") 61 ff., 82, 94, 101
Ho Chi Minh 146, 200
Holocaust 47, 54, 89 – 93, 98 f., 101, 191
"home front" 80
Honecker, Erich 156, 160, 165, 168 ff., 175
Hoover, Herbert (Hoover Moratorium/Report) 29, 34
Horn, Gyula 210
Hugenberg, Alfred 28
human rights 112, 210, 219, 221
Hungary 122, 169, 177, 186, 193, 198, 206 f., 210 ff., 218, 224
hyperinflation 24, 27, 34, 45

ideology 47 – 51, 56, 60 ff., 75, 82, 88, 140, 189
IMF, International Monetary Fund 185
immigration 33, 50, 186
independence 69 ff., 73, 116, 122, 132, 156, 174, 182, 186, 200, 206, 211, 217 ff.
India 202, 214
Indochina 200
Industrial Revolution, industrialization 8, 24, 156
inflation 7, 17, 24, 27, 34, 45, 118, 153, 156 f., 182
integration 71, 107, 110 f., 129, 136
internet 224, 227
intervention 194, 207 f.
invasion 26, 69 f., 72 – 75, 77 f., 81, 89, 150, 164, 192, 195, 206 f., 221
Iraq 173, 218, 221 – 224
Irish Question 186
Iron Curtain 115, 144, 169, 188, 206 f., 210 f.
ISAF, International Security Assistance Force 220
Islam 80, 218, 220, 222 ff.
"Islamic State" 223 f.
Islamism 220 – 223 f.
Israel 136, 156, 220, 223
Italy 28, 43, 68, 70, 74 f., 137, 139, 180, 185, 198

Jaruzelski, Wojciech 211
Jazz music 30
Jews 31, 47 ff., 51, 56, 61 f., 75, 81, 84, 88 – 93, 97 – 101, 111, 222
jihad 218, 222
Johnson, Lyndon B. 200
Jom Kippur War 156

INDEX

Kahr, Gustav von   23
Kapp Putsch   23
KdF, "Kraft durch Freude" ("Strenght through Joy")   57 f.
Kellog-Briand Pact   28
Kennedy, John F.   196–200
Khrushchev, Nikita Sergeyevich   73, 151, 194, 196–199, 206
Kiesinger, Kurt Georg   146, 153
Kim Il Sung   192 ff.
Kohl, Helmut   164 ff., 168, 172–176
Korea, Korean War   78, 132 f., 191–195, 215, 227
Kosovo   93
KPD, Kommunistische Partei Deutschlands (Communist Party of Germany)   12, 41, 53, 118, 123
Kreisauer Kreis (Kreisau Circle)   94
Krenz, Egon   169, 175
"Kristallnacht" (Night of Broken Glass) see November pogroms
KZ, Konzentrationslager see concentration camps

"**l**eadership principle" see "Führer"
League of Expellees   110 f.
League of Nations   15, 19, 28, 45, 68, 72
"Lebensraum" ("Living Space")   49, 60, 66, 68, 71, 75, 81
Leber, Julius   94
Leipzig   169, 171 f., 210
Lenin   8, 12, 213, 225
Leningrad blockade   75, 81
Ley, Robert   57
Liberalism   43, 62, 86, 147, 152 f., 208
liberation   79, 81, 90, 92, 170, 221, 227
Libya   223 f.
Liebknecht, Karl   9, 12 f., 45
Lindbergh, Charles   31
Lloyd George, David   14, 16
Locarno see Conference of Locarno
London Documents see Frankfurt Documents
Ludendorff, Erich   9
Luxemburg, Rosa   9, 12, 45

Maastricht Treaty see Treaty of Maastricht
Majdanek   92
Mann, Thomas and Heinrich   30, 33
Mao Zedong   192, 194
market economy   137 f., 158, 172, 176
Marshall Plan   102, 115 ff., 129, 137
martial law   211
Marx, Karl (Marxism)   48, 54, 114, 122, 127, 136
mass media   30 f., 50, 56, 151, 160, 191, 211
Max von Baden   9 f.
McCloy, John   134
MfS, Ministerium für Staatssicherheit (Ministry of State Security)   123, 133, 150, 160 ff., 176
migration, mass migration   50, 111, 139, 186, 216, 223 f., 227

militarism   12
Ministry of State Security (Stasi) see MfS
missiles   164 f., 196–199
Mitterrand, François   166
monarchy   7, 9, 11, 28, 193
Monday Demonstrations   169, 171, 210
monetary crisis   26, 38, 156
monetary union   172 f.
Montanunion see ECSC
Moscow Treaty see Treaty of Moscow
MSPD, Majority Social Democrats   9
Mujahideen   220
Müller, Hermann   38, 45
Munich Agreement see Conference of Munich
Muslims see Islam
Mussolini, Benito   194

Nagasaki   77 ff., 192
napalm   200 f., 203 f.
National Assembly   9, 11, 20 f., 23, 41, 45, 172
National Socialism, Nazis   31, 38 ff., 47–76, 82–85, 88–97, 101
nationalism   23, 28, 38, 49, 146, 174, 184, 186, 218
NATO, North Atlantic Treaty Organization   132, 136, 172 ff., 181, 191, 206, 212, 215, 218 f.
neo-Nazism   171, 174
neutrality   70, 74, 76, 132 ff., 174, 189, 200, 206
New Deal   34
Niemöller, Martin   94, 97
"Night of Broken Glass" ("Reichskristallnacht") see November pogroms
"Night of the Long Knives"   53
Nobel Peace Prize   28, 45, 152, 173, 210 f.
Nobel Prize   30 f.
Non-Aggression Pact   68, 75
"November criminals"   23, 48
November pogroms   88 f.
November Revolution   8–12, 20
NSDAP, „Nationalsozialistische Deutsche Arbeiterpartei" ("National Socialist German Worker's Party")   28, 41, 49 f., 52 f., 56, 90
nuclear power see atomic energy
nuclear weapons   see atomic bomb
Nuremberg Race Laws   88
Nuremberg Party Rallies   56 ff.
Nuremberg Trials   112 f.

Obama, Barack Hussein   78 f., 197
occupation   19, 24, 26, 28, 38, 45, 81, 103, 107, 112, 114 ff., 121, 128 f., 164, 192, 206, 208
October Revolution see Russian Revolution
oil, oil crisis   65, 75 f., 153, 156, 158, 168, 217, 220, 225
Olympic Games   57, 164, 192, 210, 227
Oradour   81

"Orange Revolution"   218
Ostpolitik   152 ff., 165

Palestine   80, 157, 223
Papen, Franz von   39 f., 45
Paris Conference see Treaty of Versailles
Parliamentary Council (Parlamentarischer Rat)   121 f.
partisan warfare   82, 85
passive resistance   24
peace movement   157
Peace Treaty of Brest-Litovsk see Treaty of Brest-Litovsk
Peace Treaty of Geneva see Conference of Geneva
Pearl Harbor   76 f.
People's Chamber   123 f., 140 f.
"People's Community" see "Volksgemeinschaft"
perestroika   210
Pieck, Wilhelm   123, 133
planned economy   133, 137, 140, 176
plebiscite   15, 21, 28, 45, 53, 69
pogroms   88
Polish-British Common Defence Pact   68
Politburo   140, 169
Potsdam Agreement see Conference of Potsdam
poverty   116, 139, 217
Prague Spring   207 f., 211, 215
proclamation of the German republic   6, 9, 12 f.
propaganda   53, 56, 58, 60, 64 f., 80, 83, 101, 144, 176, 209
proportional representation   20 ff., 45, 122
"protective custody" ("Schutzhaft")   56
"protectorate"   44, 68, 70
Protestantism   94, 164
Prussia   11 f., 15, 17, 33, 39, 52, 178
Putin, Vladimir   219
putsch see coup d'état

Quadripartite Agreement see Four Power Agreement

racism   47 ff., 93, 101
RAD, "Reichsarbeitsdienst" ("National Labour Service")   65
RAF, Rote Armee Fraktion (Red Army Faction)   147, 157, 159
rapprochement   152, 160
Rat der Volksbeauftragten see Council of People's Representatives
Rathenau, Walther   23
Reagan, Ronald Wilson   201, 210 f.
rearmamanet   65, 71, 104, 132, 164
reconciliation   87, 110 f., 129, 136, 183
Red Army   81, 92, 106 f., 133
Red Orchestra   94
referendum   20 ff., 29, 38, 45, 68 f., 121, 153, 182, 186
refugees   47, 89, 103, 106–110, 136, 142, 144, 152, 201, 203 f., 216, 223 f.
■ refugee crisis   224

Reichstag 9, 12, 21 ff., 38–41, 52, 101
- Reichstag fire 52 ff.
Remarque, Erich Maria 30
reparations 15, 17, 24, 28 f., 36, 45, 112, 114, 129, 206
representation 9, 20 ff., 45, 94, 122
repression 94 f., 200 f., 211
republic 7–10, 13 f., 20–23, 38–42, 121–125
resistance 24, 81 f., 94–97
reunification 98, 131 ff., 141, 151, 156, 165 f., 174, 177, 189
revision, revisionism 44, 68, 70 ff., 101, 110
Rhineland 24, 26, 28, 38, 45, 69
Ribbentrop, Joachim von 70, 73
Röhm, Ernst ("Röhm Putsch") 53
Roosevelt, Franklin Delano 34, 85, 87, 104, 112, 114
Roosevelt, Theodore 229
Rote Kapelle (Red Orchestra) 94
Ruhr, Ruhr Occupation 23 f., 26, 45, 115, 118
Russian Revolution 7 f.

SA, "Sturmabteilung" ("Assault Division", "Brownshirts") 38 f., 53 f., 56, 67
sabotage 81 f., 94
Saddam Hussein 173, 218, 221
SALT, Strategic Arms Limitation Talks 210
satellite states 123, 206–209
Scheidemann, Philipp 6, 9, 14, 20, 23
Schirach, Baldur von 61
Schleicher, Kurt von 39 f., 45
Schmidt, Helmut 146, 156 f., 159
Scholl, Hans and Sophie 46, 94 f.
Schumacher, Kurt 132
Schuman, Robert 180
SDS, Sozialistischer Deutscher Studentenbund (Socialist German Student Association) 147
Security Council 192, 220
SED, Sozialistische Einheitspartei Deutschlands (Socialist Unity Party of Germany) 122 f., 133, 140 f., 144, 150, 168 ff., 172, 176, 189
Seeckt, Hans von 23
"Seizure of power" 52 ff., 72, 88
separation of powers 20, 53
separatism 24, 26
Six-Power Conference see Conference of London
Social Darwinism 48 f.
Social Democrats see SPD
Socialism, Socialists 9 f., 12, 122, 133, 137, 140, 151, 160, 170 f., 207, 209, 215
Solidarność 211
sovereignty 132 f., 146, 173, 212
soviets 8 f.
Soviet Russia, Soviet Union see USSR
Spartacists, Spartacist Uprising 9, 12, 20, 45
SPD, Sozialdemokratische Partei Deutschlands (Social Democratic Party of Germany) 9, 20, 24, 35, 38 f., 41, 45, 53 f., 66, 94, 110, 122, 129, 132, 146, 152 f., 156, 164 f., 172, 189
spheres of influence 68, 74, 115, 123, 164, 192 f., 196, 209 f.
SS, "Schutzstaffel" ("Protection Squadron") 53 f., 56, 60, 67, 89–92, 96
"Stab in the Back" myth 23, 25
Stalin 78, 82, 102, 104, 112, 123, 133 f., 141, 206
Stalin note 133 f.
Stalingrad 76, 96
starvation 37, 81, 84, 89
Stasi, State Security Service see MfS
Stasi Records Act 176
Stauffenberg, Claus Schenk von 95 ff.
stock market crash 34
Stresemann, Gustav 24, 28 f., 45, 180
strike 23 f., 39, 53, 141, 211
Sudetenland 69 f., 72, 108
Swing Kids 61, 94
Sykes Picot Agreement 223
Syria 216, 220, 223 f.

taliban 220 f.
taxes 17, 24, 34 ff., 48, 66, 176, 182, 185
technological revolution 225
terror 11, 53, 56, 59, 81, 85, 94, 96 f., 111, 208, 218
terrorism 23, 147, 157, 159, 189, 220–224
Thälmann, Ernst 39, 140
Thatcher, Margaret 174 f.
thaw 206 f.
"Third Reich" 52, 68, 88, 98, 100
Tiananmen 169
total war 80
trade unions 35, 40, 53, 97, 133, 137, 141, 153, 164, 211
Treaty
- of Brest-Litovsk 8 f.
- of Friendship, Cooperation and Mutual Assistance (Warsaw Pact) 133, 150, 168, 171, 191, 206 f., 209, 211 f., 215, 217
- German-French Friendship Treaty 136
- of Maastricht 184
- of Moscow 152 f.
- of Non-Aggression see German-Polish-/German-Soviet Non-Aggression Pact
- of Unification 173
- of Versailles 7, 14 ff, 18 f., 23, 45, 48, 50, 65, 68–71
- of Warsaw 153
- on the Final Settlement with Respect to Germany see Two plus Four Agreement
Treblinka 90, 92
Trizone 115, 119, 123
Truman, Harry S. (Truman Doctrine) 77 f., 102, 112 ff., 116, 129, 192–195
Tucholsky, Kurt 30
Two plus Four Agreement 173

Ukraine 92, 164, 218
Ulbricht, Walter 122 f., 129, 133, 140–143, 150 f., 160
ultimatum 14, 78
unemployment 17, 24, 34 ff., 38 f., 42 f., 47, 57, 60, 64 ff., 101, 138 f., 157, 174, 176, 182, 185
Unification Treaty see Treaty of Unification
UNO, United Nations Organization 15, 47, 107, 114, 152, 156, 160, 192, 195, 218, 220, 224, 227
unrest 8, 20, 23, 146 f., 149, 182
uprising 9, 12, 24, 69, 81, 94, 123, 141, 150, 155, 209, 211, 215, 223
USPD, Independent Social Democrats 123

Versailles Treaty see Treaty of Versailles
Vichy 74, 81
Vietcong 200
Vietnam, Vietnam War 146 ff., 156, 191, 200–205, 215
"Volksgemeinschaft" ("People's Community") 49, 56, 101
Volkskammer see People's Chamber
Volkswagen 57, 137

Wałęsa, Lech 211
Wall Street 28, 34
Wannsee see Conference at the Wannsee
war crimes 15, 84 f., 101, 103, 112 f.
war guilt 14, 23
"war on terror" 220 ff.
Warsaw Ghetto 81, 89, 152, 155
Warsaw Pact see Treaty of Friendship, Cooperation and Mutual Assistance
Warsaw Treaty see Treaty of Warsaw
Weimar Coalition 20
Weimar Constitution 7, 20 ff., 38, 45, 54, 147
White Rose 94 ff.
Wels, Otto 53 f.
western integration 132 ff., 165, 172, 180 f., 183 ff., 189
William II (German Emperor) 9 ff., 15
Wilson, Thomas Woodrow 14 ff.
Wirth, Joseph 23
women, women's rights 20 f., 30, 60, 62, 65, 80, 82, 108, 160
World Trade Center 220
World War I 7 f., 14, 18 f., 24, 28, 30, 44, 48, 73, 180
World War II 34, 74–88, 101–112, 129, 132, 136, 144, 146, 180, 200

xenophobia 174, 186, 224

Yalta see Conference of Yalta
Yeltsin, Boris 211 ff., 217 f.
Young Plan 28 f., 38

Zentrum (Centre Party) 9, 20, 24, 38, 41, 122

akg-images GmbH, Berlin: 3.1, 3.2, 6.4, 9.2, 12.1, 20.2, 21.1, 21.2, 23.1, 25.1, 27.1, 30.2, 31.1, 33.1, 38.1, 46.1, 48.1, 50.1, 52.1, 53.1, 54.1, 55.1, 56.1, 57.2, 58.3, 60.1, 62.1, 63.1, 75.1, 91.1, 92.2, 94.3, 96.2, 102.1, 102.2, 112.1, 118.1, 123.1, 123.2, 126.1, 130.3, 133.1, 136.1, 137.2, 141.2, 143.1, 160.1, 165.1, 180.1, 181.1, 203.1; AKG Pressebild 32.2; AP 4.2, 204.1; Erik Bohr 31.2; H. Asemissen 89.1; Jürgen Georg Wittenstein 46.6; Lange, Karl-Ludwig Titel; Sewcz 168.2; Vaccaro, Tony 109.1; Wittenstein, Jürgen Georg 95.1; © VG BILD-KUNST, Bonn 2019/ The Heartfield Community of Heirs 67.1. |Alamy Stock Photo, Abingdon/ Oxfordshire: John Kellerman/Kinder, Birgit © VG Bild-Kunst, Bonn 2019 Titel. |Alamy Stock Photo (RMB), Abingdon/ Oxfordshire: 41.2; The Advertising Archives 32.1. |Archiv Gedenkstätte Geschlossener Jugendwerkhof, Torgau: 102/238, Erdmute Bräunlich 150.2. |Baaske Cartoons, Müllheim: Fritz Alfred Behrendt 227.2. |bpk-Bildagentur, Berlin: 12.2, 14.1, 18.1, 24.1, 26.2, 28.2, 34.2, 42.1, 57.1, 60.2, 64.1, 80.1, 115.1, 155.1; Deutsches Historisches Museum 6.2; Deutsches Historisches Museum/ Ahlers, Sebastian 83.3; Deutsches Historisches Museum/Desnica, Indra 49.1; Deutsches Historisches Museum/ Orgel-Köhne, Liselotte 49.2; Deutsches Historisches Museum/Psille, Arne 130.1; Dietmar Katz 46.4; Engel, V. 106.1; Germin 132.3; H. Noack 9.1; H. Pabel 107.2; Hans Brunswig 82.2; Hoffmann, Herbert 35.1; Katz, Dietmar 16.1, 17.1; L. Aufsberg 60.3; Lauterwasser, Siegfried 58.1; Riess, Henry 4.1, 119.1; SMB/Kunstbibliothek 58.2; Wolff, Paul Dr. 84.1; © VG Bild-Kunst, Bonn 2019/Arnold, Karl 40.1. |Bridgeman Images, Berlin: © DACS/P. Willi 194.1. |Das Bundesarchiv, Koblenz: Bild 152-21-05 59.1; Bild 183-J0908-0600-002 10.1; Bild 183-R04103/Scherl 8.2. |ddp images GmbH, Hamburg: Cornelius Meffert/Stern 148.1; Michael Kappeler 121.1. |Domke, Franz-Josef, Hannover: 184.1. |dreamstime.com, Brentwood: Yavuz, Naci 227.1. |DuMont Mediengruppe GmbH & Co. KG, Köln: KSTA/Walter Hanel 187.2. |Getty Images, München:

Bettmann 109.2; Spencer Platt 79.1; Taylor, Jack 186.1; Wally McNamme 195.1. |Getty Images (RF), München: Knaupe, Ulrich 178.1. |Haitzinger, Horst, München: 153.1, 182.1, 190.1. |Hanel, Walter, Bergisch Gladbach: 175.1, 177.1. |Haus der Geschichte der Bundesrepublik Deutschland, Bonn: Peter Leger 209.1; Szewczuk, Mirko 134.1. |Janson, Jürgen, Landau: 219.1. |Kelley, Steve, San Diego: 167.1. |Keystone Pressedienst, Hamburg: 28.1, 88.2, 198.2, 201.1. |Konrad-Adenauer-Stiftung e. V., Berlin: 164.1. |Lagatz, Uwe Dr., Wernigerode: 141.1. |Leibing, Peter, Hamburg: Hamburg 145.3. |Milla & Partner GmbH, Stuttgart: 179.1. |Nachlass Felix Mussil, Frankfurt/M.: 135.1. |Österreichische Nationalbibliothek, Wien: ÖNB/Bernhard, Fritz/Morocutti, Ottokar 83.2. |Picture-Alliance GmbH, Frankfurt/M.: 132.1; AA/abaca 224.1; abaca 223.1; AFP 211.1; AFP/McCoy 221.2; akg-images 6.3, 41.1, 85.1, 122.1, 140.2, 157.1; AP 171.1; AP Photo 5.2, 198.1; AP/Chuzavkov, Sergei 218.1; AP/J.Scott Applewhite 222.1; AP/Ng Han Guan 193.1; Arco Images/Schoening 13.1; Arco Images/Schoening Berlin 12.3; Burgi, Arno 162.1; Dirk Brockmann/HU Berlin 228.1; dpa 77.3, 78.1, 116.1, 130.2, 130.7, 144.1, 155.2, 159.1, 170.2, 225.1; dpa/afp 173.1; dpa/Athenstädt, Martin 164.2; dpa/Azubel, Diego 225.2; dpa/Burgi, Arno 185.1; dpa/Eilmes, Wolfgang 166.1; dpa/F. von Stackelberg 205.1; dpa/Geoff Green 4232907 220.1; dpa/H.-J. Goettert 121.2; dpa/Hollemann, H. 172.1; dpa/Janssen 211.2; dpa/Kneffel, Peter 176.1; dpa/PEACE_MEMORIAL_MUSEUM 77.2; dpa/Schilling 201.2; dpa/Scholz 5.1; dpa/Stein, Fred 132.2; dpa/Tewes 207.1; dpa/Weihs, Wolfgang 172.2; empics/Stillwell, John 86.1; Illingworth, Leslie/Daily Mail/SOLO Syndication 199.1; Kumm, Wolfgang 110.1; Kunstsammlung/VG Bild-Kunst, Bonn 2019/The Heartfield Community of Heirs 53.2; Picture Press 210.1; SCHROEWIG/Oertwig, Bernd 13.2; The Advertising Archives 83.1; UPI 193.2, 196.1; WORLD PRESS PHOTO/Warren Richardson 216.1; ZB/H. Link 168.1. |Presse- und Informationsamt

der Bundesregierung, Berlin: Siegmann 145.2. |Schoenfeld, Karl-Heinz, Potsdam: 183.1, 190.2. |Stuttmann, Klaus, Berlin: 224.2. |Süddeutsche Zeitung - Photo, München: 72.1, 107.1, 114.1, 114.2, 130.4; ap/dpa/picture alliance 89.2, 137.1; AP/dpa/picture alliance 145.1; Associated Press 121.3; Scherl 30.1, 34.1, 46.3, 46.5, 61.1; SZ photo 104.1; SZ Photo/imagebroker/Michalke, Norbert 130.6. |Tauber, Kurt, Plech: www.kameramuseum.de/Haus der Geschichte, Bonn 130.5, 161.1. |Thumser, Harald, Frankfurt/M.: 202.1. |Tonn, Dieter, Bovenden-Lenglern: 44.1, 44.2, 44.3, 44.4, 45.1, 45.2, 45.3, 100.1, 100.2, 101.1, 101.2, 101.3, 128.1, 128.2, 128.3, 129.1, 129.2, 129.3, 188.1, 188.2, 188.3, 189.1, 189.2, 189.3, 189.4, 189.5, 214.1, 214.2, 215.1, 215.2, 215.3. |toonpool.com, Berlin, Castrop-Rauxel: Martin Erl 187.1. |Travelstock44, Berlin: Jürgen Held 98.1. |ullstein bild, Berlin: 8.1, 20.1, 39.1, 39.2, 39.3, 46.2, 65.1, 69.1, 76.1, 82.1, 90.2, 96.1, 109.3, 140.1, 169.1, 170.1, 206.1; AP 221.1; Archiv Gerstenberg 26.1, 29.1, 43.1, 81.1, 88.1, 94.1, 102.4, 105.1; Boom 163.1; Borgas 94.2; BPA 156.1; Brauer 156.2; DHM/Schwarzer 160.2; dpa 146.1; Fotoagentur imo 217.1; Granger Collection 77.1; imageBROKER/Michalke, Norbert 169.2; Low, D. 71.1; Mehner 147.1; Nowosti 92.1, 212.1; Probst 150.1; Roger Viollet 198.3; Schlemmer, H. 173.2; Stary 102.3; TopFoto 157.2; ullstein bild 6.1; Voller, Ernst 81.2. |VG BILD-KUNST, Bonn: © VG Bild-Kunst, Bonn 2019 90.1. |Walter Ballhause-Archiv, Plauen: 35.2. |Wilhelm-Busch-Gesellschaft e.V., Hannover: Hanns Erich Köhler 154.1. |Zöllner, R., Berlin: 176.2.

Wir arbeiten sehr sorgfältig daran, für alle verwendeten Abbildungen die Rechteinhaberinnen und Rechteinhaber zu ermitteln. Sollte uns dies im Einzelfall nicht vollständig gelungen sein, werden berechtigte Ansprüche selbstverständlich im Rahmen der üblichen Vereinbarungen abgegolten.

Terms for Discussion

War and peace

- to be responsible for the outbreak of the war
- to set off / trigger a war
- to enter / join the war
- to declare war
- to win / lose a battle / war
- to occupy / take control of / invade / annex / conquer a country / territory
- to volunteer for military service / join the army
- to mobilize / demobilize troops / an army
- to fight for sovereignty / independence
- to demand / pay reparations
- to establish peace / to stabilize a country

Diplomacy

- to send / serve as an ambassador / (an envoy)
- to have / break off diplomatic relations with a country
- to achieve a diplomatic triumph
- to guarantee neutrality
- to negotiate / sign an agreement / a pact / a treaty
- to stir up / settle a dispute over
- to cause / create rising tensions
- to issue / deliver an ultimatum
- to sign / negotiate an armistice / a peace treaty
- to proclaim a republic

Economy

- to make an invention / to invent sth.
- to be a pioneer
- to start a business
- to invest money / to go bankrupt
- to increase production / to grow crops / to breed animals
- to exploit natural resources / exploitation
- to open new markets
- to be employed / unemployed / a skilled / unskilled worker
- to enjoy economic benefits
- to suffer from food shortages